Evangelicals and the Continental Divi

MCGILL-QUEEN'S STUDIES IN THE HISTORY OF RELIGION

Volumes in this series have been supported by the Jackman Foundation
of Toronto.

SERIES TWO   In memory of George Rawlyk
Donald Harman Akenson, Editor

SERIES ONE
G.A. Rawlyk, Editor

Evangelicals and the Continental Divide

The Conservative Protestant Subculture in Canada and the United States

SAM REIMER

McGill-Queen's University Press
Montreal & Kingston · London · Ithaca

© McGill-Queen's University Press 2003
ISBN 0-7735-2592-0 (cloth)
ISBN 0-7735-2624-2 (paper)

Legal deposit third quarter 2003
Bibliothèque nationale du Québec

Printed in Canada on acid-free paper.

This book has been published with the help of a grant
from the Canadian Federation for the Humanities
and Social Sciences, through the Aid to Scholarly
Publications Programme, using funds provided by
the Social Sciences and Humanities Research Council
of Canada.

McGill-Queen's University Press acknowledges the
support of the Canada Council for the Arts for our
publishing program. We also acknowledge the financial
support of the Government of Canada through the Book
Publishing Industry Development Program (BPIDP)
for our publishing activities.

National Library of Canada Cataloguing in Publication

Reimer, Sam
　　Evangelicals and the continental divide: the conservative
　　protestant subculture in Canada and the United States /
　　Sam Reimer.
　　(History of religion series)
　　Includes bibliographical references and index.
　　ISBN 0-7735-2592-0 (bnd); ISBN 0-7735-2624-2 (pbk)
　　1. Evangelicalism–United States. 2. Evangelicalism–
　　Canada. 3. Evangelicalism–Comparative studies. I. Title.
　　II. Series: History of religion (Montréal, Quebec)

BR1642.C3R44 2003　　　　277.3'082　　　C2003-901024-4

Typeset in Palatino 10/12
by Caractéra inc., Quebec City

To my wife, Mary Beth

Contents

Tables

Preface

This project began in summer of 1995 when I was a doctoral student at the University of Notre Dame. A rusty 1984 Honda Accord took me from Minneapolis to Winnipeg, down to Mississippi, and finally to New Brunswick, where I spent my days interviewing evangelicals and evenings transcribing the interviews from tape. I was impressed by the similarities between active evangelicals in all four locations, and I began to speculate about why those similarities existed. This book, originally my dissertation completed in 1996, is the result. It is typical of Canadians to understand themselves in contrast to Americans, so as a Canadian sociology student in the US and the son of evangelical missionaries, a comparison of evangelicals in the two countries seemed natural.

Regardless of where I travelled, I was warmly received by the people I interviewed. A special thanks to those pastors who gave up valuable time to talk about their faith. They were trusting enough to give a stranger the phone numbers of several of their parishioners and access to their Sunday school classes. I was invited into their homes, greeted at their church services, taken out for meals, and given places to stay, and the personal questions I asked were patiently answered. The whole research process was rewarding because of the kindness and hospitality these people displayed.

Since my graduate school days, two research projects that are important to the study of evangelicals in North America have appeared. The first, used extensively in this project, is the 1996 poll "God and Society in North America: A Survey of Religion, Politics and Social

Involvement in Canada and the United States," which I refer to as the God and Society poll, the first survey on religion and politics that allowed for Canada-us comparisons. I am indebted to Andrew Grenville, senior vice-president of Angus Reid, for use of this data set. Joining Grenville as the primary researchers on this project were the George Rawlyk Research Unit on Religion and Society, based at Queen's University in Kingston (including Drs David Lyon and Marguerite Van Die). A "gang of four" of US political science, Drs John Green, Jim Guth, Lyman Kellstedt, and Corwin Smidt, also worked on the project and created the measure of evangelicalism used below. The second important project is the massive study of American evangelicalism performed by Christian Smith and his colleagues in 1996, which has resulted in three books to date (Smith 1998; Smith 2000; Emerson and Smith 2000) and many articles. Although I developed most of my own material before reading these books, it was reassuring to find that Smith's phone survey and interviews with active evangelicals brought him to similar conclusions. My study extends their excellent analysis across the forty-ninth parallel and offers another view of this religious subculture.

The original dissertation was guided by Mark Chaves (now at the University of Arizona), and I am indebted to him for his encouragement and direction. My dissertation committee – Chaves, Lyn Spillman, Robert Fishman, and Kevin Christiano – was the sort of committee that many graduate students wish for: prompt, encouraging, and constructively critical. Chaves and Spillman also gave helpful comments on a recent draft of this manuscript. Others who deserve thanks are fellow graduate students Vince Neal, Lynda Nyce, and James Cavendish for their help and encouragement. My dissertation research was funded by research grants from the Society for the Scientific Study of Religion and Religious Research Association. The Helen Kellogg Institute for International Studies provided funding during the writing process. I also made use of the Project Canada data series, generously provided by Reginald Bibby.

More recently, this book has benefited from comments by Benne Faber and Dan Goodwin at Atlantic Baptist University where I now teach. I gratefully acknowledge the editorial help of Roger Martin and Claire Gigantes of McGill-Queen's University Press. Thanks also to Mary Beth Clements for proofreading and Mitchel Mealey for his help in creating the index. While the input of others has made this a better book, I alone am responsible for the analysis and conclusions contained herein.

Finally, I wish to thank the following editors/publishers for graciously granting me permission to integrate previously published material into this book: The *Journal for the Scientific Study of Religion*, for permission to include in chapter 7 material from Sam Reimer, "A Look at Cultural Effects on Religiosity," in vol. 34, no 4: 445–57; and University of Toronto Press for permission to include in chapter 8 material from Sam Reimer, "A Generic Evangelicalism," in *Rethinking Church, State, and Modernity: Canada between Europe and America*, edited by David Lyon and Marguerite Van Die, 228–46 (2000).

Evangelicals and the Continental Divide

1 Examining Evangelicals in Canada and the US

INTRODUCTION

Two stories illustrate a common Canadian attitude towards American evangelicals. The first story received significant press coverage in Canada. On 8 July 2000, Stockwell Day became the leader of the recently formed Canadian Alliance Party, Canada's official opposition. Day is unabashed about his evangelical faith and his social and fiscal conservatism. The 8 July run-off featured another evangelical, party founder Preston Manning, son of radio evangelist and one-time Albertan premier Ernest Manning, whom Day defeated soundly by a sixty-three-to-thirty-seven percent margin. About a month later, a journalist from the Toronto *Globe and Mail*, a national newspaper, contacted me. "Are we seeing the Americanization of Canadian politics?" he wondered.

The mixing of conservative faith and politics, characteristic of the famed Religious Right in the US, is not well received by many Canadians, who value distinctiveness from Americans. Writes Dennis Hoover, "The formula 'religious right = un-Canadian' has been a point of national pride among many Canadians, in keeping with the country's image as the 'kinder, gentler' North American country" (2000, 2). The success of evangelicals like Day and Manning sparked widespread speculation from the media: are evangelicals gaining (political) power in Canada? Have American influences erased the continental divide? Since 2000, Day has lost the leadership of the Canadian Alliance (formerly the Reform party) and the support of many Canadians, including several of his party's members of Parliament. Still, talk of growing American influences in Canada began long before Day and continue into the present.

The second story comes from the Canadian edition of the May 2002 *Reader's Digest*, featuring an article about "The Preacher Who Conned the Town." Richard Minard was an American con-artist who moved to the northern logging town of Smithers, British Columbia, under the guise of an Assemblies of God pastor. Expecting the rural yokels in Canada to be easy prey, Minard was surprised to find the town rallying behind a local Pentecostal pastor who sought to expose his fraudulent business of selling timeshares for a resort. Minard started a popular radio program and smooth-talked the locals out of their money, all the while cloaking his schemes in authentic religious talk. He was brought to justice in February 2000 and faced charges in Idaho.

A disproportionate amount of what Canadians know of American evangelicalism comes from images of slick charismatic televangelists, some of whom have widely publicized moral failings. Like the residents of Smithers, Canadians are wary of American evangelicals as a result. The story probably made the cover of a popular Canadian magazine because it gives further reason to be sceptical of glitzy American-style religion, and because it is a Canadian feel-good story in which the small-town locals were not too naive to see through the American Minard's schemes.

By comparison, American evangelicals know little about their Canadian counterparts, just as Americans seem to know little about Canada more broadly. Rick Mercer, a Canadian comedian well known (in Canada) for his roles on satirical TV shows like *This Hour Has 22 Minutes* and *Made in Canada*, enjoys exposing American ignorance about Canada in his feature "Talking to Americans." Since most Americans know virtually nothing about Canadian evangelicalism, it is fitting that both stories present Canadian attitudes towards Americans, and not the reverse.

But evangelical politicians like Day and con-artist wolves in religious sheep's clothing like Minard are not representative of the average evangelical. Nor are the front-page issues of evangelical politics and scandal – although given significant space in chapter 7 – the main focus of this book. Instead, I focus on understanding the realities of grass-roots Canadian and American evangelicalism. The more mundane topics of evangelical beliefs, practices, and attitudes occupy most of the pages that follow. Still, a careful comparative study provides a context for understanding the media hype about evangelicalism in North America and answers important questions. What are the differences between American and Canadian evangelicals?

Do the media-supported stereotypes of American evangelicals hold true? Are Canadian evangelicals carbon copies of their American counterparts?

This book also provides an inside look at a vigorous subculture that many think is growing in influence. Recent decades have witnessed the resurgence of evangelicalism, most notably south of the forty-ninth parallel. After spending a few decades encapsulated in their fundamentalist enclaves, evangelicals in the United States have regrouped and re-entered public life in the second half of the twentieth century. Various manifestations of this resurgence – "Religious Right" political activity, "born-again" presidents, televangelists, and aggressive pro-life campaigns – have generated the most media interest and created public awareness of American evangelicalism. The Canadian resurgence has been less well publicized, but it is significant nonetheless. Canadian evangelicals have been led back into the spotlight not only by politicians like Manning and Day but also by the politically active Evangelical Fellowship of Canada, and the acclaimed "Toronto Blessing," a recent spiritual renewal that spread across the globe from a church in Toronto, the Airport Christian Fellowship.

Away from the cameras and spotlights, evangelical resurgence is most notable in the quiet growth and vitality of the evangelical subculture in both countries. If we look only at those evangelicals who attend conservative Protestant denominations, evangelicals account for roughly one-quarter of the American population and one-tenth of the Canadian population. In both countries, there are more conservative Protestants in church on any given Sunday than mainline Protestants, and from all indicators, evangelicals are more likely to experience continued growth than any other Christian group.[1] At a time when mainline Protestant and Catholic participation is declining, evangelical church attendance is growing slowly. Somehow evangelicalism manages to hold the allegiance of a sizable proportion of North Americans in spite of societal pressures to abandon orthodox beliefs and practices. In short, evangelicalism is thriving in modern North America (Smith et al. 1998).

What about the continental divide? Is American-style evangelicalism coming to Canada? Many researchers and future prophets suggest that global forces produce homogenizing transnational effects. Evangelicalism has no shortage of transnational influences. It produces an abundance of institutions and cultural paraphernalia, which move freely across the border. In addition to sharing denominations and parachurch organizations such as Focus on the Family and Promise Keepers, evangelicals in both countries shop at Christian bookstores that market the same books, the same Christian music, and the same array of evangelical kitsch. One mainline Protestant academic who recently immersed herself in the evangelical subculture concluded, "Today's evangelicals are culture-makers." Not only do they have a distinctive set of beliefs and behaviours, they "have a vast and distinctive material culture. Almost anything that you can imagine they make, they probably do" (Wheeler 1995, 292). Furthermore, evangelicals can be quickly mobilized, particularly towards political ends. In sum, there is a plethora of institutions and cultural "stuff" that links North American evangelicals together.

One of my central arguments is that the institutions and commodities of evangelicalism provide an adequate base to maintain a distinctive subculture that spans national boundaries. Distinctive beliefs, practices, attitudes, and consumer "products" set evangelicalism apart from the larger national milieus that house it. If the arrival of the "religious right" in Canada blurs political distinctions between the two countries, the transnational nature of the evangelical subculture blurs differences between evangelicals in the two countries. Evangelicals, particularly active evangelicals, in both countries resemble each other far more than they resemble their fellow countrymen. A transnational evangelical subculture seems to have a greater influence on them than their national cultures.

To make sense of the distinctiveness and vitality of the evangelical subculture, I focus on active, or "core," evangelicals. Core evangelicals are actively involved in the evangelical subculture and committed to the basic tenets of evangelicalism. In addition, I look for international and intranational variation within evangelicalism in North America. Do evangelicals differ in important ways between Canada and the US? Studying variation within evangelicalism is a fruitful way to explore the subculture's relationship with the broader society and is necessary to get an accurate picture of the nature and future direction of the movement.

In any study of evangelicalism, it is necessary to say a brief word on how evangelicals are defined. They are not easy to categorize, and a variety of definitional strategies have been used. Denominational definitions, belief-based definitions, and self-identification measures have all been used in previous research to distinguish evangelicals from other Christian traditions. For my purposes, a denominationally based definition is best since churches in conservative Protestant denominations are the institutional "carriers" of the evangelical subculture. A belief-based definition – which typically defines an evangelical as one who believes in a personal God, in the divinity and unique saving work of Jesus, and in the unique authority and inspiration of Scripture – would include conservatives in Catholic and mainline Protestant churches, but they would not be part of the evangelical subculture to the same degree. For the same reason, self-identification is insufficient for this study, since some claim to be evangelical who are not involved in evangelical institutions, while others who are actively involved do not espouse the evangelical label. Finally, this study is limited to white evangelicals since African American (or African Canadian) evangelicals have always constituted a separate subculture (for more information on measurement, see appendix 2).

Two themes, then, are prominent throughout this book. The *subculture* theme focuses on the identity, boundaries, beliefs, morals, practices, and commitment of those embedded in the evangelical subculture, the core evangelicals. It illuminates questions regarding the vitality and distinctiveness of evangelicalism. In terms of *geographic variation*, I analyze the similarities and differences among evangelicals in different regions of Canada and the US to explain why such similarities and differences exist. Within this second theme, I examine the issue of how evangelicals are influenced by their larger cultural milieu. These two themes are interwoven in the chapters that follow because they inform each other. The way evangelicals are similar across regions tells us what is distinctive about the subculture, and where "symbolic boundaries" used to distinguish evangelicals from non-evangelicals have been created. As we shall see, the two themes interrelate in many other ways as well.

Core evangelicals are the most devoted in a subculture that is already strong in commitment. They regularly attend worship services and other events sponsored by conservative Protestant churches, read the Bible and pray regularly, give money to evangelical organizations, and interact regularly with other evangelicals. In other words, core evangelicals are immersed in the evangelical subculture. They are therefore most familiar with the inner workings of the subculture and the influence of the broader evangelical subculture is likely to have a significant impact on them. Of course, focusing on core evangelicals misses those evangelicals who are not as steadfast in evangelical conviction and commitment. This focus is warranted, however, for several reasons.

Some who affiliate with evangelical churches rarely attend church, spend little time reading their Bible and praying, and prefer the company of nonevangelicals. Some would argue that less-active evangelicals who distance themselves from evangelical subculture are in danger of accommodating to secular society, a process the eminent sociologist Peter Berger refers to as "cognitive contamination" (Berger 1992, 38). Berger argues that social and cultural forces in a heterogeneous and urbanized society call into question traditional religious explanations of the world, reducing what were once givens to mere possibilities. As a result, evangelicals who are not securely anchored in the subculture may succumb to secularizing pressures, thus weakening their orthodoxy, and some may accommodate completely to the secular culture. Researchers disagree on the extent to which this is happening among evangelicals, although Quebedeaux thought the tendency was significant enough to title his 1978 book *The Worldly Evangelicals*. Evangelicals who accommodate to secular culture may differ in important ways from the core evangelicals. Thus, indiscriminately treating all evangelicals as a single entity may skew our understanding of the essence of evangelicalism, clouding the distinction between the evangelical subculture and the larger national culture. The inclusion of marginal evangelicals in a sample may affect our understanding of evangelical characteristics. Certain attributes or attitudes that some assume to be the natural consequence of evangelical beliefs – intolerance, for example – may better represent those on the periphery than active evangelicals.[2] Focusing on core evangelicals will partially control for differences based on involvement, so that the most active evangelicals are compared across geographic boundaries.

Why compare American and Canadian evangelicals? Basically, it is because our understanding of both American and Canadian evangelicalism will be enhanced by doing so. Canada is often hidden beneath the shadow of the American eagle, and what is true on a national scale is also true of evangelicalism. Because American evangelicalism is roughly twenty times more extensive, and attracts considerably more media attention, Canadian evangelicalism can easily be conflated with its American counterpart.

Furthermore, American evangelicalism, though more visible, lacks a comparative case. What is exceptional about American evangelicalism? Seymour Martin Lipset (1990; 1996), the best-known advocate of American exceptionalism, suggests that part of what distinguishes the US from other nations is its unique brand of evangelicalism. The traditional moralism and individualism of American evangelicalism is thought to infuse American culture with some of the ideologies and values that make it exceptional. Exactly what is uniquely American about American evangelicalism can only be answered through international comparison. The two countries are well suited for comparison because basic similarities make it easier to isolate key differences. Religiously, they share an open pluralistic environment and many matching denominations. However, they are distinct in important historical and cultural ways.[3]

With this in mind, the central questions of this book can now be presented. What characterizes evangelicalism at its core? Does the study of core evangelicals shed light on what is truly distinctive about evangelicals as compared to nonevangelicals in their cultural environments? In what ways, if any, do Canadian and American evangelicals differ? What aspects of their national (or possibly regional) context help explain such differences? In turn, how do these aspects help us understand the influence of the broader culture on evangelicalism?[4]

THE DATA

In order to answer these research questions, I spent about one month observing, interviewing, and surveying evangelicals in each of four locations – Minneapolis, Minnesota; Winnipeg, Manitoba; Jackson, Mississippi; and Saint John/Moncton, New Brunswick. Winnipeg and Minneapolis were chosen because of their many similarities. Manitoba and Minnesota are both about ten percent conservative Protestant, half of which belong to a single religious tradition, Mennonite and Lutheran – Missouri Synod (LMS) respectively. Both locations are about twenty-five percent Catholic, have a dominant mainline Protestant denomination, are predominately white, and about two-thirds urban. Finally, they both have histories of strong health-and-welfare programs, high voter turnout, farmer-led political parties, and similar industries. If evangelicals in these locations differed in the ways one might predict based on national differences, then the forty-ninth parallel remains a significant boundary for evangelicals. Alternatively, if they showed few differences, it would suggest that the national border has less cultural significance. The second pair of locations, Saint John/Moncton, New Brunswick, and Jackson, Mississippi, represents the "hot-bed" of evangelicalism. They are not as well matched as the first pair but were chosen because they represent the quintessential evangelical locations in their respective countries. Both lead, or nearly lead, their countries in the percentage that affiliates with conservative Protestant churches. They are similar in other interesting ways as well. Both also lead or nearly lead their countries in the percentages that are under the poverty line. Both have the largest percentage of the largest minority group in their countries (New Brunswick is thirty-five percent Acadian French and Mississippi is thirty-five percent African American). In addition, both places are centres of Baptist strength and have histories of racial or ethnic tension (Hodgson 1992). In each of these four locations I interviewed and surveyed pastors and active church attendees from the denominations indicated in Table 1.1. Only evangelicals from white suburban churches of matching denominations were surveyed.

Table 1.1
Denominations Selected in Each Research Site

Family	Minnesota	Manitoba	Mississippi	New Brunswick
Baptist	Southern Baptist Convention	Canadian Baptist Ministries Canadian Conference of Southern Baptists	Southern Baptist Convention	Canadian Baptist Ministries (United Baptist Convention of the Atlantic Provinces)
Holiness	Church of the Nazarene	Church of the Nazarene	Church of the Nazarene	Church of the Nazarene
Pentecostal	Assemblies of God	Pentecostal Assemblies of Canada	Assemblies of God	Pentecostal Assemblies of Canada
Other	Lutheran – Missouri Synod	Mennonite Brethren	Lutheran- Missouri Synod	Mennonite Brethren / Lutheran Church Canada

Note: The Canadian Conference of Southern Baptists, the Lutheran Church Canada, and the Pentecostal Assemblies of Canada were originally part of the Southern Baptist Convention, Missouri Synod Lutherans, and Assemblies of God respectively.

In sum, pastors from thirty-eight churches and eighty parishioners from sixteen churches were interviewed, for a total of 118 interviews. In each of the sixteen churches, pastors recommended five active church attendees according to certain age and gender requirements. Interviews averaged eighty-three minutes in length. In addition, 268 survey forms were completed in adult Sunday school classes in the sixteen churches and returned in usable form, resulting in a total sample of 386. These data are called the Core Evangelical (CE) sample below. (For more detail on the sampling strategy and the CE data, see appendix one.) Very few pastors and almost no parishioners refused interviews. Those interviewed spoke at length about their religiosity, and no interviewee refused to answer a question. The richness of these interview data reflect the gracious and willing participation of active evangelicals in all four locales.

Of course, the interview data are not random and cannot be said to be representative of all North American evangelicals. In addition to the CE sample, nationally representative polls of Americans and Canadians with significant religious components were analyzed. The best poll in this regard is a 1996 "God and Society in North America" poll, which is a representative sample of roughly 3,000 Canadians and 3,000 Americans (see appendix 2 for details). The strong quantitative data from this and other polls, along with the rich qualitative interview data and observations in the churches create an excellent data source for the investigation of the evangelical core and for comparing evangelicals on both sides of the forty-ninth parallel.

PORTRAITS OF CORE EVANGELICALS

To provide a taste of the interview data, here is a look at four core evangelicals, one from each region where interviews took place. While all evangelical interviewees have unique profiles, these portraits provide an opportunity to introduce some of the themes developed in this book. To protect anonymity, the church names and personal names given here are pseudonyms.

Brian Carter. Holy Trinity Church (LMS) is nestled between middle-class homes in a Twin Cities suburb. The sign on the door informs the passerby that services are held Sunday mornings at 8:15, 9:30, and 11:00, and on Thursday night in the summer (for those who leave for cottage country on the weekends). As the multiple services suggest, this church is bursting at the seams, with 550 to 600 attending weekly in a sanctuary that holds three hundred. Sunday school runs concurrently with the 9:30 service, and small groups meet during the week for adults. Pastor Brian Carter is a middle-aged man, stylishly dressed with carefully groomed blonde hair. He informs me that they have already purchased land for a larger sanctuary. An electric bass, a drum set, and an assortment of amps, speakers, and wires clutter the stage of the relatively austere sanctuary. The church services feature both modern and traditional styles of music, but Carter hopes to have only modern music in the near future.

While the LMS is known as a liturgical confessional tradition, the modern style did not surprise me because of my previous interviews with Lutheran–Missouri Synod pastors. Holy Trinity is more traditional in style than Good Shepherd, a large LMS church in the area, but far more trendy than Our Redeemer, whose pastor referred to the Good Shepherd people as "raving Pentecostals." As the pastor of Good Shepherd argued, however, the differences between the extremes of Our Redeemer and Good Shepherd are mostly stylistic: "I would say that the differences [between Holy Trinity and Our Redeemer] are not primarily theological; the differences are more in the area of practice. Quite honestly, when you interview Missouri Synod Lutheran pastors and other church workers, I think you will find that, by and large, they are very conservative in their approach

to the Scriptures, maintaining a strong bond in terms of the fundamentals of the faith ... We do not rigidly adhere to particular worship
forms or formats, instead it is much more [of a] – if I can use an
overworked term – 'user-friendly' kind of worship format. We use a
lot of drama, a variety of music." This variation in style, he told me,
was common among LMS churches in other areas. It was clear that
the two churches on the "modern" end of the spectrum were growing
rapidly, while traditional Our Redeemer was both greying and
shrinking, a pattern that Pastor Carter said was true on a larger scale.

Like most pastor interviewees, Pastor Carter spoke in a language
that could be considered broadly evangelical. While explaining his
role in the conversion of an aging alcoholic, he used terms like "the
Spirit broke through" and "he received Christ." For Carter, the conversion process involved "spiritual warfare" and "claiming the blood
of Christ," phrases one would expect to hear from those in charis-
matic/Pentecostal denominations. As an example of a recent answer
to prayer, he spoke of the physical healing of his son. Carter identified
himself as a Christian, which he defines as "one who believes in
Christ as their personal Saviour and is committed to following him,
and to sharing him [evangelism]." Also characteristic of evangelicals
was his concern for what he saw as the moral breakdown of the
country, and particularly the low value placed on human life as indicated by the widespread practice of abortion. When asked how Christians could bring about positive change in society, his answer was
typical of evangelicals in its dedication to evangelism and its lack of
clarity on how community change might practically be accomplished:
"[We] need to pray for the Spirit to change [people] and model positive things ... [Some churches] think its time to retrench, time to ...
wait for God to come back. I never read in Scripture that its time to
dig a foxhole and wait for him to return, never ... If our security and
meaning for life is in Christ, there is nothing this world can do to us ...
I think we need to get bolder [in evangelism], not less. Where do they
put a diamond they are trying to sell? Against a black background,
because it makes it shine brighter. The darker the society gets the
brighter we should shine." LMS respondents like Brian Carter differed from most evangelicals, however, in considering their infant
baptism – the time of their salvation – to be their most significant
religious experience. Pastor Carter did not like the use of the term
"born again" in modern parlance, though he did consider himself to
have been born again in the "biblical use of the term." Overall, Pastor
Carter showed signs of embracing the larger evangelical subculture
in his beliefs and behaviour, and he is making stylistic changes to his
church services so they will be more appealing to the modern seeker.

Naomi MacDonald. Naomi MacDonald looks younger than her senventy-one years, in spite of her recent bout with cancer. The chemotherapy she endured had not sapped her religious fervour. Originally from the New York area, she and her recently retired husband George moved to Winnipeg many years ago when he found employment as a maintenance man. I found several Americans like the MacDonalds in Canadian evangelical churches. Particularly common were Americans pastoring churches of denominations recently transplanted to Canada, like the Southern Baptists, Lutheran Church – Canada (which had been the Lutheran – Missouri Synod), or the Pentecostal Assemblies (formerly the Assemblies of God). Canadian influences in American churches were predictably less common, although several in the US spoke of the "Toronto Blessing."

Like a typical grandmother and mother, Naomi spoke highly of her godly children and grandchildren, pointing to large pictures that decorated their modest apartment. Naomi is a longtime member of Pineglen Nazarene. She has held just about every position in the church except pastor, although she has on occasion filled the pulpit at short notice. She has played piano, sung in the choir, chaired church boards, and been involved with the street mission downtown. Recently, her health has not allowed her to keep these commitments. It was not rare for women interviewees to hold positions of influence in their churches, although I interviewed no female senior pastors.

Like most evangelicals, Naomi identifies herself foremost as a Christian, which she defines by emphasizing commitment to Christ. Naomi considered the labels "Christian" and "evangelical" to be synonymous. After defining an evangelical, I asked her to define a Christian: "I just said, a Christian is one who lets the Lord be the Lord of his life, not just the Christian movement as such. People say that if you're not a Muslim or a Buddhist you are a Christian. I don't mean Christian in that sense. A Christian to me is a follower of Christ and one where Christ is Lord of his life." It was primarily the Canadian evangelicals who felt the need to define a Christian more narrowly, in opposition to the broad definition they believed was common in Canadian society. In comparison, it seemed the general understanding of the term Christian was more closely aligned with the evangelical understanding in the US, particularly the South.

I asked Naomi if she could recall an incident during which she received an answer to prayer. "Oh, yes," she laughed, and looked knowingly at her husband. "In fact, I have had a number of experiences where I believe God healed me just like that." She went on to describe at length how she was cured of "polio of the throat" by being anointed with oil during a Wednesday-night Bible study, and of her miraculous recovery from her chemotherapy treatments. She also described incidences when George was out of work and they were not able to buy food, and someone would bring them groceries without knowing their situation: "We just prayed and God would bring it in or supply him [her husband] a job or do something, right?" She looked at George, who agreed. "This cancer I had in my liver ... by the way, my blood test came back and [it] was good, and I had a CAT scan and it showed that the tumours had shrunk way down ... So I feel God's presence very close." Committed evangelicals reported that life's trials – sickness, death, suffering – strengthened their faith instead of weakening it. They were able to see God sustaining, healing, and working through difficult circumstances even to the point where, often in retrospect, they interpreted trials as blessings.

Although she is an American citizen, Naomi's greatest national concern was Canada's financial problems, particularly the loss of jobs, a response more representative of Canadian than American evangelicals. American evangelicals overwhelmingly point to moral problems as their greatest concern for their country, while economic issues are more salient to Canadians. However, Naomi was willing to accept the "fundamentalist" label (even though she preferred "evangelical"), a trait more common among evangelicals south of the border. The interview with Naomi demonstrated a mixing of Canadian and American evangelical traits, a microcosm of what seems to be happening on a larger scale. As people become more transient and (mostly American) media influences find a home on both sides of the border, evangelical differences based on geography may be diminishing. This theme is developed in later chapters.

Trey Johnson. Mississippi Baptist Trey Johnson invited me to interview him at his office in Jackson, where he served as vice-president of Operations for an insurance company. My wife and I had been in Mississippi for two weeks, and I was acclimatizing to the August weather and finding my way around the lower-class neighbourhoods near our small apartment, which lacked air conditioning. As I stepped out of the stifling heat into the air-conditioned office building, the cool air was more of a shock than the plush carpet and the pricey wooden furniture of Trey's office. Jackson is a city of contrasts: wealth and poverty, white flight from black neighbourhoods, violent crime and southern hospitality.

Trey's affluence matches the well-to-do Southern Baptist congregation he is a part of. About 3,000 attend the two morning services each Sunday in a lavish sanctuary that the pastor said could squeeze in 2,500 people. The church has some fifty paid staff members, half of whom are professionals with seminary training. Senior Pastor Greg Smith, whom I also interviewed, admitted that the church was known for its wealth but stated that they try to put it to good use. He highlighted their outreach to single parents (there were many single parents attending the church) and to homosexuals (several attend, including five suffering from AIDS). They employ a pastor whose sole task is to find urban ministries created by African Americans for African Americans so they can funnel money into them. When I attended, I saw no African Americans at the church. Pastor Smith told me that they have tried hard to integrate African Americans into their church, but they would not stay because they wanted to be involved in helping African congregations. Thus, said Smith, they stopped trying to recruit African Americans or to create programs for the urban poor and switched to the strategy of financing worthwhile projects.

Pastor Smith, Trey, and most of the active evangelicals I interviewed in Jackson were not fundamentalists. Pastor Smith has an earned a PhD and felt that the "fundamentalist movement was wrong headed." He is not a strict premillennialist – a typical fundamentalist eschatology emphasizing Christ's return for the saints prior to his millennial reign on earth – nor did he believe that the Bible was a word-for-word literal translation of what God said. When I did find a Southern Baptist pastor who espoused the fundamentalist label (the only fundamentalist pastor interviewed), he told me there were only three other churches in the Jackson area, besides his, that would be considered fundamentalist. It appeared to me that, at least in the large cities I visited, a brand of "generic evangelicalism" held sway, an idea that is explored in later chapters.

Trey's attitude towards African Americans was common among the committed evangelicals in the South. He was aware that he likely had hidden prejudices and did his best to free himself from them. His discussion about his concerns for society touched on racism, an issue obviously at the forefront in a city where "white flight" is common. While Trey stated that the "best solution for community problems" was spiritual revival, he revealed his conservative political leanings by mixing the racial and welfare issues in the same discussion:

[While] I don't harbour any great prejudice against blacks – I guess here again my experience, I grew up the tough way [in poverty] and I've overcome ... I didn't depend on others, I just decided to go to college, no one else in my family had ever gone to college, but I did – so where I come from, I didn't need anybody's help so ... this is my prejudice: Why can't everybody else do that? ... Why should I pay high, high, exorbitant taxes so somebody else can have a free ride? That's my prejudice, not against blacks, but against a system where people aren't encouraged or allowed or required to overcome like I did ... I don't care if they're black or white ... Its not a black-white issue, it just that we built a society on the basis of dependency ... If somebody is trying and I know they are trying, I'll be the first one to help them. I've spent a lot of bucks on people who are really trying and struggling 'cause I know what they are going through.

Trey also stated that he wished Mississippi could "progress fifty years overnight" so that they could get over their racist past and "get on with creating a better life for everybody." While he thinks that Mississippi is making advances in this regard, progress is inhibited by the lingering perception that the state is racist and backward. "We are further ahead than most people give us credit for."

Trey's most "significant religious experience" was his conversion. Regardless of whether a conversion was gradual and uneventful or sudden and traumatic, most evangelicals considered their conversion, or "born again" experience, of the highest significance. Trey's conversion, however, was unique. During his upbringing by a poor single mother who refused welfare, he started dating a girl in his teen years who insisted he go to church with her. Under the impression that he needed to wear a suit to church and not having the money to buy one, he began stealing food from the local grocery store and pocketing the extra grocery money given to him by his mother. One fatal day, the storeowner stopped him at the door and ushered him into a back room where he was commanded to sit facing the owner's desk: "[On the desk] he had a Bible here and a pistol here [he gestures] and said to me, 'Now I am going to give you two choices. I am either going to call the police or you're going to let me read this Bible to you' ... so he read some Scripture and told me about God and Jesus, course I knew all that ... When he got through, I was under what I call conviction from the Holy Spirit and I started running home ... I had such an urge to read the Bible ... so I got the Bible down and just started flipping pages ... looking for something that would mean something to me ... The circumstances were right for it so I just asked God to come into my heart and change my life. So that's how I became a Christian." Trey did finally save the money to buy a suit and, upon arriving at Sunday school with his girlfriend, found he was the only teen wearing one.

Nancy Leblanc. Nancy Leblanc is a petite and timid twenty-two-year-old native of New Brunswick, Canada. She attends Queensway Church, a downtown church affiliated with the Pentecostal Assemblies of

Canada. Queensway bought their historic church building from the United Church, though the church was originally built by Presbyterians before the 1925 union of Methodists, Presbyterians, and Congregationalists that became the United Church of Canada. "We bought the pipe organ and they threw in the building," joked Queensway's pastor, James O'Brien, since he said the best organ in the Maritimes is housed in the large church. The ornate woodwork, high ceilings, and huge pipe organ remained, although the area around the pulpit was redone, and the stained-glass windows were replaced with clear glass, presumably to give the sanctuary more light. On the right side of the stage, a few pews have been removed to make room for a worship band, and the overhead light shines over the pipes of the organ. The juxtaposition of the modern and traditional reflects an equally awkward attempt on the part of the congregation to please both modern and traditional tastes. The church's music minister was recently laid off because of a disagreement over styles of worship, a tension that is presently handled with traditional worship in the morning and contemporary in the evening. It was not hard to conclude which side of the debate Nancy was on, as she was a member of the worship band and had a love for music put out by Vineyard churches, a rapidly growing charismatic denomination that produces a disproportionate amount of contemporary worship music. Many evangelicals in North America, like those at Queensway, are reluctant to embrace modern musical styles on Sunday morning, although the influences of modernity are not always resisted. In their personal lives, there is little reluctance to adopt modern technological advances and consumerism.

Like other young evangelicals I encountered, Nancy was uninterested in the theological distinctiveness of her Pentecostal roots, identifying herself simply as a Christian. Her definition of a Christian – "a follower of Jesus, someone who wants to be like him" – lacked the clear boundaries of most answers, though after prompting, she did say that a Christian must "believe that Jesus died on the cross for you ... [so that] your sins are gone." Although Nancy showed that she had put little thought into doctrinal and ethical questions, she nonetheless tended to give typical answers to moral questions and questions of belief, indicating that her evangelical upbringing produced a set of boundaries in her mind that divided "Christians" from "non-Christians" and right from wrong.

Nancy found questions about religious experience much easier to answer. While most Pentecostals spoke of such experiences as receiving the baptism of the Spirit, healings, speaking in tongues, and being slain in the Spirit – experiences we explore in a later chapter – Nancy placed religious significance in her dreams. Nancy felt that she had recently reconnected with God. Part of the reconnecting involved breaking off a relationship with a young man who attended church but "was not serving God," which was a very difficult process for her. At the time, she was attending a Vineyard church in a nearby town where she had undergone a spiritual transformation. In the course of a month, she experienced God "taking a lot of garbage out of my life." It was after these events that her dreams became more numerous, although she had been dreaming all her life. For example, when she was seventeen years old and feeling friendless and alone, she dreamt that "Jesus and I were walking and it was like a big party, there were a lot of people around, and in the dream it showed him holding my hand and walking through the party, and I remember that he was wearing a jeans jacket and it was just kind of funny because it showed me he was my friend. I woke up and read a verse ... I wish I wrote it down ... but it was really encouraging ... I had some big dreams that really helped me in my life." Evangelicals see their spiritual journeys as a relationship with God, a divine friend, even a divine lover, as Nancy's dream aptly demonstrates.

Like other members of her church, Nancy is concerned about the poverty in her area. Her church, which runs a food pantry, wants to meet physical needs so as to have the opportunity to address spiritual needs as well, said her pastor. Her greatest concern for the community is unemployment, and she wanted to reach out to the people: "If I had money like a lot of people do, I would reach out more. If I had a million dollars, I would open up a shelter."

Though soft spoken, Nancy tries to carry her faith into the workplace. When I asked what effect her faith has on her at work, she described to me a situation that was typical of the nonaggressive personal approach to evangelism that modern evangelicals espouse: "The girl who worked right behind me was an atheist, and everyone knew she was an atheist and everyone knew I was a Christian, and the funny thing was we got along really well. I could see how God was actually allowing me to share things with her ... my Christian beliefs and by the time I left, she was kind of open to it [Christianity]." How did she become known as a Christian? "I think people realize you are different ... People are saying to you, 'want to go drinking or do this or that,' 'no,' 'well, why don't you?' People see you differently."

Like Nancy's, the faith of many evangelicals affected their private behaviour at work (in terms of honesty, a positive attitude, hard work, etc.), although some seek opportunities for low-key evangelism. As noted in a later chapter, no committed evangelical was able to articulate how faith should affect the public structural levels of organizations or society.

SUMMARY

These portraits of core evangelicals suggest multiple similarities and some differences between evangelicals in different parts of North America. In chapter 2, I examine arguments for both similarities and differences across the forty-ninth parallel. On the one hand, historical and cultural differences between the US and Canada, and between American and Canadian evangelicalism, lead one to expect differences in areas outside of the central tenets of evangelicalism. On the other hand, transnational forces and globalizing flows lead some to conclude that differences between Canada and the US are diminishing; hence, too, the differences between evangelicals in these countries.

As the interview with Lutheran pastor Brian Carter shows, the evangelical subculture is influential and pervasive, even among conservative Protestant denominations that remain somewhat separate from the evangelical mainstream. While denominational differences remain, similarities between evangelicals from different denominations are surprising. Furthermore, similarities between denominations do not end at significant national or regional borders. Naomi MacDonald's interview points to a significant American presence in Canadian evangelicalism, and to a lesser extent, Canadian evangelicals are influential in the South. In addition, a significant number of material cultural "carriers" – evangelical books, magazines, music, videos, seminars, denominations, and parachurch organizations – have moved across geographical borders. The permeability of national boundaries to evangelicalism, along with increases in the communication and networking among evangelicals, has resulted in similarities among core evangelicals. In chapters 3 through 6, similarities between denominations and across geographical boundaries are examined.

In chapter 3, I examine evangelical identity and subcultural boundaries. Besides the question of variation within and between Canada and the US, this research focuses on the characteristics of those most actively involved in the subculture. Just as Nancy Leblanc, Naomi MacDonald, and Pastor Brian Carter chose to identify themselves as Christians (as they define it) instead of by a denominational label, so it is true that evangelicals tend to see themselves as part of something bigger than their church or denomination. They share a strong subcultural identity, which has clear boundaries. They know who qualifies as an evangelical "Christian" and who does not. Chapter 3 seeks to identify the central characteristics of evangelicalism, from the views of core evangelicals themselves.

In addition, respondents in all regions emphasize the same defining characteristics of evangelicals. Religious experience is a necessary ingredient, particularly conversion. Trey Johnson's colourful conversion account is an indication of its foundational significance for evangelicals, and Nancy Leblanc's dreams made her faith "real" to her and strengthened her commitment. I explore the varieties and significance of religious experience in chapter 4 and emphasize its centrality in evangelicalism. Evangelicals embrace and maintain their faith partly because of religious experiences that assure them of its validity.

Also emphasized consistently by core evangelicals is the importance of orthodoxy, or correct beliefs, without which one cannot enter the evangelical fold. As noted in chapter 5, beliefs about the authority of the Bible and the unique salvific work of Christ on the cross were frequently emphasized in the interviews. Morally, beliefs about sexual ethics – particularly regarding sex outside marriage, homosexuality, and abortion – are salient. This chapter discusses the possibility of waning orthodoxy or accommodation to the "secular" culture. Are evangelicals losing their orthodox moorings in the secular sea of modernity?

In chapter 6, evangelical practice and commitment, or orthopraxy, is examined. Church attendance and private devotionalism are important practices evangelicals identified. Evangelicals also seek to influence the "world." As my interview with Nancy Leblanc indicated, evangelistic techniques have taken on a nonconfrontational nature, and as was the case for Pastor Carter, evangelicals could not articulate a clear strategy for world transformation. In each chapter, evidence indicates similarity. Evangelical identity, boundaries, experience, beliefs, morals, or behaviours – in short, the evangelical subculture – is distinctive and similar in Canada and the US.

Of course, there are important differences, whether between denominations, countries, or otherwise. Trey Johnson's open discussion about community problems brings up the possibility of differences in racial attitudes and political affiliations, whereas Naomi MacDonald's interview suggests differences in the area of national concerns. In chapter 7, I explore differences among evangelicals with particular attention to differences that follow national lines. The differences are most pronounced in the areas of political attitudes and what can be called irenicism, a tendency towards tolerance and civility among Canadian evangelicals. Two other differences, incongruity and national concerns, are also noted. The issue of incongruity between verbalized standards and actual practice is framed by recent disclosure of scandalous behaviour among prominent evangelicals, particularly televangelists. Such publicized scandals call into question the congruity between the "talk" (beliefs and morals) and the "walk" (behaviour) of evangelicals. Does the rank-and-file evangelical walk the talk? Regarding national concerns, evangelicals see significant problems in their respective countries and seek societal change that aligns with biblical standards. In this area as well, Canadian and American evangelicals show interesting differences. Although the significance of geographical differences may be waning, some evangelical differences follow national lines, and regional differences do not account for the national differences that I observed.

To recap, this book examines variation in evangelical beliefs, practices, and attitudes in North America. In general, similarities far outnumber differences, prompting the major conclusions of this book: that there exists a transdenominational transnational evangelical subculture in North America. This subculture is distinctive, and those active in it have a clear sense of identity, a clear understanding of the subcultural boundaries, and knowledge of the norms and values associated with it. What differences there are point to the continued cultural significance of the forty-ninth parallel. Still to be answered are some obvious questions: Why so much similarity? Why have certain differences persisted? How do we explain them? How has evangelicalism remained distinctive and vibrant in the face of secularizing forces? These questions, and many others, deserve thorough examination.

2 Evangelicalism and the Continental Divide

The late Canadian historian G.A. Rawlyk, himself an evangelical, spent the winter of 1994–95 in South Carolina writing his book *Is Jesus Your Personal Saviour?* in which he sought to capture the essence of Canadian evangelicalism in the 1990s. Rawlyk expected to find the southern evangelical-fundamentalist environment of South Carolina conducive to his work; instead he found the atmosphere "depressing and profoundly alienating" (1996, 7). The tirades of fundamentalist televangelists and the right-wing polemics of southern churches made him want to distance himself not only from southern evangelicals but from evangelicalism in general. As he immersed himself in his research, however, he was relieved to find what he considered to be a more accommodating and irenic northern brand of evangelicalism. He concluded that "there has always been a powerful populist/spiritual/irenic quality to Canadian evangelicalism" that gives it a more "accommodating quality" (ibid.). Rawlyk is not the only Canadian evangelical who finds American evangelicalism alienating. For that matter, several American evangelicals I interviewed in Minnesota want to distance themselves from what they think of as a fundamentalist and racist brand of evangelicalism in the southern states. If evangelicals hold to stereotypes of southern evangelicalism as dogmatic, aggressive, intolerant, brash, and anti-modern, then it is likely that those perceptions are more widely held, and possibly true. Alternatively, stereotypes might be based on media perceptions, and evangelicals in the American South might be equally incensed by their publicized image. Are perceived differences real?

A certain amount of flawed thinking underlies the perception of differences between Canadian and American evangelicals, and even between evangelicals in the southern states and elsewhere. First of all, there is the desire of Canadians to distance themselves from American excesses. Poll data show that Canadians in general do not feel as warmly about Americans as Americans feel about them. A *Maclean's*/Decima poll of 1989 concluded that Canadians view Americans as "obnoxious, pig-headed snobs" and that Canadians show an "increasing determination ... to preserve their independence from their superpower neighbour" (*Maclean's* 1989, 32). Historically, Canadians rejected revolution, protected their borders against American expansionist efforts, and maintained a notable degree of anti-American sentiment (Noll 1997; Lipset 1990). If Canadians distinguish themselves from Americans, it is the American tendency to distinguish themselves from all nations, which means people on both sides of the border are biased towards distinctiveness. Furthermore, scandals involving evangelical leaders have been more prominent south of the border, though evangelicals in Canada have not been exempt from scandal (Bibby 1993). Interviews indicated that this increased the desire for Canadian evangelicals to separate themselves from American evangelicalism. As Rawlyk was well aware, perceived differences that stem from these biases may be more wishful thinking than fact.

Second, it is easy to assume that evangelicals in the two countries mirror national cultural differences. Put another way, perceived evangelical differences may be no more than an extrapolation of national differences, which may or may not be accurate. If it is perceived (at least by Canadians) that Canadians are culturally distinct from Americans, it is easy to assume that American evangelicals differ from Canadian evangelicals in the same ways Canadians (think they) differ from Americans. Since evangelicals have historically resisted outside "worldly" influences, the tendency to parallel their national environment should at least remain an open question.

Third, it is easy to assume that the loudest southern evangelical voices are representative of the whole. The personalities and opinions of televangelists and evangelical spokespersons tend to give rise to stereotypes, even though it is likely that rank-and-file American evangelicals are very different from their spokespersons. Smith argues that most American evangelicals are moderate compared to the "noisy, entrepreneurial activists" who claim to represent them (1996, 1). Further, evangelicals in Canada may appear more peaceable in part because there are no dominant evangelical voices.[1]

Previous arguments aside, however, there are good reasons to expect differences between Canadian and American evangelicals.

One common line of argument is that evangelicals in Canada and the US differ because of their different national contexts. It is reasonable to assume that there are (still) some national differences that affect religious subcultures. Furthermore, it is likely that evangelicals on both sides of the border are influenced by their cultural milieus, at least to some degree. Both assumptions – that national differences persist and that evangelicals are affected by those differences – are reasonable but not definite, and both need to be true in order to find measurable differences between Canadian and American brands of evangelicalism. A quick look at arguments for and against both assumptions is helpful. Regarding the first assumption, most authors argue that national cultural differences exist, and that they stem from historical differences. I turn now to a brief historical and cultural comparison with a focus on the history of Christianity and evangelicalism, leaving the obvious similarities between the two countries for a later discussion.

HISTORICAL AND CULTURAL DIFFERENCES

In 1848 an English Methodist preacher, the Reverend James Dixon, made a fraternal visit to the US and Canada and was impressed by the cultural differences between the two countries. Here are excerpts from his observations, which he published the following year:

Every book I have read, and every person with whom I had conversed, after visiting America and Canada, united in their testimony as the great difference instantly felt on passing the boundary-line … the fact is indisputable … On the American side, the people are all life, elasticity, buoyancy, activity; on the Canadian side we have people who appear subdued, tame, spiritless, as if living much more under the spirit of fear than of hope. Again: on the American territory we behold men moving as if they had the idea that their calling was to act, to choose, to govern – at any rate to govern themselves; on the Canada soil we see a race, perhaps more polite than the other, but who seem to live under the impression that their vocation is to receive orders, and obey. Then on the American side, you are placed in the midst of incessant bustle, agitation; … On the Canada shore we have comparatively still life; delicate, genteel, formal.

In relative agreement with the Reverend Mr. Dixon are three contemporary historians – Canadian George A. Rawlyk, American Mark A. Noll, and Englishman David W. Bebbington[2] – whose work makes a comparative history of evangelicalism in the United States and Canada possible. For these scholars, Canadian evangelicalism is distinct from its American counterpart. This is in part because of evangelicalism's "chameleon-like ability to adapt" to its cultural surroundings, thus taking on the attributes of its local surroundings (Noll 1997, 11). Evangelicalism has "altered its nature enormously over time" and space (Bebbington 1994, 184).

Typically, Canadian evangelicals are seen as differing from American evangelicals because of their stronger ties with Britain, ties that now place them somewhere between British and American evangelicalism. From Britain, they have inherited tradition and decorum, in contrast to the sectarianism and enthusiasm brought up from the South. Thus, Canadian evangelicals presumably differ from their American counterparts in much the same way as American and British evangelicals differ. This is partly true, but as historians are quick to emphasize, Canadian evangelicalism is more than a combination of British and American influences (cf. Bebbington 1997). It has developed a character of its own based on Canada's unique history and culture. In determining the historical sources of difference between branches of North American evangelicalism, then, one important question is: What historically can be attributed to the embracing of British evangelical influences, and what to the development of unique Canadian influences among Canadian evangelicals?

In the first centuries of European colonization in North America, the most important difference for religious comparisons was that from the outset the Catholic presence in Canada was significant, whereas it was comparatively insignificant in the early United States. Early Canadian Catholic settlements resulted in a time of relative religious toleration between Catholics and Protestants, in spite of British-French conflicts. After the British took control of Acadia in 1710, they guaranteed religious freedom to the Acadian French in the Atlantic region in the Treaty of Utrecht in 1713. Although conflict increased in 1740 and persisted up to the expulsion in 1755 of the Acadians from Nova Scotia, surprisingly good Catholic-Protestant relations endured (Noll 1992). Similarly, when France ceded Quebec to Britain in 1763, it was soon recognized that efforts to anglicize the French inhabitants were unlikely to succeed, and the Quebec Act of 1774 led to peaceful relations between the Catholic French and the British governors.

Catholic establishment in early French Canada also meant that church-state relations loomed large from the start in British North America. By contrast, the comparatively weak Catholic presence in the thirteen colonies that would later become the United States allowed for a Protestant hegemony that remained until the twentieth century. Church-state separation was agreed upon as early as 1639 by the first Baptist congregation in America, which was formed on

Rhode Island with the help of Roger Williams (Noll 1992). Furthermore, the relative religious diversity in the US compared to Canada meant that attempts to create an established church failed earlier in the US, and decisively in the Declaration of Independence.

In later centuries, three conflicts bolstered the resolve of Canadians to distance themselves from the US, thus opening the way for British influence. First, the War of Independence south of the border sent loyal British subjects fleeing to Canada, strengthening loyalism and increasing resistance to the anti-establishment tendencies of American patriots in Canada. In Quebec, resistance to American ways was strengthened by American invasions in 1775. In the Maritimes, the apolitical gospel of influential preacher Henry Alline along with the influx of American loyalists cemented anti-independence (Noll 1992). Second, the War of 1812 also focused Canadian anti-Americanism and nationalism. Canadians wanted to maintain ties with the old country. Loyalty, tradition, and respect for the past were virtues they espoused. Finally, the Civil War in the US further warned Canadians of the dangers of "extreme" democracy. The anti-slavery movement in the northern states divided religious groups along the Mason-Dixon line, most notably the Baptists in 1845, but also the Methodists (1844) and the Presbyterians (1837). These divisions were part of a greater trend towards schism in the southern country, contrasted with ecumenical tendencies in the North. The Civil War also fuelled the fires of civil religion, as Americans on both sides of the Mason-Dixon line clothed the conflict in religious terms. The tendency to use the Bible and millennialist language to legitimize national or regional causes is comparatively rare in Canada.

Although Canada was not free of anti-British sentiment, the minor rebellions against British control led by Louis-Joseph Papineau and William Lyon Mackenzie in the 1830s were most notable for the lack of support they received and their decisive defeat. The rebellions had the net effect of strengthening loyalism. The British North America Act itself, signed in 1867, hardly represented a decisive break from Britain but had much to do with the Canadian fear of assimilation to the US and Britain's cold feelings towards the colonies. In sum, these conflicts had the combined effect of distancing Canadians from American extremes and strengthening Canadian resolve to remain loyal to Britain. The general loyalist tone also affected churches and church leaders, who sought to maintain the religious traditions and decorum better suited to faithful British subjects. Furthermore, anti-establishment sentiment and civil religion were weaker in Canada.

In the nineteenth century a broad evangelicalism held sway in both countries, so the period is less important for national differences than the twentieth century. The latter brought at least three events that are significant to a discussion of US-Canada religious differences: the fundamentalist-modernist debate, the formation of the United Church of Canada, and the alignment of religious and political conservatism in the US. The fundamentalist-modernist debate heated up in the first decade of the twentieth century. In the wake of changes in higher education – including the prominence of evolutionary theory, adherence to the scientific method, and the loss of church control over universities – theologians began to question traditional views of the authority of the Bible, subjecting it to critical methods. The backlash from the conservatives included the writing of *The Fundamentals* between 1910 and 1915. This series of booklets, from which the movement fundamentalism received its name, defended traditional doctrine and biblical authority. By the 1920s, fiery spokespersons such as Presbyterian William Jennings Bryan on the fundamentalist side and Baptist Harry Emerson Fosdick on the modernist side fuelled the antagonism. The results of the modernist-fundamentalist conflict were significantly more widespread and longer lasting in the US than in Canada. Some US fundamentalist groups split from their denominations to form independent bodies, like the orthodox Presbyterians led by J. Gresham Machen. Fundamentalism's separatist tendencies were brought to a head in the US in the wake of the 1925 Scopes trial, where the conservative William Jennings Bryan opposed the teaching of evolution in schools, while attorney Clarence Darrow defended it. Although Bryan won the trial and evolution was banned in Tennessee for a time, the fundamentalists were presented as backward intolerant anti-intellectuals by the press, further alienating fundamentalists from the rapidly changing society. Fundamentalists in the US recoiled into separate enclaves, seeking to protect themselves from the evils of modernism. It was not until the 1940s that a group of more moderate neoevangelicals emerged from these enclaves and began to re-engage with society. In Canada there was no systemic fundamentalist-modernist division, and evangelicals did not polarize or encapsulate to such an extent. The Canadian T.T. Shields, a militant Canadian Baptist, succeeded in leading a group of dissenting churches out of the Baptist Convention of Ontario and Quebec but failed to create a national fundamentalist movement. Even though there were networks of self-identifying fundamentalists in Canada during this time, they were on the whole less militant and sectarian than their American counterparts.

While fundamentalism fuelled tension and schism in the South, Canadian Protestants were gathering to form the United Church of Canada, uniting Methodists, Congregationalists, and some Presbyterians in

1925. David Plaxton argues that the formation was possible because of a broadly shared moderate evangelical consensus, which tended to reject both the extremes of militant fundamentalism and of liberalism (1997, 108). The union illustrates the Canadian ecumenical spirit and the tendency to avoid perceived American extremes.

In the later twentieth century, evangelical engagement with society included more involvement in politics, goaded by politically active television preachers such as Pat Robertson, Jerry Falwell, and Jim Bakker. These and other evangelical spokespersons energized political debate about religious freedom, conservative economics, abortion, homosexuality, pornography, school prayer, and other issues in the 1980s. Evangelical voters were mobilized to align with certain presidential candidates who supported their causes, notably Ronald Reagan, George Bush, and Robertson himself, all Republicans. In recent decades, white evangelicals have tended to align themselves with the Republican party in the US, a correlation that is stronger among more active evangelicals (Kellstedt et al. 1996). Canadian evangelicals supported the socialist government of Tommy Douglas in Saskatchewan in 1944 as well as the conservative Social Credit party of William Aberhart in Alberta in 1935. More recently, the conservative Reform party – now part of the Canadian Alliance – has failed to attract the majority of evangelical voters in spite of its ties to evangelicalism. Evangelical political alignment is less clear in Canada.

Any discussion of differences between Canada and the US must take into account the effects of geography and demography. In Canada, an expansive terrain coupled with a small population encouraged cooperation between churches and denominations. Churches found it necessary to pool resources to christianize the western provinces in particular. In 1924 only sixty-two percent of Presbyterian congregations in Ontario voted to join the United Church of Canada, whereas ninety-five percent of Presbyterian congregations in the sparsely populated West supported the union (Bebbington 1997, 40). A degree of anti-Americanism and anti-Catholicism also encouraged unity among Protestants, who believed that it was necessary to work together to establish a presence on the frontier lest the Catholics or Americans get there first. In the US, a larger population on a smaller land mass spawned a less-cooperative spirit.

Demographic differences, especially to do with religious affiliation, are also important. In Canada, deference to traditional religious forms meant more attempts towards religious establishment and less success for the sectarian Methodists and Baptists at the start of the nineteenth century. Presently in Canada, the Anglican, United, and

Catholic churches hold the allegiance of approximately two-thirds of Canadians, whereas in the US, Catholics, Methodists, Presbyterians, Congregationalists, and Episcopalians (sister denominations to Canada's big three) account for less than forty percent of Americans. To quote the historian Mark Noll: "Compared to Christianity in the States, Christianity in Canada was less fragmented, more culturally conservative, more closely tied to Europe, more respectful of tradition, more ecumenical, and less prone to separate evangelical theology and social outreach" (1992, 284).

quote this

Later (1997), Noll summarized evangelical differences in a systemic comparison. First, because Canadian evangelicalism is a smaller movement and less concerned about "ideological boundary-marking," Canadian evangelicals show greater *"flexibility of rapid deployment"* in that they can cooperate on projects that take less time and bureaucracy. Second, American *"myths of national origin,"* which include civil religion, individualism, and liberalism, have resulted in greater suspicion of inherited institutions and traditionalism, more entrepreneurial innovation, and the "exalted role of the language of freedom" in southern religion (1997, 14). Third, Canadian evangelicalism has the effect of *"moderating the political extremes."* Finally, Canadian evangelicalism is less polemical and features a "somewhat more accommodating spirit," which Noll calls *"mediating evangelicalism"* (1997, 17; italics in original). While he recognizes that these differences may have been diminishing since World War II, he argues that they still exist. The differences fit the common perception that Canadian evangelicals differ from American evangelicals in the same ways that Canadians differ from Americans, and also that Canadian evangelicalism is "more British" than the American brand.

These historical considerations inform present national cultural differences. Popular cultural commentators, including Lipset (*Continental Divide*), Malcohm (*The Canadians*), Berton (*Why We Act Like Canadians*), and others, have written rich national cultural comparisons of the two countries. Canadians are more "law-abiding, deferential to authority, cautious, prudent, elitist, moralistic, tolerant (of ethnic differences), cool, unemotional, and solemn," says Berton (quoted in Lipset 1990, 44). Lipset adds that they are less aggressive, that they prefer stronger central government, and that they are moderate, reliable but a bit dull, quiet, and less reactionary (1990, 42–5). These cultural commentators also agree that cultural differences exist, and that they stem from national historical differences. For Lipset, the key differences between the two nations are the disestablishmentarianism and revolution south of the border, contrasted with the northern tendency towards deference to authority and counterrevolution. This central difference results in greater individualism, populism, liberalism, and meritocracy in the US.

Besides these national cultural differences, there are many contemporary religious differences that likely effect evangelicalism.[3] One key difference is that Americans have higher levels of religious practice. Roughly forty percent of Americans claim to be in church on any given weekend, a number that has changed little in the last fifty years. By contrast, Canadian church attendance has fallen from over fifty percent in the 1950s to about twenty percent today. What accounts for this difference? There are explanations for religious vitality. Sociologist Reginald Bibby suggests that the cultural "rules" for the religious marketplace are different in the two countries: "In Canada, a pluralistic ideal means that religious groups are expected to co-exist for servicing. In the United States, the pursuit of truth means that religious groups are allowed to compete for truth" (1987, 217). American religious groups are more aggressive and entrepreneurial in expanding their markets. In Canada denominations prefer to meet the needs of their own in a spirit of tolerance and mutual respect for religious differences. Some argue that a more competitive pluralistic religious market makes for greater vitality, whereas religious lethargy and indifference are the natural results of weak competition.[4]

Other religious differences exist. The US has more religious groups than Canada, the result not only of schism but also of innovation – like the Latter Day Saints or Scientology. Canadian Christians have historically connected with social concerns to a greater extent than American Christians, who tend to emphasize individualistic virtues and morality, leaving public decisions and structural change to politics. The lack of loyalty to traditional denominations and a revolutionary anti-establishment culture results in greater voluntarism – the tendency to switch denominations – south of the border. There is less of an open market for religious innovation in Canada. As Bibby notes (1987), even Canadians who rarely participate in organized religion still identify with a religious tradition and call on it for religious rites like baptisms, weddings, and funerals. Congregational polity, where the power of the churches lies in the hands of the congregation, is predictably more common in American where populism, sectarianism, and a general distrust for established institutions runs high. Religious schools find state support in Canada but not in the US, where church-state separation is more decisive. Fundamentalists in Canada are comparatively rare. Finally, American churches are still more likely to embrace civil religious symbols and rhetoric than Canadian churches.

There is, of course, some debate over the historical or contemporary differences given above. To what extent are historical differences, which are assumed to give rise to current national cultural-religious differences, eroded by globalizing forces? The extent to which these differences ever resulted in widespread differences in beliefs, practices, and attitudes remains an open question. As we shall see below, some contemporary research undercuts assumed national cultural differences.

To this point, my discussion has focused on national differences. But scholars have noted regional cultural and religious differences within each country as well. Wilson and Ferris (1989) and Reed (1972) emphasize the enduring cultural distinctiveness of the American South, which is related to the predominance of evangelical religion, especially its Baptist brand, in that region. Elazar (1966), Gastil (1975), Lieske (1992), Zhu (1992), and others have all argued for distinctive regional differences within the US. Zhu demonstrates that regional cultural differences have important effects on individual beliefs, practices and norms.

In Canada, regionalism is often juxtaposed to nationalism in debates over Canadian identity. Canadian scholars argue that Canadians have a weaker national identity than Americans, but that stronger regional differences exist in Canada. Studies have shown that residents of the Prairies and the Atlantic Provinces have a sense of regional uniqueness, stemming largely from their perception of themselves as an inferior economic "hinterland" compared to the Ontario/Quebec "heartland" and a sense of isolation, exploitation, and alienation from the national government whose policies appear to favour the wealthy central provinces (Hiller 1991). The Prairies and the Maritimes are known to be more conservative socially than Ontario, Quebec, and British Columbia. These regional differences lead one to predict a greater evangelical conservatism in the American "Old South" and the Canadian Maritimes. However, such a prediction may be incorrect. The evangelicals in the American South or the Maritimes and Canadian Prairies are not necessarily more conservative vis-à-vis other evangelicals, but their relative size may give those regions a conservative tone.

Examining regional differences is important because perceived national differences may in fact be caused by regional distinctiveness. Put another way, American evangelicals may appear distinct from Canadian evangelicals, not because all Americans differ from all Canadians but because southern US evangelicals (or evangelicals in another region) are unique. If evangelicals in the American South are aggregated with northern American evangelicals, then the southern uniqueness may account for Canada-US differences.

In fact, it may be that the forty-ninth parallel is a relatively insignificant cultural boundary in comparison to regional differences within each country. Some recent research suggests that regional differences are more important than national differences (Baer, Grabb, and Johnston 1990; Garreau 1981). Works comparing Canada and the US must pay particular attention to the unique contribution of French Canada as well. However, in this particular study French Canada gets little attention because (Protestant) evangelicals in Quebec are too small a proportion of the population to analyze accurately based on national survey data.[5] I examine regional explanations throughout this research, but in the main I found them to be minimal (see appendix 3 for further discussion).

OUTSIDE INFLUENCES ON EVANGELICALISM

The second assumption that we need to consider is that the evangelical subculture in both countries (or at least one of the countries) is influenced by the larger national cultures in substantial ways. Do secular external influences infiltrate North American evangelicalism to a significant degree? The question relates to whether or not evangelicalism as a subculture is maintaining its orthodoxy (conservative beliefs) and orthopraxy (conservative practices) under significant secular pressure to accommodate. Leading all voices in a negative response has been James Davison Hunter.[6] Hunter finds evidence of significant secularization within American evangelicals as beliefs and morals have softened. In his view, the forces of modernity are too strong for the traditional boundaries of orthodoxy.

However, Hunter's evidence of weakening orthodoxy or orthopraxy has been called into question. Some argue for cyclical patterns of "resacralization" and secularization. For instance, Hunter's finding that young evangelicals are less orthodox than older evangelicals may not mean linear secularization but may simply indicate that evangelicals become more conservative as they age. Others argue for a continuous repositioning vis-à-vis secular society as evangelicalism engages its environment. The pattern of reformulating orthodoxies while maintaining the central tenets of the faith is typical.[7] Thus, the debate is not over whether evangelicals are unaffected by their cultural milieu but between linear secularization and a repositioning that leaves central tenets intact while allowing for certain (peripheral) beliefs and practices to be swayed by popular culture. This debate suggests that one cannot consider only linear accommodation away from orthodoxy as evidence of significant external influence. Of course, it is easiest to attribute internal changes to external forces if the changes take the same direction as societal trends.

If linear accommodation over time (in the direction of secularity) is not the only measure of external influence, then change over time may not be the only or best way to look for external influences. The primacy of internal or external influences can also be tested geographically. Any evidence that variation in evangelical beliefs, attitudes, and practices parallels national and regional variation lends support to the notion of significant external influences. In this regard it is helpful to compare evangelicals to nonevangelicals in their region (within-region differences), as well as to compare evangelicals across regions (between-region differences).

Alternative Causes of Variation

It is natural to assume that if there are differences between American and Canadian evangelicals, it is because North American evangelicals are not only evangelicals but also Canadians or Americans. Cultural differences between the two countries may help to explain evangelical differences. National-level influences, however, are not the only important source of variation. There is a complex array of interacting forces that influence any religious or social group, whether national, regional, institutional, or individual. To further complicate the issue, national-level differences may have regional, institutional, or individual causes. Alternative explanations include regional cultures, denominational uniqueness or the uniqueness of an individual church, demographic differences, and local contextual differences. These possibilities are examined where data are available. For an examination of possible regional and institutional sources of variation, see appendix 3.

WHENCE SIMILARITIES?

Canadian evangelicals may differ from American evangelicals in the same ways that Canadians differ from Americans. Evangelicals involve themselves in the everyday life of their society, and it is likely that some of the broader cultural differences rub off on them. But there are two sides to the coin. Just as there are reasons to suspect that evangelicals are influenced by their social surroundings, so there are good reasons to suspect that evangelicals resist societal influences. If there is anything at all to being an evangelical, data will reveal beliefs, behaviours, and attitudes that are unique to evangelicals, whereby they show little inclination to buckle under social pressure. After all, evangelicals take seriously the biblical command "Do not conform to this world" (Romans 12:2). While it is true, as Hunter found, that most evangelicals no longer think it is sinful to play cards, dance, or go to the movies, it is also true that most evangelicals do think it is sinful to engage in premarital sex or view pornographic materials. Unlike most of their American and Canadian counterparts, nearly all active evangelicals believe that Jesus Christ was miraculously born to a virgin, that the Bible is God's authoritative word, and that those who reject Jesus as Saviour will go to everlasting torment in hell. In spite of modern influences, therefore, evangelicals – particularly core evangelicals – will show substantial similarities.

What factors help explain similarities? The question is crucial to an understanding of geographic variation – or the lack thereof – within North American evangelicalism. Similarities can stem from historical similarities between the two nations, global forces, institutional influences, and subcultural strength.

Historical Similarities

Historians give at least three broad reasons for predicting similarities between evangelicals in both countries. First, early European settlers brought similar ideologies and religious affinities to both countries. Second, there was and is a significant flow of evangelical influences across the border. Third, British influences have taken a back seat to American influences in Canada in recent years.

Both Canada and the US received similar religious forms from Europe (largely Britain) because early immigration was primarily European. Imported religious groups included Congregationalists, Presbyterians, Anglicans, Methodists, and Catholics, though their distribution and density varied considerably. Evangelicals have also been influenced by popular Western intellectual and theological currents, including the "commonsense" reasoning of the Enlightenment and the scientific method, pragmatism, romanticism, premillennialism, inerrancy, holiness, fundamentalism, and the charismatic movement (Noll 1992; 1997).

Both countries lay claim to an "evangelical century" (the nineteenth), during which time evangelical Protestantism held sway in English North America until the start of the twentieth century, when evangelistic energy ran high in both countries in an effort to create a "Christian America" in the South and "God's Dominion" in the North. In the attempt to create a moral society, North American evangelicals led similar moral crusades, including those for temperance and sabbatarianism, in which nineteenth-century evangelical women were prominent catalysts. The Woman's Christian Temperance Union formed in both countries only a few years apart (Noll 1992, 278). Both countries also had significant anti-Catholic movements.

The two-way flow between countries was significant. Particularly from 1870 to 1950, fundamentalist and evangelical networks developed as ideas and spokespersons crossed the border. Moving north to south were such prominent leaders as A.B. Simpson, founder of the Christian and Missionary Alliance, and Aimee Semple McPherson, founder of the International Church of the Foursquare Gospel (Elliot 1993). In the other direction crossings were more frequent as leaders like Henry Alline and, more recently, Billy Graham and John Wimber, carried southern evangelicalism to the North. In addition, conservative Protestant loyalists, pacifists, escaping African slaves, and large numbers of prairie farmers moved in a northern direction (Westfall 1997). Many denominations and parachurch groups have moved from south to north as well. The Lutheran Church – Canada, Pentecostal Assemblies of Canada, and Canadian Conference of Southern Baptists are fairly recent denominational "branch-plants" from south of the border, and groups like Focus on the Family and Promise Keepers are American initiatives that have landed on Canadian soil.

Most commentators agree that American influences have surpassed British influences in Canada in the last fifty years, which suggests that historically recognized differences might be diminishing. Canada and the US seem to be moving closer together. Economically, they are now each other's biggest trading partner, forming the largest trading dyad in the world. American investment in the Canadian economy is massive, and Canadian investment in the US is growing (Nevitte 1996). The 1989 North American Free Trade Agreement is seen by some as a turning point in US-Canada relations, such that nationalism is curbed and economic links strengthened (Bromke and Nossal 1987). The adoption of the Charter of Rights and Freedoms in Canada is also seen as evidence of "Americanization." Culturally, the lion's share of anglophone television is imported from south of the border, and Canadian content laws have done little to save Canadian shows from the margins of prime-time viewing (Ferguson 1993; Anderson, Swimmer, and Suen 1997). John Meisel, sometime chairman of the Canadian Radio-Television and Telecommunication Commission, stated that, "inside every Canadian whether she or he knows it or not, there is, in fact, an American. The magnitude and effect of this American presence in us varies considerably from person to person, but it is ubiquitous and inescapable" because of the predominance of American media north of the border (quoted in Taras 2000, 192). Regarding social policy, some have observed patterns of convergence in American and Canadian policies because of increased networking and similar environments (Bennett 1991; Howlett 1994).[8]

While several trends suggest convergence, many commentators, Noll (1997) and Lipset (1990) among them, argue that important differences remain. To quote historian William Westfall, it seems that the two countries have "a long history of putting similar materials together in different ways," creating "two compatible but different religious cultures" (1997, 192).

One wonders, however, whether religious and cultural differences are diminishing as networking, communication, and border crossings increase. Recent survey evidence contradicts the conventional wisdom on cultural differences between Canada and the US. In contrast to Lipset, Nevitte (1996) argues that Canadians are not more deferential to authority than Americans, while Grabb and Curtis (2002) find no evidence that Americans place higher priority on "individualism and related democratic values" than do Canadians (2002, 45). Baer, Grabb, and Johnstone find "virtually no support" for the cultural differences posited by Lipset (1990, 693).

Globalizing Forces

Most of the historical-cultural comparisons discussed above limit their focus to North America. Others see similarities between Canada and the US within a broader context of international change. Inglehart (1990; 1997) and Nevitte (1996) see parallel "value" changes in advanced industrial societies, where the US and Canada are two countries in a much larger pattern. Using Maslow's well-known hierarchy of needs, Inglehart argues that those (older) segments of the population that have experienced such traumas as World War II and the Great Depression prioritize the "lower" needs of economic security and safety because they have experienced economic scarcity. Those born after 1945, who have enjoyed relative prosperity throughout their lives, take the fulfilment of economic needs for granted and are thus free to focus on the "higher" aesthetic, intellectual, and "self-actualization" needs. Inglehart uses evidence from the World Values Survey to show a shift from materialist values to post-materialist values. This shift has wide-ranging effects on people's orientation towards work, politics, family, morality, and of course religion.[9]

With industrialization and economic development, argue Inglehart and Baker (2000), societies tend to become increasingly secular and rational. However, this does not mean that people are secular. Instead, advanced industrial societies show the contrasting trends of decreasing allegiance to established religious institutions and "growing interest in spiritual concerns at the individual level" (2000, 41). Like Bibby's findings in Canada (1993, 2002), Inglehart sees a growing interest in spiritual things in the US and widespread concern about the meaning and purpose of life. While the trajectory towards self-expression and away from institutionalized religion is the dominant trend for advanced industrial societies, one should not assume that such countries are set on a path towards cultural convergence or that a new set of "global values" holds sway. The historical dominance of Christianity or Islam or Communism, for example, creates distinct cultural zones, differentiating between even the most advanced nations. The US is an anomaly, in fact, maintaining a high level of traditional values and religiosity in spite of being among the wealthiest nations in the world. Most other advanced industrial democracies including Canada (with the obvious exceptions of Ireland and Northern Ireland) are drifting away from traditional values and established religion to a greater degree.

For globalization theorists,[10] the late twentieth century was characterized, even transformed, by a dramatic increase in the international flow of goods, communication, and people across geographic, cultural, and political boundaries by which the "constraints of geography on social and cultural arrangements recede" (Waters 1995, 3). Transnational organizations, internet communication, and "virtual communities" make geographic borders less significant. Technological advances facilitate the movement of people, goods, and ideas, which in turn promotes the internationalization of economic, political, and religious organizations and movements (Coleman 1993). Not only are there "macro" changes such as global markets, international treaties, and international organizations but individuals develop global consciousness on the "micro" level as well. With the increased flow of people, goods, organizations, and ideas across the Canada-us border and within each country in recent decades, one might expect to find less national and regional distinctiveness in religiosity and thus considerable convergence in areas of belief, attitudes, and practice among evangelicals across North America.

While some transnational flows spawn homogeneity, certain proponents of globalization argue that increased border crossing does not necessarily predict or explain convergence between nations or religious groups. The encroachment of foreign goods, people, and media into one's world can cause a crisis of identity, such that identity is recreated and sometimes protected. Canadian national identity has often been strengthened by the perception that US influences will swallow up Canadian uniqueness. In Robertson's words, the process of globalization results in increased global consciousness coupled with a universalized expectation of "identity declarations" (1992, 27). For Robertson, globalization is a "twofold process involving the inter-penetration of the universalization of particularism and the particu-larization of universalism" (ibid., 100). By this he means that particular identities are maintained (though challenged) in globalized societies and that ways of identification become shared. For example, various modern fundamentalist movements – whether Islamic, Hindu, Jewish, or Christian – can be seen as a reaction to a bombardment of external forces, which threaten to undermine religious boundaries. For this reason globalization theory does not necessarily predict an under-mining of the identity of religious groups, since an international emphasis on individual and collective self-identity is embedded in the globalization process.

One might expect evangelicals to resist globalizing and moderniz-ing influences to some extent, particularly in those areas that form the basis of their collective identity. Differences may appear in mat-ters that are perceived to be less important. As Hexham and Poewe have argued, international religious movements maintain the mini-mum of elements – an "ecology of tradition" – that are uniform across countries, while other elements "take on local colour" (1997, 43; Poewe 1994, 17). Evangelicals on both sides of the border are likely to show minimal variation in central tenets of the faith but may vary on peripheral issues.[11]

New Institutionalism

There is much more to be said about the undermining effects of global forces on geographic or religious boundaries, but globalization is not the only helpful theoretical lens. Proponents of the "new institution-alism" (Powell and DiMaggio 1991; Scott and Meyer 1994) focus on institutions and their environments. The argument, in a nutshell, is that organizations now rationalize and bureaucratize less for reasons of efficiency and competition (as purported by the "old" paradigm in institutional theory) and more for reasons related to the "structuration of organizational fields" (DiMaggio and Powell 1991, 64). Organiza-tional fields – or recognized areas of institutional life (e.g., schools, hospitals, car manufacturing plants, etc.) – pressure organizations to orient or adapt themselves towards the "structure" (the taken-for-granted scripts and prescriptions for action) that defines the organi-zational field, leading to homogeneity within the field, which is called "isomorphism" (ibid., 66; Meyer and Rowan 1991, 50). New Institu-tionalists focus their attention on the environments that shape the organization more than on the inner dynamics of the organizations themselves. In doing so, they emphasize that the norms and scripts that shape institutions are superorganizational, and that organizational fields are often national and international in scope. The boundaries of a field are defined by function, not by geography (Scott and Meyer 1991, 117–18).

According to DiMaggio (1983), an organizational field is defined by "1) increased interaction between organizations in the field; 2) the emergence of interorganizational structures of domination and patterns of coalition; 3) an increase in the information load in the field; and 4) the development of mutual awareness among participants in the organizations that they are involved in a common enterprise."

One could argue that these traits are present in evangelicalism in North America. The prominence of evangelical organizations like the National Association of Evangelicals, Christian Coalition, Focus on the Family, Evangelical Fellowship of Canada, and other groups has created new patterns of coalition and domination within evangelicalism. Ecumenical efforts like Promise Keepers, March for Jesus, Vision 2000, groups that promote "concerts of prayer," Billy Graham Crusades, and many other national and international organizations bring evangelicals of every stripe together in increasing frequency. The result has been an increased awareness among evangelicals that they are involved in a common enterprise, which in turn increases cooperation between them.

In addition, others have noticed a generic evangelicalism promoted by evangelical institutions. Wagner (1997), for instance, finds a "generic" panconservative Christianity in the Christian schools she studied. With the proliferation of religious special interest groups (Wuthnow 1988), Wagner suggests that denominational differences are honed down because the support base from one denomination is too small, and curricula and teachers need to be drawn from the wider evangelical pool.

Growing interaction between evangelical organizations is evident as well. Poewe demonstrates increased international networking among Pentecostal organizations. She notes that some megachurches function much like international corporations in the exporting of religious products (Poewe 1994, 5). Coleman (1993) shows how one aspect of conservative Protestant ideology was imported from the US and diffused by an organization in Sweden. Recent research by Michael Wilkinson on the global interconnectedness of ethnic Pentecostals (2000) and Mark Chapman's work on networks between evangelical organizations in one Ontario city (1998) indicate that evangelicals are interconnected. Hunter (1987, 172–8) has documented the dissemination of (less-orthodox) evangelical beliefs and attitudes through evangelical colleges and universities, while Shibley (1996) has demonstrated that evangelicalism in the US has been southernized by the spread of southern-style evangelicalism into the North.

Distinctive Subculture

One final approach to understanding similarities between Canadian and American evangelicals revolves around the notion of a distinctive subculture. The argument, which overlaps with the previous two, is that evangelicals are similar across geographical boundaries because they are part of a powerful and pervasive subculture, which overrides differences that may exist in the broader cultural environments.

As already noted, evangelicals are prolific producers and disseminators of popular religious culture.[12] Over the years, evangelicals have established their own educational institutions, special interest groups, denominations, radio and TV programs, music, books, and magazines. Children are socialized by attending evangelical schools, listening to evangelical contemporary music, reading evangelical comic books and magazines, buying evangelical toys and games, attending social events with other evangelicals, even attending evangelical colleges and graduate schools. In other words, evangelicals have created the institutional base and the cultural commodities necessary for a distinctive culture and plausibility structure (Hammond and Hunter 1984; Berger 1967). In 1995, some 2,500 Christian bookstores in the US sold over three billion dollars' worth of evangelical literature, music, videos, T-shirts, greeting cards, and a host of other items (Christopherson 1997).

Olson (1993) and Smith et al. (1998) make this argument in their efforts to explain religious vitality. Smith promotes a subcultural identity theory in which he argues that evangelicals have a strong sense of identity and boundaries that distinguish them from other groups. He concludes more generally: "Religion survives and can thrive in pluralistic, modern society by embedding itself in subcultures that offer satisfying morally orienting collective identities which provide adherents meaning and belonging" (1998, 118).

In sum, previous research suggests that evangelicals evidence a strong subculture with clear identities and moral and doctrinal boundaries. It is the content of that identity and the scope of those boundaries that I now examine. Cultures, or subcultures, have at least three components: identity, boundary maintenance, and norms (Welch et al. 1995; Leege 1993). If the components are powerful and pervasive, strong, clear identities and boundaries should be evident.

3 A Distinctive Evangelical Subculture?

Evangelicals are known to be distinctive in North America, and much of what is considered distinctive about evangelicals is less than complimentary. According to Smith, "The dominant image that many nonevangelical Americans hold of American evangelicals can be characterized as contentiously exclusivist, self-congratulatory, and intolerant of diversity. And many of the spokespeople for the Christian Right certainly provide evidence to substantiate that view" (2000, 21). Smith dedicates his book to refuting these stereotypes, arguing for a more ambivalent, tolerant, and nonthreatening rank-and-file evangelical. He demonstrates the importance of listening to evangelicals themselves to gain a clear picture of what they espouse. What do evangelicals say are the central characteristics of an evangelical, and what do they say distinguishes them from nonevangelicals?

Not surprisingly, core evangelicals evinced strong attachments to their evangelicalism. "I am a Christian first and foremost" was the decisive self-identity of one elderly Baptist in Minnesota. Like core members of any group, she internalized a group identity as part of her personal identity. Scholars of identity creation tell us that the groups to which we feel connected shape much of our sense of who we are – that is, our self-concept or self-identity. Individuals may identify with social groups based on gender, nationality, religion, politics, and other social categories. Group identity has emotive aspects (emotional attachment to the group) and cognitive aspects (knowledge of being part of the group). Tajfel defines group identity as "the individual's knowledge that he/she belongs to certain social groups together with some emotional and value significance to

him/her of the group membership" (cited in Turner 1982, 18). Therefore, people with an evangelical group identity have been influenced
by the evangelical subculture to the extent that they have internalized
the evangelical identity into their self-concept and place some affective or emotive significance on that identity.

Furthermore, group members are often "group conscious," or committed to action to realize group interests. They also exhibit "group
affect," the positive or negative valence attached to other groups in
their environment (Conover 1988, 53). People tend to give a positive
valence to groups they identify with and a negative valence to groups
that resist their group interests (or at least are perceived to do so).
Core evangelicals have a clear group identity, they are group conscious, and they share negative (and positive) opinions towards certain groups. Group identity and boundary maintenance allow for the
creation of cognitive and social categories that distinguish between
groups. As Lamont and Fournier suggest, these cultural differences
become part of the "institutionalized repertoires" that structure social
life. Cultural signals (stemming from the social significance applied
to racial, class, gender, religious, and other differences) are mobilized
in exclusionary practices that affect the social positioning of individuals. Subcultures then institutionalize differences that have a powerful effect on the structuring of everyday life (1992, 7).

If it is true that evangelicals are a distinctive subculture with clear
boundaries, then core evangelicals should be able to articulate a clear
religious identity that is distinguishable from other religious identities. During my 118 face-to-face interviews, respondents were asked
open-ended identity questions, allowing the core evangelicals to
identify themselves religiously with minimal structure or prompting
(see appendix 1, questions 12 to 16). Responses showed striking similarity in all four regions where interviews took place. To illustrate,
answers from four typical respondents are given below. They were
each asked how they would identify themselves religiously to an
acquaintance:

"I would say I am a conservative Bible-centred Christian, evangelistic, with
a world vision" (Lutheran pastor, Minnesota).

"I would identify myself as being a Christian based on the authority of the
word of God and what it says about a person's relationship with Him [God]"
(retired Pentecostal man, New Brunswick).

"I think I would start off by saying that I'm a Bible-believing Christian, that
Jesus Christ has made a difference in my life" (middle-aged Baptist mother,
Mississippi).

"As an evangelical Christian" (elderly Mennonite woman, Manitoba).

There is nothing in these responses that might help to identify the location of the interview, or the denomination or personal demographics of the respondents. Such is the case of most responses to questions about religious identity. Denominationally distinctive answers (e.g., "I would say I am a Nazarene"), while not uncommon, were a clear minority. There was no way to distinguish responses on the basis of country or region in which the interview was held.

These examples also illustrate the common themes in evangelical identity responses, such as emphasis on the Bible, the work of Christ, evangelism, and a divine relationship with God. A content analysis of interview responses revealed two types of response, those related to the "scope" of the individual's religious identity and those related to its "content." Responses in the "scope" category indicated how broadly or narrowly the person identified himself or herself religiously. Responses like "I am a Christian," "I am a Pentecostal," or "I am a member of the Assemblies of God" indicate three concentric circles of scope – religion, tradition, and denomination. In the first response, evangelicals place themselves in the broadest category, identifying with all Christians, and in the last response, they identify with the narrowest category of denomination. Other evangelicals identify themselves along the "content" dimension. "Content" responses usually include a list of beliefs, experiences, or practices by which evangelicals define themselves religiously. For example: "Well, I would say that I believed the Bible is the true word of God and that Jesus is God's Son." Content responses fall into four subcategories, which seem to fit best into David Bebbington's "quadrilateral" (1989). Bebbington argues that throughout its history evangelicalism has been defined by four components: biblicism, which asserts the ultimate authority of the Bible; activism, or the importance of evangelism and religious involvement; conversionism, which stresses being "born again"; and crucicentrism, or the centrality of Christ's work on the cross (1989, 2–17). These four components are emphatically upheld in nearly all the interviews. Table 3.1 presents the frequency of scope and content responses.[1]

Looking at the content responses, we see that conversionism is the most common ingredient in evangelical identity responses. Active evangelicals emphasize their "born again," or conversion, experience as central to their religious identity. Many evangelicals consider their conversion the most significant event in their lives and can as readily state the date and time of their "rebirth" as their natural birth. Ninety-four percent of the respondents claim to have been born again, and eighty percent stated that they experienced a one-time

Table 3.1
Content and Scope Responses to Identity Questions

Content	%	Scope	%
Conversionism	37.9	Christian	49.3
Crucicentrism	27.6	Tradition	24
Biblicism	23.7	Denomination	26.7
Activism	10.8		

Source: CE sample, interviews only (N = 118), 1995.
* The percent of content and scope responses is based on the percent of the cumulative total
of responses to questions 12, 14, and 16 (see appendix 1). More than one content response may be
given in each question. For example, a person may make reference both to the need for conversion
and belief in the Bible in one response.

conversion.[2] The next most frequent categories are the belief-based items of crucicentrism and biblicism. In order to be an evangelical, one must believe that Jesus' death on the cross is the only means to salvation, and one must hold a high view of the Bible. While conversion allows an evangelical entry into the evangelical fold, true converts will adhere to these certain doctrines. Beliefs and conversion themes were much more common than the practice-based activism themes. In fact, only one respondent mentioned a specific behaviour – "prayer and Bible study" – when identifying himself initially, while all the others identified themselves by conversion and beliefs. Obviously, the evangelical identity has more to do with what one believes than with what one does.[3]

Activism responses may be relatively rare because behavioural requirements for inclusion in the "evangelical" fold are troublesome for core evangelicals. This ambiguity became evident when respondents were asked to define "Christian" and "evangelical." Many respondents wanted some sort of behavioural evidence of conversion, but most were not specific about the sort of behaviours they had in mind. Only a few mentioned church attendance, Bible reading or prayer; most responded in terms of general lifestyle, like this young Baptist woman: "I would say someone [is a Christian] who has identified Jesus as the true son of God, who has given their life to Him, and yielded their will and has asked God to be their Lord and Saviour, and, um, I think that if that is true you will see a change, that their lives will be changed for the good." For many, then, the salvation experience alone is not enough: a Christian needs to "walk the walk," or "follow the teachings of Christ."

Some respondents seemed to think that adding a behavioural element to their definition of a Christian compromised their belief that salvation is "by grace through faith alone." When asked whether he would add any specific beliefs or practices to his definition of a Christian, one retired salesman from New Brunswick simply stated, "You can't add anything to the finished work of Christ." Evangelicals don't believe that salvation is gained through good works, yet they do believe that true conversion will lead to godly living. One perceptive Mennonite pastor, when asked whether he would add beliefs or practices to his conversionist definition of a Christian, said: "Um, if that question is in the behavioural sense, my tendency would be to say no. Theologically, most definitely. But I think the question is often meant behaviourally, do you have to look, smell, or feel a certain way, and I say no." He seems to suggest that truly converted Christians do certain things in obedience to the imperatives of the Bible, but he realized that conservatives often put legalistic requirements on converts that are peripheral to salvation. Evangelicals want to say that salvation is not based on what one does, but that, as Weber pointed out in *The Protestant Ethic and the Spirit of Capitalism* (1958), there is behavioural evidence of salvation.

The self-identity of evangelicals includes one other emphasis, that of a divine relationship. As described by an elderly Maritime Baptist man: "I would say that I was a child of God, that Jesus Christ was the only way to receive eternal life, and that religion will not be important when you get to heaven, but a relationship with Jesus Christ is the only way." Over one-third of the interviewees emphasize that their faith is a "relationship" (getting to know God personally through Bible reading, prayer, and fellowship with other believers), not a "religion" (ritual or religious tradition). For the evangelical, this divine relationship begins at conversion. While believing the right things is important, it is not enough; for the individual must enter into a relationship through the conversion process and then cultivate it through worship, Bible study, and prayer. In his survey of 1,215 evangelical laity, pastors, and leaders at Vision 2000 Canada Consultations on Evangelism across Canada, Reginald Bibby states that when "asked about the aspects of their faith that are most important to them personally ... these leaders fairly uniformly tended to emphasize their relationship to God, confessing Christ as Saviour and Lord, prayer, caring for others, and sharing their faith" (Bibby 1995, 3). With so strong a tendency among church leaders, it is not surprising that the same emphases cropped up in my sample.

Based on the content analysis of all identity responses, I conclude that for evangelicals, their identity is relational (that is, it involves a relationship with God in which conversion is the necessary first step), with doctrinal boundaries. Thus, conversion and correct beliefs determine whether someone is or is not a truly converted evangelical.

We move now to the question of scope. As shown in Table 3.1, most evangelicals identify themselves as part of the broad category of "Christian." In a follow-up question, respondents were asked if they would identify themselves by a tradition (evangelical, Pentecostal, fundamentalist, etc.), as a Protestant, or as a Christian. Seventy-five percent chose the final category. This suggests that evangelicals consider themselves part of a group of believers that encompasses more than conservative Protestantism. But does this mean that evangelicals categorize themselves with all Christians, including liberal Protestants and Catholics? Not necessarily. As the respondent Naomi MacDonald made clear (see chapter 1), the Christian and evangelical labels are synonyms in the minds of most interviewees.

The uniformity in identity responses is notable. Evangelicals in all regions and denominations use similar language to discuss their identity and to define what they mean by "Christian." Whether Canadian or American, Baptist or Lutheran, they all emphasize biblicism, crucicentrism, conversionism, and, to a lesser extent, activism. There are no significant regional or national differences between respondents in any of these identity items, indicating that the basic aspects of evangelical identity is widely shared in North America, at least among active evangelicals. In each region, roughly two-thirds of interviewees preferred to identify as evangelical, instead of Pentecostal, charismatic, fundamentalist, or mainline Protestant.

However, there is an interesting national difference in emphasis. The American evangelicals I interviewed, especially those in Mississippi, stressed that some who claim to be Christian don't live like Christians, while Canadian evangelicals held that the label "Christian" is too broadly applied. As indicated in chapter 1, the difference seems to suggest that the term Christian is more widely understood in the evangelical sense (emphasizing orthodox beliefs and conversion) in the US, than in Canada. While American respondents did not decry the meaninglessness of the term Christian, they lamented the fact that people did not live like Christians. In Canada, respondents tried to establish that their definition of Christian differs from the accepted definition of non-evangelicals. The evangelical definition seems to hold sway in the US particularly in the South, likely because of their regional dominance. Compare these responses, first from a Baptist woman in Mississippi and the second from a Nazarene man in Manitoba.

[A Christian is] one that has accepted Jesus Christ as Lord and Saviour of their lives and that fact has made a difference in their life, they are changed. [Are there specific beliefs and practices that are essential to a Christian?] Yes there are. Just the very fact that they've accepted the Lord should influence how they treat others, in their showing love to others and in their actions and reactions to things ... Not that you can always judge somebody if someone is a Christian by their behaviour, but I think it's an indication.

[To identify myself religiously], I would start by telling him "Look, I'm a Christian," and we would have to start talking about what that means because the word Christian has been seriously used and abused ... and it [has] become almost meaningless ... There are plenty of people who say they are Christians – "I'm a Christian, I don't believe what the Bible says, I think its all a bunch of hogwash but I'm a Christian" – ... so what the heck is a Christian these days? We used to know but we don't know any more.

The Canadian respondent went on to define a Christian as a "follower of Jesus Christ" and explained that a follower of Christ is someone who obeys the central teachings of Christ and believes in the truth of the Bible. His definition allowed him to infuse the identity "Christian" with meaning and behavioural requirements.

To sum up, when evangelicals are asked to define themselves, they usually indicate that they are Christian, which they define according to certain orthodox beliefs about the work of Christ and the Bible, and on the strength of a conversion experience and, to a lesser extent, a godly lifestyle. For evangelicals, not all people who identify themselves as Christians or affiliate with evangelical or mainline Christian churches are "true" Christians, only those who meet these requirements, which are fundamental to the evangelical identity. While there was no perceivable variation in how the content and scope of the evangelical identity are articulated interviews did reveal some minor variation in how the scope dimension is applied.

While it is clear that evangelicals do not share as wide a definition of the "Christian" category as nonevangelicals (except where numerical dominance has meant that their narrower definitions holds sway), it is not yet clear exactly how they determine where the division between Christian and non-Christian is drawn. Is inclusion in the Christian category based solely on correct beliefs and a conversion experience, or do evangelicals further limit the scope of possible Christians based on denominational, behavioural or attitudinal boundaries?

BOUNDARY MAINTENANCE

Evangelicals maintain group boundaries primarily through their theological and moral orthodoxy (Hunter 1987). We have seen much of what makes them theologically distinctive in their emphasis on conversionism, crucicentrism, biblicism, and activism. As we shall see in later chapters, evangelicals also maintain boundaries through their strict morality, especially in the area of traditional family values. Based on these distinctions, evangelicals may see certain individuals or groups of individuals as non-Christian because they do not hold positions or agendas that mesh with the evangelical identity. Below we test the status of three loosely defined groups. The respondents were simply asked whether Catholics, racists, or homosexuals could be Christians. The unprompted responses are categorized in Table 3.2 below. Regional percentages are not given because regional differences are minimal.

All the evangelicals I interviewed agree that Catholics could be included in their understanding of what a Christian is. "Yes, some are [Christian]," or, "Definitely, I have Catholic friends who I know are Christian," are common emphatic responses. A few have reservations; one elderly Pentecostal in Manitoba, for example, agreed that Catholics could be saved but admitted he had difficulty with some points of Catholic doctrine, such as "allegiance to Mary." He went on to say that people in any denomination could be saved and that not even all Pentecostals were saved. These responses are consistent with a belief- and conversion-based "Christian" identity that transcends denominational divisions and even the division between Protestant and Catholic. None of the core evangelicals suggested that their definition of Christian was restricted to certain denominations or even to Protestants.

Respondents were for more hesitant to include racists or homosexuals in the Christian category. Most often respondents gave qualified positive or qualified negative responses, indicating that they thought that a racist or a homosexual could be a Christian based on the belief/conversion criteria, but that these types pushed the limits of evangelical behavioural norms. Respondents made it clear that all Christians struggle with sin, yet they wanted to see an effort on the part of homosexuals (at least the sexually active ones) or racists to purge themselves of those attributes, which nearly all agreed were sinful.

The most common qualified response with regard to homosexuals was that those with a homosexual orientation could be Christian, but only "if they are not practising." One Mennonite pastor said that Christians tend to be judgmental about homosexuality and that he would be more judgmental where homosexuality was "flaunted." He believed, however, that people can have homosexual tendencies, just as people can have alcoholic tendencies, yet such tendencies are not in themselves necessarily sinful. The vagueness of the behavioural

Table 3.2
Groups That Could Be Considered Christian by Evangelicals

"Could a ___ be a Christian?" (N = 119)	Catholic	Racist	Homosexual
% Yes	96.6	43.5	30.5
% Yes, qualified ("Yes, if ...")	3.4	31.3	39.9
% No, qualified ("No, unless ...")		4.3	12.7
% No		20.9	16.9

Source: CE sample, interviews only (N = 118), 1995.

requirements for acceptance into the "Christian" category is related to the wide variation in answers that I received.

The division between Christian and non-Christian is not the only salient boundary for evangelicals. Evangelicals are also concerned about reaching their group goals in the public spheres of politics, education, and economics, despite resistance from other groups. How do evangelicals draw boundaries between groups in these spheres? It is difficult to apply the private criteria of belief and conversion, on which their category "Christian" is based, to the public sector. Evangelicals must evaluate groups based on publicly available information about group goals and on their own experiences with those groups.

Group Consciousness and Affect

Core evangelicals, through their socialization in the evangelical subculture, develop group consciousness, which includes a sense of group goals as well as knowledge of other groups' positions with respect to their goals. Groups that are perceived to hold agendas that oppose evangelical goals are "outgroups," and those that hold similar positions or are at least empathetic to evangelical positions are given "ingroup" status (Conover 1988, 54). Naturally, group members tend to feel positively towards ingroups and antagonistic towards outgroups.

In many cases, evangelicals develop opinions about groups based on cues from the pulpit, from evangelical spokespersons and other evangelicals, from the pronouncements of the group itself, or even from personal experience with group members (Welch et al., 1995). These evangelical spokespersons are often connected to a bulwark of special-interest groups that lobby for orthodoxy in political policies and institutions. Often their efforts rotate around protecting the traditional family, moral education, and religious and economic freedom (Hunter 1984; 1991). One does not need to travel in evangelical circles for long to hear pronouncements against groups that support homosexual rights or prochoice agendas. Such cues can lead to strong affective opinions, especially if the issue has prompted heated debate in the past.[4] The strength of the reaction to the group is affected by the salience of issues associated with the group – do they attack or support important group goals? – and by the clarity of the group's positions – does the group publicize its agenda, and do leaders and activists vilify or promote the group? (Conover 1988, 60).

One indication that pastors speak about the issues that influence opinions towards groups is available from the survey. I asked pastors how often they spoke on various subjects in their sermons on a scale from nearly weekly to hardly ever/never. The thirty-nine pastors I interviewed were most likely to speak (monthly or more) on biblical authority, family breakdown, heterosexual morality, drugs and violence, and media. They were likely to speak on poverty, cults, abortion, and homosexuality several times a year, and less often on public education, patriotism, and the environment. They rarely if ever spoke on political candidates. Not surprisingly, evangelicals hear more often about family values and traditional morality from the pulpit than about social-justice issues or other agendas. As a result, evangelicals tend to view certain doctrinal and moral issues as salient and worth protecting.

Interview respondents often indicate by their responses that they connect affective labels to social groups in their minds. One Manitoba Baptist stated: "I don't know what a secular humanist is, but I am probably against it." Negative or positive attitudes towards a group do not necessitate even a minimal familiarity with the actual goals or positions of the group (cf. Conover and Feldman 1981). Even some of the pastors that I interviewed were at a loss as to what "secular humanists" or "new agers" were, yet nearly all respondents gave them negative ratings without hesitation. What is important to group affect is that the evangelical has internalized cues about the group.

To explore how group affect influences evangelical boundary creation and maintenance, I asked evangelicals "how close or how far" they felt towards a variety of groups, including Right to Life, Catholics, feminists, the American Civil Liberties Union (ACLU) and many others. Table 3.3 gives the percentage of those who stated that they felt close or very close to the group in question. Groups like Right to Life and various evangelical groups received predominately "close" ratings, while groups like the new age movement, movie producers, and secular humanists received "far" ratings. While there was some variation in responses between US and Canadian evangelicals, there was overall agreement.

Table 3.3 also gives the results of an exploratory factor analysis performed on these close/far questions. Factor analysis is used to determine whether a large number of questions could be grouped into fewer factors that made theoretical sense. Put simply, it identifies groups of items that tap into the same factor or concept.[5] The close far questions were grouped according to five factors, given with their factor loadings in the table. A factor loading simply indicates the strength of the connection between the item and the underlying factor.

The factor analysis groupings seem to be divided according to their ingroup-outgroup status and by the type of organization (religious body and special-interest group). The Right to Life (factor 5) and Co-evangelicals (factor 2) can be interpreted to be consensus ingroups for evangelicals, and most evangelicals feel close to these groups. The Ecumenism factor (factor 3) includes religious bodies towards which evangelicals generally feel indifferent, neither too close nor too far from them, and which evangelicals probably view as neither a threat nor a strong ally. Most evangelicals feel far from what they perceive to be the political establishment (factor 1) and very far from the perceived cultural establishment (factor 4), indicating that these groups receive outgroup status from most evangelicals. Not all evangelicals feel equally far from the political groups (factor 1), however. Canadian and politically liberal American evangelicals feel closer to the groups in factor 1. It may be that the groups in factor 1 are more disturbing to politically conservative evangelicals (who constiture the majority in the us), but that the groups in factor 4 are seen as a threat to moral and theological orthodoxy on which all evangelicals agree. Thus, factor analysis supports the contention that evangelicals create group boundaries on which there is relative agreement across national and denominational boundaries.

Evidence presented to this point suggests that core evangelicals maintain distinctiveness with their "Christian" identity and the clear requirements they have for inclusion into the "Christian" category on the individual level. On the group level, many evangelicals have affective labels for other social groups, giving them a set of ingroup-outgroup boundaries and a sense of distinctiveness. Another way evangelicals maintain their distinctiveness is through tension with the world.[6] This tension is not fixed on any particular social group but is based on an evaluation of the general state of the society around them. If evangelicals perceive antagonism from nonevangelicals, or feel that society is deteriorating around them, such feelings will increase their sense of distinctiveness from the rest of the world

Table 3.3
Factor Analysis of Group Distance Items

FACTOR 1 – Political Establishment	Loading	% close*
NCC/CCC	0.756	12.6
ACLU	0.689	0.8
Environmentalists	0.668	21.2
Feminists	0.643	7.2
Government	0.557	4.8
FACTOR 2 – Co-Evangelicals		
NAE/EFC	0.763	60.3
Canadian Evangelicals	0.743	65.7
US Evangelicals	0.742	74.6
Southern Baptists	0.614	60.9
Fundamentalists	0.552	46.5
Pentecostals	0.551	58.3
FACTOR 3 – Ecumenism		
Jews	0.775	25.3
Catholics	0.681	29.0
Episcopalians	0.448	24.9
FACTOR 4 – Cultural Establishment		
Secular Humanists	0.829	1.9
New Age Movement	0.778	0
Movie Producers	0.624	0
Homosexuals	0.51	3.0
FACTOR – 5		
Right to Life	0.806	76.8

Source: CE sample, 1995.
*Percent who feel close or very close to the group.
NCC – National Council of Churches (US)
CCC – Canadian Council of Churches
ACLU – American Civil Liberities Union
NAE – National Association of Evangelicals (US)
EFC – Evangelical Fellowship of Canada

and encourage the use of affective labels and the creation and maintenance of boundaries. I asked all CE respondents whether they had been "put down or ridiculed" because of their Christian faith and I asked whether they could recount an example. Roughly seventy percent of respondents said they had been ridiculed, and about sixty percent of interviewees gave an example.[7] Evangelicals stated that they are most commonly criticized for what they believe or for their moral prohibitions. Some respondents were only able to recall vague instances of ridicule while other accounts were recent and salient. The difference likely relates to the degree to which the evangelical verbalized displeasure with unorthodoxy, as was the case for this Pentecostal Minnesotan: "Oh, when was it – two weeks ago? A bunch of guys and girls were sitting around my desk [at work] talking about how they were going to go off and get drunk that weekend – parties they were going to, the dates they were getting and each of them was reserving a hotel room for the weekend. I spoke up against it – 'Why are you guys doing that?' 'Well, it will be fun.' 'Well, don't you think it's wrong?' ... 'Why?' They are totally devoid of right and wrong ... they called me a 'Jesus freak' or something like that and swore at me and said, 'oh, shut up.' That was the most recent one."

Respondents were also asked: "Have you ever felt pressure from people around you to do things you feel are wrong?" Again, nearly seventy percent of the total sample said they have felt pressured, and about half of the interviewees gave examples. Some of those who indicated that they did not feel pressured to do wrong seem to mean not that they had never been pressured but that they did not feel strongly tempted to succumb to the pressure. Others indicated that they had been pressured to stretch their moral boundaries, but that it was not important to them. Still others gave pointed examples. A pastor in Manitoba described the following instance: "Just had a fellow come into my office [at church] the other day and fix my photocopier, and he gave me his home phone number and he said, 'Next time you need your photocopier fixed call me, I will give it to you cheaper.' I'm sure that is against company policy, and I was shocked that he would suggest it to me, a pastor ..."

Many respondents indicated that encounters such as these were not isolated events. Since the majority of core evangelicals had negative encounters with nonevangelicals, the boundaries that separate them are more salient. In addition, more than ninety percent of respondents believed that the "values in this country" are "becoming worse." It is likely that the distinctiveness of being an evangelical is enhanced by a sense that much of the rest of society is deteriorating.[8]

If evangelicals feel tension with society, they will most likely prefer to interact with their own. The tendency for groups that experience such tension with the larger society to minimize relationships outside their religious group is called "social encapsulation" (Stark and Bainbridge 1985, 60). Olson has found that conservative Protestants tend to have closer fellowship ties with their own kind than do mainline Protestants, which increases their sense of distinctiveness (1993). Frequent interaction with those of like faith also allows evangelicals to maintain the plausibility of their distinctive faith (Berger 1967, 1992) and increases commitment.[9] Do core evangelicals interact primarily with other evangelicals? On average, core evangelicals stated that between two and three of their five closest friends attended their congregation. When asked how many of these friends were non-Christian, nearly sixty percent stated that none of them were, while only ten percent had three or more non-Christian friends among the five. These findings reinforce the distinctiveness of the core evangelicals as indicated by their social encapsulation.[10]

In this chapter, I have argued that evangelicalism is a subculture with clear boundaries and identities that allow evangelicals to maintain their distinctiveness. The mechanisms by which their distinctiveness is maintained are the same mechanisms that explain similarities between regions. Their distinctive character maintains salience through tension with the outside world and frequent ingroup interactions. Their "Christian" identity is most important, which they define according to certain beliefs, experiences, and behaviours, specifically biblicism, crucicentrism, conversionism, and activism. These identities mean that their most important boundaries follow the "Christian/non-Christian" fault-line, but that line can be difficult to identify because of the private nature of the criteria. As a result, various groups receive ingroup or outgroup status based on affective labels and personal experience. Yet to be demonstrated is the degree to which evangelicals show uniformity in experiences, beliefs, attitudes, and practices across geographical boundaries.

4 Evangelical Religious Experience

Religious experience has played a central role in the emergence and growth of evangelicalism in North America. Many of the revivals of the eighteenth and nineteenth centuries that shaped modern evangelicalism were characterized by intense religious experiences. The leaders of these revivals – Whitefield, Wesley, Edwards, Finney, Alline, and others – spoke of "being ravished by a divine ecstasy" and overwhelmed by "a lively sense of the excellency of Christ" (cited in Rawlyk and Noll 1994, 17). The displays of frenzied behaviour that typified some US camp meetings and revivals were not as common north of the border, but the experience of being "moved by the spirit" was central in Canadian revivals led by Henry Alline and others (Rawlyk 1984; 1990). These revivals provided models for a wide variety of evangelical experiences, from conversion to "being slain in the Spirit," where individuals collapse and fall to the floor under the power of the Holy Spirit. The patterns of experience became widespread in North America, such that religious experience has been an important element in evangelical religiosity up to the present (Noll et al. 1994, 3–5).

There are signs that experience is vitally important to evangelicals today. The continued growth of Pentecostal denominations and charismatic movements in North America and worldwide indicates this. Poloma (1989) suggests that religious experience is a key component of that vitality. On the national level, Bibby in Canada (1987; 1993) and Greeley in the US (1987) have found surprisingly high levels of religious experience. Some twenty studies conducted between 1962 and 1990 in the US found that between twenty percent and fifty percent of Americans claim to have had a religious experience (Spilka et al. 1985, 182; Yamane and Polzer 1994, 2). In Canada, nearly half the population claims to have felt sustained by an outside power (Bibby 1987, 70). Among evangelicals, there is interest in the widespread and often bizarre religious experiences associated with the Toronto Airport Christian Fellowship (formerly the Toronto Airport Vineyard Church). Barking, roaring, laughing, and being slain in the spirit are among the typical manifestations (Poloma 1995). Several core evangelical interviewees in both Canada and the US had experienced renewal connected with the Toronto church. In this chapter I look at the religious experiences reported in the interviews through the lens of sociology. The significance, frequency, and range of religious experiences are discussed and specific attention paid to variation of evangelical experience by region. I also analyze the importance of evangelical religious experience to commitment.

RELIGIOUS EXPERIENCE AND SOCIOLOGY

For many years, social scientists gave little thought to religious experience, even though some of the "founding fathers" of its various fields (e.g. Troeltsch 1931; James 1902) paid it much attention. The lack of sociological research on the subject may stem from the fact that religious experience is viewed primarily as an individual or subjective phenomenon. Or, it may be that the groups within which religious experiences are most common have received so little attention because the secularization thesis – which indicated that those religious groups were losing importance – held sway for many years. Whatever the reason, recent scholarship in the area holds that religious experience is eminently social.[1] This is not to say that religious experiences are nothing more than a social construction. That is, the "raw" experiences reported by those I interviewed may be real outside of the social reality applied to them (see Yamane and Polzer 1994, 11n6 and appendix). Debating the possibility of spiritual realities is beyond the scope of social science and is neither confirmed nor denied here. The point is that whatever else they are, religious experiences are socially mediated and culturally understood. Hence they are important to a sociological understanding of evangelicals. I do not wish, however, to make light of the passionate accounts of religious experiences among the evangelicals I interviewed.

Religious experience is social, first of all, because such experiences are interpreted on the basis of culturally available symbols and meanings.

Once an experience happens, individuals (or other group members) make sense of it by locating it within the range of experiences that are considered appropriate by the group they are involved in. The language used by the group to describe the experiences they sanction allows the individual to make sense of the experience by applying a name to it and by defining its characteristics. In doing so, meaning and significance are applied to the experience. Alternatively, an experience may not be readily interpretable within a person's frame of reference, which may lead the individual to search for an explanation elsewhere or ignore the experience as trivial. Regardless, the point is that the experience is "culturally transformed" after the fact, which is a social process (Neitz and Spickard 1990, 24–5).

Second, religious experiences can be evoked by certain religious settings (Yamane and Polzer 1994, 10–11). Certain rituals (communion, worship, baptism) together with various sensory stimuli (music, incense, ornamentation) invoke experiences, such as sensing a divine presence. As Neitz (1987) has argued from her study of charismatic Catholics, individuals learn to speak in tongues, prophesy, and engage in other authorized religious group activities through socialization into the religious group. It is not surprising, then, that religious experiences are reported most often by those who are active in religious groups that promote religious experiences.[2] In this way, social factors have an effect prior to the religious experience.

Third, religious experiences are shared experiences. In his classic book *The Elementary Forms of the Religious Life*, Durkheim argues that religious experiences are necessarily social because the power behind such experiences is society experienced through collective ritual and symbolism (1915, 257). In the same vein, Neitz and Spickard argue that religious experiences are not simply personal experiences, nor are they just outward expressions of inner experiences. Rather, religious experiences are shared, similar to the way music is shared between the composer, performers, conductor, and audience. For Neitz and Spickard, an individual with a religious experience shares "inner time" with a supernatural "other" and those who have had similar experiences, in much the same way that someone shares "inner time" with a composer and performers of a musical piece, regardless of whether the music is listened to in solitude or in a concert hall. Even private religious experiences are social because those who have such experiences share "inner time" with those past and future who have had or will have similar experiences, just as the musician or listener connects with the composer by experiencing the music, even though they may be separated by time and space (1990, 29–30; see also Spickard 1991).

Neitz and Spickard suggest that this is one way to understand the "otherness" of religious experiences. That is, the analogy helps us understand from a social scientific perspective why individuals say that their experience stems from a force outside themselves. As Durkheim states, a religious force often "appears to be outside of the individuals and to be endowed with a sort of transcendence over them, it, like the clan of which it is the symbol, can be realized only in and through them; in this sense, it is imminent in them and they necessarily represent it as such" (1915, 253). The private religious experience, then, is social in that the individual connects with "an other" even when no one is present. This allows Neitz and Spickard to argue that private religious experiences are social as experienced, not only in their interpretation or when they are publicly expressed. Thus, religious experience, whether private or public, is social because it can be socially evoked and interpreted, and because it is a shared experience.

Finally, religious experience has social consequences. As Poloma[3] has argued, religious experience affects institutional change and growth and, on the personal level, motivates evangelism and correlates positively with religiosity and a sense of well-being. Religious experience is shaped by social forces and has social consequences. In light of a sociological understanding of religious experience, this chapter will attend to the ways in which the evangelical subculture supplies the cultural "tools" (Swidler 1986) needed to evoke and interpret religious experience, and how religious experience strengthens identity and commitment to evangelicalism. In this way, the religious experience and the subculture that supports it are mutually reinforcing.

For evangelicals, whether Pentecostal, Baptist, Nazarene, or Lutheran, the importance of religious experience is difficult to overemphasize. The salvation experience is fundamental and central to their identity. Recall from chapter 3 that evangelicals are more likely to identify themselves by conversion than by any other theme. All the salvation accounts presented below represent the respondents' most significant religious experience. Many referred to those experiences as life changing. What's more, religious experience is the basis of the divine relationship. As previously noted, evangelicals understood their faith as a "relationship with God." In explaining situations where they have felt God's presence and received answers to prayer, respondents bring out the relational side of sharing time with God. In devotional practices, private or corporate worship, and ecstatic experiences, evangelicals "talk to," "meet with," "feel," and are "intimate" with God. In the second part of this chapter, I will discuss accounts of feeling close to God and answers to prayer. Finally, religious experience strengthens commitment. The last section of this chapter will demonstrate statistically that religious experience is connected to evangelical commitment, and that they reinforce each other.

Nearly all the interview respondents (ninety-eight percent) reported significant religious experiences and have felt the presence of God. For most, religious experiences are common, and this is true regardless of denomination. Although the content of the experiences are often very personal, respondents felt free to discuss them. It was often at this point in the interview that brusque answers ended and restless respondents relaxed. For core evangelicals, opportunities to speak about religious experiences come in the form of testimonies, or "sharing" times, often in small group settings, or even recounting their faith journey as a form of evangelism. As Gerlach and Hine state in their discussion of the conversion process, "testifying objectifies a subjective experience and 'fixes' it as a reality" (1970, 136). The many opportunities evangelicals have to "testify" enhance the reality of their experiences and add credence to their worldview, both in their eyes and in the eyes of the group. Retelling experiences allows evangelicals to have a sense of belonging that comes from sharing similar experiences. In brief, core evangelicals were comfortable discussing their religious experiences.

CONVERSION

Most evangelicals, across all denominations and regions, considered conversion to be their most significant religious experience. Prior to conversion, a person is spiritually dead, without hope of reconnecting with a holy God based on personal merit or virtue. One is "saved," or converted, when one accepts the atoning work of Christ as the sole means of salvation. Conversion often involves the "sinner's prayer," in which the unconverted ask Christ to forgive their sins, recognize him as Saviour, and submit their life to God's lordship. This simple act is the means by which converts pass from spiritual death into spiritual life and are given access to a personal relationship with God. The conversion experience, accompanied by the necessary beliefs about Christ and his atoning death as recorded in the Bible, is the only requirement for membership into the evangelical subculture. Conversion is the basis of the evangelical faith.

Sociologists[4] have written much on conversion, preferring theories that emphasize process, social ties, and the active role of the convert in conversion over deterministic and passive models (brainwashing, social drift) or individual and psychological models (underdeveloped egos, addictive personalities). The accounts of conversion given by evangelicals, however, did not always fit sociological models of conversion, since conversion for a sociologist "entails the displacement of one's universe of discourse by another or the ascendance of a formerly peripheral universe of discourse to the status of primary authority" (Snow and Machalek 1984, 169–70). For evangelicals, "conversion" refers to a broader set of experiences (which I call salvation experiences below). Some Missouri Synod Lutherans referred to their infant baptism as a "conversion," a time when they were "born again," or "saved." Even though they did not recall their infant baptism, forty-four percent pointed to it as their most significant religious experience. This Lutheran pastor is typical: "Well, um, theologically I would have to say my baptism, realizing I am Lutheran and there is infant baptism. It's the most significant event in my life but it's not an experience I remember." Some less-dramatic born-again experiences reported by respondents would not qualify for conversions in the sociological sense but could be referred to as "alternation" or "regeneration" (Snow and Machalek 1984, 169), like this report from a Mississippi pastor: "When I came to know Jesus Christ as my savior … I was fourteen years old. [Was it a crisis?] No, I just came to realize that if I was going to live with him [God] something was going to have to happen in my life that was different. So I simply asked him [Jesus] to come into my heart and he did. [Where was this?] It was at the church. I grew up in a Christian family. I don't believe you have to have a 'Damascus road' experience [a traumatic experience like the apostle Paul's sudden conversion on the road to Damascus]. Jesus came into my heart when I asked him to and saved me." Regardless of whether or not their salvation experience was dramatic, or whether or not they could remember it, evangelicals considered it to be of fundamental significance.

It was not difficult to find examples of ways in which ritual or evangelical group members evoked salvation experiences. One young Pentecostal, however, insisted that he had had no prior evangelical influences. Because he did not have the wherewithal to interpret his salvation experience, it wasn't until he went to an evangelical church that he understood its meaning:

I had no religious anything, I had no one to lead me in a "sinner's prayer," no bible, no church or anything, so I just cried out to God and said, "You have got to bail me out. If you are there, I need help bad" – you know I was a drug addict – I said "I am not even sure I believe in you but if you are there I need help bad." That's how I got saved. Then I went to church and the church helped me understand what happened … but I was saved just by calling on the name of the Lord. [You were by yourself in your home?] Yeah, I mean the power and the presence of God came down in my living-room, it was unreal. Yeah, it was not a one-two-three-repeat-after-me. God just came down, it was amazing ... I'm saying as far as someone going out and witnessing and knocking on our door and asking us if we want Jesus, it didn't happen ... I know one person who turned the Lord down when it came to witnessing to me, so I guess God decided that if [he] was going to [save me], he was going to have to do it [himself].

Most respondents grew up in the church, or had strong religious ties, indicating that conversion was a natural consequence of religious socialization. About sixty-five percent of salvation experiences happened during childhood and teenage years. Respondents reported that they were saved as early as age six. A Maritime Pentecostal gave this salvation account, which he considered his most significant experience: "I was very young. I realized the importance of it when I grew older. I don't think at that time I realized how significant it was but there was a point when I definitely passed from death unto life, was born of the spirit. I was very young because I had the privilege of growing up in a Christian home." In this case a childhood salvation experience is interpreted as significant later in life. The evangelical subculture applies meaning to diverse experiences, which come to be understood as central to the evangelical identity.

Unlike stereotypical revival conversions, some twenty percent of respondents considered that their born-again experience had been a gradual change over time. Some respondents said their conversion was both a one-time experience (they can point to an actual conversion event) and a change over time (a process of encounters and changes that lead to conversion and then a gradual spiritual growth after that). A New Brunswick Nazarene said: "I always grew up in the church so there is not one particular point [of change], I just always went [to church] and agreed. I remember when I was a young girl, probably six or seven, that was the first time I went to the altar and really felt the need to ask God into my heart, so that stands out in my mind and [was] the first commitment I really actually made. Since then it has just been an ongoing thing." Several others reported that they were "saved" at evangelistic meetings like crusades or camp meetings, or at summer camps or church programs for children such as Sunday school, Boys Brigade or AWANA (Approved Workmen Are Not Ashamed) clubs. Through these means and others, evangelical churches and organizations schedule times for salvation experiences to take place. Altar calls, during which the preacher invites the unsaved to come to the "altar" (or platform) to receive salvation, are given weekly in some evangelical churches I visited (especially in Pentecostal evening services) and less often in others. A scheduled time for salvation experiences legitimates and encourages the experience. Rituals surround these scheduled salvation times, which evoke strong feelings and elicit responses. In this way members share "inner time," through which group bonds are strengthened and the centrality of salvation is reinforced. In addition to corporate rituals and events, salvation experiences are evoked by proselytizing the unconverted.

The powerful "otherness" experienced by the respondents was striking. Some reported powerful life-changing encounters with the transcendent. Note the experience of this Manitoba pastor:

Well, there are many [significant experiences]. I would say the most significant was [in my] early university years where the murder/suicide of two fellows I knew ... led to my conversion. It was one of the few times in my life I have heard God audibly speak ... that whole experience just shattered my whole worldview. [I had a] kind of cavalier approach to life, cynical of faith and religion in general. When I was standing at the graveside and watching the family ... so grief stricken they couldn't even cry properly, that's when I heard God speak. All he said was "as much as they are unable to grieve over the loss of their sons, what do you think I feel like over how you are wasting your life?" That's it ... I heard that audibly, and that sent me into a weeklong wrestling match with God (that ended in conversion) ...

The powerful "otherness" of this event was traumatic enough to prompt a major life change and eventually led to the respondent's call to the pastorate. Such encounters with the transcendent, when retold, reinforce the experiences of others and add legitimacy to the evangelical worldview. Salvation experiences strengthen the subculture. As Berger states, "The experience of conversion to a meaning system that is capable of ordering the scattered data of one's biography is liberating and profoundly satisfying" (1963, 63).

Few regional differences emerged in salvation accounts. Mississippi respondents seem to have had considerable evangelical influences, and their salvation experiences emphasize reaching a point where they accept what they have previously heard many times before, rather than responding to something new. The salvation account of this elderly Pentecostal was typical: "Well, as I said before, I was born and raised Assemblies of God ... I loved the Lord all through my elementary, young teen years, but I did not truly commit to the Lord as my personal Savior until I was eighteen. [Where was that?] It was at an Assemblies of God school in ... Texas." Repeated contact with the evangelical subculture was the norm, even though Mississippi respondents were significantly less likely to have attended church regularly while growing up than those in other regions.[5]

EXPERIENCING GOD'S PRESENCE

We now turn to religious experiences that emphasize the divine relationship. When asked, "Have there been times in your life when you have felt the presence of God or felt very close to God?" ninety-eight percent answered in the affirmative, and nearly all interviewees gave examples. I also asked respondents how often they felt the presence of God, and under what conditions they were most likely to feel God's presence. The results of these questions are given in Table 4.1.

For both questions, there are no significant differences by region, although there are denominational differences. For those who claim to feel the presence of God weekly or more, Lutherans have the highest percentage (85.7 percent), followed by Pentecostals (79.4 percent), Southern Baptists (71.7 percent), Mennonites (65 percent), Nazarenes (60 percent), and Canadian Baptists (53.2 percent). Considering that the Lutherans in the CE sample offered brief and unspectacular accounts of experiences – most reported feeling God's presence during communion, baptism, or confirmation – the result is surprising. These rituals, though not ecstatic, have special significance for the Lutheran and are thus imbued with an aura of divine presence. If other evangelicals look for more dramatic experiences with God, it is not surprising that they feel God's presence less often.

It is clear that a sense of the presence of God is a frequent occurrence among the evangelicals I interviewed. Many suggested that they had felt God's presence in significant ways so frequently that it was difficult to report just one instance. One Pentecostal Canadian pastor said: "Yes, [I have felt God's presence] many times. Oh, I could write a book. I just came back from Russia Wednesday night after three weeks of night-after-night, three to four services a day, grassroots evangelism and preaching to crowds and seeing people flock [forward] – seventy-five percent of the congregation coming for conversion, praying for the sick and seeing miracles of healing, weeping and sensing God's presence in a way that I find difficult to explain so that it would be meaningful to anyone else. God has been very, very gracious to me by making his presence real many, many times in my life. That's only one answer I could give you." Interview respondents felt God's presence during devotional times such as private prayer

Table 4.1
How Often and Where Respondent Felt the Presence of God

23. How often would you say you feel the presence of God, or feel very close to God? Would you say:	%	24. Under what conditions are you most likely to experiences God's presence or feel very close to God?	%
Once or twice in my life	1.9	In a church service or in a large group of believers	13
Several times in my life	10.4	In a small group or Bible study	3
A few times a year	10.2	In times of private prayer or Bible reading	14.9
Once a month or so	7.4	Throughout my day	8.2
Every week or nearly every week	19.2	All of these or at any time	53.5
Daily or nearly every day	50.8	Other (describe)	7.3

Source: CE sample, 1995.

(14.5 percent), trials like a death or illness (14 percent), special meetings or corporate worship (10 percent), ecstatic experiences such as the baptism of the Spirit or visions (7.6 percent), or even in nature (4 percent). These "shared" times provide the evangelical with comfort in trials, "intimacy with God" in corporate worship, and ecstasy in certain experiences. As with salvation experiences evangelical church services and events encourage other experiences that deepen faith and strengthen affective bonds with God and other group members. Below are examples of common experiences from responses to the question: "Can you describe a situation where you felt God's presence in a special way?" A Lutheran man from Mississippi described his experiences during private worship: "Yes ... particularly in prayer time, reading Scripture and prayer, there is a sense of peace – 'hey, you are all right,' and [I] have a sense of sin and confess that sin, 'you are still all right, God still loves you.' God's love doesn't change, and that truth will come to me when I feel bad, you know, undone." Religious experiences like this one can provide encouragement, peace, joy, and assurance of salvation for the evangelical.

Many evangelicals reported that God's presence was especially real to them in *times of trial*. Berger states that a religion's ability to make painful or marginal situations meaningful provides legitimation for that religious worldview (1967, 55f). In this way, evangelicals are able to reconcile troubling experiences with their view of God's love, which results in strengthened faith. A Nazarene pastor from New Brunswick had this experience: "Um, it may seem odd, but my mother was killed in a car accident eighteen months ago, at her bedside just moments before she died [she died ten days after the accident] ... our family was surrounding her bedside at the hospital. There was a very clear recognition that we weren't alone, God was there, in a way that brought healing to the family, to relationships in the family, as well as the assurance that even though we had to let her go, that was not the end of our relationship. I think that was probably one of the most vivid recent experiences."

Corporate worship and special meetings invoke experiences for many evangelicals. A Baptist pastor in New Brunswick had an experience during group worship that gave him unshakeable faith in God's love for him and strengthened his commitment:

It was probably an experience in a Vineyard conference in Edmonton ... just a powerful time of meeting God, and on the experiential level, coming into an experience of what I believed in doctrinally about the father love of God. From that experience, no matter what happens, I know that God loves me, and I know that I know what I know, no matter how much life falls apart. I was converted sometime before that ... but it was sort of the good Baptist faith – dutiful, obey the book [Bible], know that God loves you because the book says so – but on the experiential level ... [I gained] intimacy with God ... I went home from that weekend just completely transformed in terms of worship. I take my guitar from my office over to the church and sing to God for an hour and half the time end up on the floor crying.

Evangelicals make it clear that experiences to do with *baptism of the Spirit* are not based on human effort or the situation but on "God's timing." They note that they are often in situations where others have experiences and they do not and are sometimes surprised by "God's presence." In a service described by a Pentecostal woman from Mississippi, the worship leader sanctioned a time for ecstatic experience:

I had been seeking the baptism [of the Spirit] and was asking God for it, but I had this preconceived idea of how it was going to happen, it was going to be at my church, at my altar with my friends praying for me. I had made up my mind how it was going to sound and everything, it was going to be very earth-shattering, a very religious experience [laughs]. The guy leading worship [at the revival meetings] ... said "The women danced before the Lord" and I am a very balanced person ... "No, we were not going to dance, no, we were not going to do that." [I thought] the Spirit just had to take you and move you, and I thought that when you were baptized in the Holy Ghost that the Spirit was actually going to move my mouth and my tongue for me [when I spoke in tongues] ... it was just going to take me over ... [When] he said "We are going to dance before the Lord," the whole city auditorium began jumping up and down, and I thought, "There are some other people from my church who are not jumping up and down." He [the worship leader] said, "Hold on just a minute, people, this is Scriptural" ... and he read how David danced before the Lord ... He started playing the music again, and this couple who goes to our church – the man is very dignified and refined – raised his hands ... and he started jumping up and down, a little kind of hop, you know. I thought, well, if it's OK for him, and he's been sane for forty-five years, its OK for me [laughs]. So I started jumping up and down and I got filled with the Holy Ghost ... I was just praising the Lord and singing and I just got filled with the Holy Spirit just right there, it was the strangest thing ... it was not anything like I thought it was going to be ... You can't put God in a box, he is going to do it the opposite of what you think.

Spiritual *visions*, such as one described by a Pentecostal woman in Manitoba, validate the faith of the person experiencing them: "Yeah, I always feel the presence of God, especially when our oldest daughter was very sick. She had an operation and she almost died and I felt the peace of God carrying me every day ... Jesus showed himself to me [one night], and I tell people that and they said it was just a dream, but I know it was not just a dream. My husband said my face was aglow and he said I was speaking in tongues, and I had my hands reached out and he said, 'There was something about you that night.' He said it lasted about a minute, he said it was the most awesome holiness that just came across the room. I think that has changed my Christian walk because it was God reconfirming himself to me. He is real."

Nature gives rise to evangelical experiences as well, as this Nazarene man from New Brunswick attests: "There are times like in special services at church, vacations [in] real beautiful spots, probably times of prayer, especially when my children were born ... I am weird, though, one time I was out shovelling the driveway and it was late at night, and there had been a storm ... It was really calm by this point and the sky was clear and I just looked up and the sky was so clear and the stars and everything. Even though I was doing something like that I felt really close to God at that time. That's just one example."

In sum, these experiences provided comfort and encouragement, assured the people of divine favour, and validated their faith through experiences of God's presence. The benefits of "a relationship with God" are not limited to a sense of divine presence, however. Evangelicals believe that God is the source of material and physical blessings as well, through prayer.

Answers to Prayer

I asked interview respondents if they could point to specific answers to prayer in their lives. All respondents but one said they had had specific prayers answered and all but six (ninety-five percent) could recall an example. One-quarter of the respondents gave examples of divine healing, and respondents consider most healings miraculous. About one-third gave examples of provision, such as the provision of a church building, home, car, or money. Others (thirteen percent) asked for guidance on an important life decision and felt they received it.

Reports of healing, like other "Pentecostal" experiences, are not limited to Pentecostal denominations. Several Nazarenes felt they had been healed during healing services at Nazarene churches or revival meetings, and Baptists reported healings as well. This was the experience of on Nazarene man in Manitoba:

My father was healed from rheumatoid arthritis when we were kids. So every night we would go to bed for several years and pray [to God] to heal Daddy's arthritis. On the way back from a trip to the west coast, where one of his nieces and a small group of women had been praying for him, he was healed on the highway [going home]. We consider it a bona fide miracle in the sense that the rider was taken off his insurance and he had to go through all the associated medical tests of course. All the doctors were baffled. We are not talking about a gradual six-month, ten-month remission here; it was boom! He came back from holidays with no more arthritis. My clearest memories of him as a child was seeing him lying there on Christmas Eve, after a Christmas concert at church. We would be lying there on the couch with a bench under his knees to drain his knees, eh, so we consider that a miracle … He beat me in racquetball today [laughs].

Evangelicals claim to have had divine guidance in finding their spouses, dealing with relational problems, or making important decisions. It was common also for evangelicals to pray that God would provide money, jobs, homes, cars, even children or grandchildren, that were desired or needed. In this report, a Baptist grandmother from Mississippi prayed for grandchildren:

My husband and I lost our first child and we were told we would not have any children, and we had two sons after [that]. Then when the youngest son got married, I really wanted some grandchildren, and I prayed and prayed and they went and saw a fertility specialist and all sorts of things. They were married five years … and when the gynecologist looked at their medical history he said, "You might as well start adoption procedures, because I don't think you will ever have children" … I was praying again about that and it was as if the Lord was saying, "You don't have to pray anymore," it was going to be all right ... At the end of March she was pregnant, and then we had a grandchild every two years, and I was afraid that God had stored up all those prayers [laughs]. But after three, they called it off. That was just one of them. There have been many times when God has answered prayers.

Like this woman, many respondents stated that they had received numerous answers to prayer. Most often God "speaks" by giving an individual a "sense" of what he or she should do. Three respondents, however, along with the Mennonite pastor cited above, claimed they heard God speak to them audibly.

Examples of answers to prayer were surprisingly uniform in all four locations. Exactly six respondents in each region spoke of a physical healing as an answer to prayer, between eight and twelve mentioned a provision, and between two and four spoke of divine guidance. Denominational differences were minor as well, although Lutherans are somewhat less likely to report healing than those in other denominations.

From these responses, I conclude that religious experiences serve several functions for evangelicals. For one, they *authenticate* or confirm their beliefs and worldview (cf. Glock and Stark 1965, 43–6). Experiences that seem to be more than just coincidence confirm for the evangelical the existence of a personal God who is involved in their lives. For many evangelicals, experiences of the divine offer religious legitimations in times of tragedy (Berger 1967, 53–4). The Mennonite woman who received a vision and knew God was real during her daughter's illness is an example. Beyond simple confirmation, though, many experiences *illuminated* something about God, the individual, or the relationship between them. The Baptist pastor cited above said, "I know that I know God loves me," because he felt God's presence in a special way at a meeting. His experience allowed him to recognize the love of God in a new way. Others stated that they recognized their sinfulness or the power of God because of their experiences.

Some experiences seemed to *initiate* someone into full participation or membership with the group, or initiate change. Conversion for evangelicals and the baptism of the Spirit, evidenced for some Pentecostals and charismatics by speaking in tongues, initiates one into that group (Neitz 1987). Several Pentecostals stated that they were seeking after the baptism of the Spirit since it is emphasized as a necessary part of Christian life in their tradition. The responses also show that religious experiences are times when one can *communicate* with God and receive from God specific messages of comfort, guidance, or even reproof (as in the case of the Mennonite pastor's salvation experience). Finally, religious experiences *invigorate* evangelicals to deeper commitment and activism. Evangelicals come away from religious experiences with a renewed sense of the reality of their religious worldview and a fresh resolve to deepen their spirituality. In these ways and others, religious experience and the evangelical subculture are mutually reinforcing.

Religious experience resulted not only in personal change but in institutional change as well. In two separate cases, Baptist pastors had "Pentecostal" experiences and as a result became "charismatic Baptists." These personal experiences led to institutional changes in their churches, including more charismatic worship and an emphasis on the spiritual gifts.

EXPERIENCE ENHANCES COMMITMENT

The anecdotal evidence for the significance of religious experience to the evangelical can be verified through statistical analysis. There is much evidence to show that religious experience and religious commitment are mutually supportive. In the US, Poloma and Pendleton found that ecstatic religious experiences increased the likelihood that Assemblies of God adherents would evangelize and argued that such experiences "provide ongoing transfusions that ensured its continued vitality" (1989, 419). In Canada, Andrew Grenville of the Angus Reid polling firm found that different types of religious experience – including sensing God's presence, experiencing religious insights or awakenings, feeling close to a spiritual force, speaking in tongues, and being slain in the Spirit – encourage evangelism, prayer, and Bible reading among a sample of Canadian evangelicals (1995b).[6] Grenville found that those who claimed to have felt the presence of God or to have been close to a powerful force would evangelize more often. Using the same data, I found that the number of religious experiences a person reported correlated positively with Bible reading, prayer, and evangelism among evangelicals. Furthermore, my analysis shows no regional differences in frequency of experience.[7] Results from US data are similar. Using a sample of evangelicals from the General Social Survey – with religious experience items on feeling close to God and feeling close to a spiritual force – I once again found a positive connection between the measures of commitment and religious experience.[8] Using the CE data, frequency of experience showed no significant regional differences, whereas devotionalism, church attendance, and evangelism are all significant and positively related to religious experience. Thus, the positive relationship between commitment and experience exists even among core evangelicals, a relationship that holds true in all four regions. In sum, religious experience consistently has a positive relationship with certain measures of commitment, including church attendance, prayer, Bible reading, and evangelism. There is no clear indication that religious experience varies by region among evangelicals, other things being equal.

Along with distinctive identity and clear boundaries, religious experience helps to explain evangelical vitality. Religious experience is hardly mentioned in sociological discussions of religious vitality, likely because it is not clear whether experience causes commitment or vice versa. After all, do evangelicals have religious experiences because they are committed, or are they committed because of religious experience? The interviews and related data seem to suggest that both are true; they are mutually reinforcing. The fact that there is no neat unidirectional cause-and-effect relationship between these variables, however, does not make experience any less important in explaining religious commitment.

One could argue that religious experience is particularly important for religious vitality in modern North America. In a pluralistic cultural-religious milieu, self-identity is not socially given but achieved. As Smith points out, religious identity and lifestyle are seen as legitimate in a pluralistic religious environment if it is based on individual choice. Simply to "inherit" the faith of your parents, or to accept uncritically the teachings of a religious group without choosing it for oneself, is seen as unauthentic and shallow. Rather, the religion must be "real" to the individual; something personalized, or chosen (Smith 1998, 102–3). If Smith is right, evangelicalism's emphasis on conversion may be well suited to modern North Americans. One cannot enter the evangelical fold without making a personal choice to "accept Christ as Lord and Saviour." One is not "saved" on the strength of church membership or inheritance but by a personal conversion experience.

As the interviews demonstrate, evangelical religious experience establishes the "realness" of the individual's religious identity (or calls it into question) and endows it with meaning. Experience is personal and, in the modern world, uniquely legitimate. Experience is "spiritual," not "religious." It moves faith from the cold sterility of doctrine and duty to the heart. Largely absent from the interviews is any evidence that evangelicals became convinced of the reality of their faith through an intellectual defence of the faith in light of opposing religious claims. An intellectually defensible faith was not a key component in the salvation of any evangelical I interviewed. Evangelicals did not report changes in their theology or denomination, or any increase in their commitment for intellectual reasons. Nor did they emphasize apologetics in their accounts of witnessing to the "unsaved." In fact, it was hardly mentioned at all. Instead, evangelicals "know that they know" their faith is real because of experience. Since religious experience is a key component in evangelical vitality, researchers would be wise to look at the degree to which religious groups promote experience in seeking to explain religious vitality.

5 Orthodoxy: Evangelical Beliefs and Morals

In his various works, James Davison Hunter has focused on the maintenance of evangelical orthodoxy in light of modernity (Jelen 1990). Hunter argues that evangelicals distinguish themselves from other religious groups on theological grounds.[1] For this reason, beliefs are fundamentally important to the maintenance of boundaries. "Evangelicalism shares with the larger Protestant phenomenon a fixation with theology," he states. "Yet its concern is far more intense. Not only do Evangelicals distinguish themselves from other religions this way, they also distinguish themselves from liberal Protestants this way. Orthodoxy, strictly speaking, is a theological matter" (1987, 19).

For Hunter, not only beliefs but religious behaviour is central to evangelical religiosity. In *Evangelicalism: The Coming Generation* (1987), Hunter argues that the importance to evangelicalism of "orthopraxy," or moral behaviour, in the twentieth century "is difficult to overemphasize" (57). Moral behaviour is "an external index" for the spiritual well-being of the soul; it distinguishes those who had been transformed by salvation from those who have not (ibid.). As Weber noted in *The Protestant Ethic*, moral asceticism was evidence for salvation (1958). In addition, moral strictness maintains evangelical distinctiveness. Evangelicals separate themselves from "worldly" influences in keeping with biblical mandates to resist temptation and sin.

Much evidence supports Hunter's claim that theological beliefs are central to evangelicalism. Evangelicals, as demonstrated in chapter 3, are more likely to define themselves on the basis of religious beliefs than by religious practices, morals, or experiences. It is not surprising, then, that social scientists, including Hunter (1983), often define evangelicals on the basis of adherence to orthodox beliefs: belief in the inspiration and authority of Scripture, the divinity of Jesus, and his atoning death and resurrection as the sole means of salvation. One would expect that all core evangelicals, regardless of denomination or region, would agree with these beliefs. Other religious beliefs, however, may vary by region, even among the most active evangelicals.

Some evangelical beliefs are central, not only because they are theologically important but also because they are symbolically important. Symbolically important beliefs provide a litmus test for identifying "true" Christians – or what evangelicals sometimes call "Bible-believing" or "born again" Christians – and to distinguish them from those "Christians" who do not fit within their subcultural boundaries. For instance, belief in the Trinitarian nature of God and in the humanity of Jesus are theologically important and typically part of evangelical doctrinal statements. However, they are not as symbolically important as believing that Christ's work of atonement is the only means to salvation, since the latter belief distinguishes evangelicals from "liberal" Protestants. Similarly, certain moral issues, such as abortion and homosexuality, have added symbolic importance, whereas evangelical moral taboos like extramarital affairs are less symbolically important (Soper 1994).

For the purpose of highlighting similarities, the role of beliefs in boundary creation is central. Evangelicals not only hold similar theological beliefs, but they also *emphasize* the same beliefs as indicated in chapter 3. This emphasis suggests that evangelicals know where they draw their theological and moral lines, and that relaxing orthodoxy in peripheral areas may be less important for evangelical distinctiveness than maintaining orthodoxy in areas of symbolic importance. For this reason, similarities in symbolically salient orthodox boundaries and other doctrinal or moral standards are important for the argument presented here. To restate: evangelicalism in North America is a distinctive subculture that transcends national boundaries, and orthodox beliefs are central to that distinctiveness. In this chapter, I demonstrate that evangelicals in North America hold to core set of beliefs that vary little over space and time. While more peripheral beliefs vary geographically and by denomination, there is widespread agreement on certain beliefs that distinguish evangelicals from the nonevangelicals around them.

SYMBOLIC ORTHODOXY

Evangelical orthodoxy is well known. The conservative positions of evangelicals on premarital sex, pornography, and abortion, and their defence of the Bible, for example, are well documented by media and scholarly sources. Of all the moral issues, abortion may carry the most symbolic and affective weight and provides a good example of how orthodox boundaries are defended and maintained. Seventy-nine percent of my CE respondents said they were strongly against the legal availability of abortion, and about fourteen percent more were moderately against it. On specific instances, however, evangelicals are somewhat more lenient. Significant percentages of evangelicals thought abortions should be legally available if the mother's health was endangered (72 percent), in the case of rape (36 percent), and if there was a strong chance of a serious defect in the baby (27 percent). Only a handful of core evangelicals, however, felt that abortion should be allowed if a mother did not want any more children (3.6 percent), if a family couldn't afford more children (4.2 percent), or when the mother was not married and did not want to marry the man by whom she was pregnant (4.5 percent).[2] This suggests that it is symbolically important to evangelicals (and other religious conservatives) to take a stand on the abortion issue as an indication of their sexual conservativeness, even if they are more lenient on specifics (Welch et al. 1995).

Interviewees perceived that most abortions are performed for expedient reasons or because of pressure from others, not because of rape, defect, or the health of the mother. One Minnesotan woman who volunteers at New Life Family Services, a pro-life counselling service for pregnant women, said: "You will hardly believe how many girls come in there [New Life Family Services] and say they have to have an abortion, and when you get to the root of the problem, its 'My boyfriend will leave me if I don't, I don't want to but I have to.' We really just show them that they don't have to do anything; it is their choice. We have parents drag them kicking and screaming, 'You are having an abortion.' To give them a way out, we have homes that they can stay in if they get kicked out; we have adoption, all sorts of services to help them."

Orthodoxy Explained

When asked why they believe that abortion is wrong, most evangelicals pointed to the Bible as their moral guide, as Hunter predicted. He states that evangelicals justify their moral code with biblical precedent. It is not, of course, that the Bible directly addressed all moral issues but that "God's word ... provided clear principles for Christian living which prohibited these [immoral] kinds of activities" (Hunter 1987, 56). Without prompting, sixty-one percent of interview respondents said the Bible was their guide, and about half of the respondents gave a scriptural basis for their beliefs. Some quoted the commandment "Thou shalt not murder," others paraphrased Bible passages like "You are knit together in your mother's womb" (Psalm 139), or "before you were born I knew you" (Jeremiah 1), often giving the biblical reference as well. For the evangelical, these passages are evidence that God cares for the fetus in the womb, thus suggesting that abortion is wrong. One pastor in Minnesota said: "The Psalmist says that 'While I was still in my mother's womb you know me and had every day of my life planned' [paraphrase of Psalms 139: 15–16]. So obviously that little embryo was a living being in God's sight, so God had a dream for that child. I happen to be a product of an unwed mother, she put me up for adoption ... We have to make it very plain what the Bible does say about it. I think abortion is murder."

As these explanations for an orthodox position on abortion show, the most common defence for orthodoxy was their interpretation of particular passages of Scripture. Of course, the interpretation of a biblical text is not always clear, and interpretations based on the whole biblical account can be even more difficult in light of seemingly conflicting passages. In many cases, the correct interpretation of Scripture is debated among evangelicals themselves. Thus, to say that evangelical orthodoxy is based solely on "the Bible" is too simplistic. Several other factors come into play. Naturally, some ambiguity in the interpretation of Scripture is minimized by the influential views of evangelical friends, pastors, denominational leaders, authors, and radio and television spokespersons. That is, biblical interpretation is influenced by relational ties to significant individuals or groups. Furthermore, evangelical orthodoxy is influenced by symbolic boundary maintenance, just as it is symbolically important for the evangelical to be pro-choice. As Chaves (1997) shows in his examination of women's ordination, orthodox denominations with an inerrantist view of the Bible fall on both sides of this issue, and biblical fiat is used to defend both positions. Chaves concludes that the use of the Bible is affected by the desired "symbolic display" of a more conservative or progressive public identity (1997, 6). In sum, biblical interpretation is socially influenced.

However, biblical fiat is not the only explanation for moral standards given by core evangelicals. A second explanation had to do with issues of personal conscience. On this basis, drinking, for example, would be wrong only for certain people. A New Brunswick Pentecostal who had been "saved" as an adult said that drinking for him would be always wrong, "because I came from that lifestyle." In other words, the temptation to drink to excess is too great for him, so he avoids alcohol beverages altogether. There is, then, a subjective side to moral prohibitions. Morality is not simply based on universal moral law as recorded in the Bible: some things are wrong for some, yet not wrong for others.

One might also abstain from certain behaviours so as not to offend the moral sensibilities of another. One Minnesota pastor stated that he couldn't go "mixed" swimming (where men and women swim together) when he was in Missouri because people in his church there thought it was wrong, even though swimming with women was not wrong for him personally. For the evangelical, keeping oneself from behaviours that violate your own or another's conscience follows the biblical principle to keep clear of situations that would cause others (1 Corinthians 8:13) or yourself (Matthew 5:28–30) to sin.

GEOGRAPHICAL VARIATION IN BELIEFS

Since evangelicals consider orthodoxy central to their identity, it is not surprising that Hunter's focus on evangelicalism's ability to maintain orthodoxy against the cultural currents of society centres around beliefs and morals. Hunter finds that the boundaries of orthodoxy are unable to stand against the secular onslaught of modernity. He concludes, "Far from being untouched by the cultural trends of the post-World War II decades, *the coming generation of evangelicals ... have come to participate fully in them*" (1987; 74; italics in original). Put simply, he sees the secularization of evangelicalism. Are evangelicals becoming less orthodox?

Evidence for increased secularity is generally examined over time, where modern evangelicals are less orthodox than their staunch forebears. However, the influence of broader society on evangelicalism can also be examined geographically. Investigating geographic variation in orthodoxy is worthwhile because it informs evangelicalism's relationship with "secular" modern culture in two ways.[3] First, regional analyses reveal the *permeability* of evangelical subcultural boundaries. Have evangelicals maintained their orthodoxy equally well in all regions of North America, or are they less orthodox in less-orthodox regions? Second, regional analyses illuminate the *ubiquity* of evangelical boundaries. Are the central tenets of evangelicalism the same in all areas? If so, are those tenets equally adhered to in all regions? In this chapter, I will look at the maintenance of orthodoxy both over time and geographically in order to expand evidence of cross-national similarities into areas of belief and morals.

Among the larger population in North America, significant regional differences exist with regard to religious beliefs. In international surveys, Canadians have been found to be less orthodox in belief than Americans. Within the US, southerners are more conservative than people in other regions. Within Canada, the Maritimes is the most conservative region, then the Prairies, then Ontario. In both countries, the west coast is less orthodox.[4] If the broader culture has an important influence on evangelical orthodoxy, then one might expect a similar pattern to emerge. Evangelicals in the southern US would be most orthodox, followed by nonsouthern US evangelicals, then Maritime, Prairie, Ontario, and west coast evangelicals. As we shall see, however, the pattern does not fit.

Table 5.1 (a and b) presents the belief items that were given to all respondents in the CE sample (N=386). The percentages in the table indicate the percentage of evangelicals who gave the more orthodox or conservative responses, and the items are listed from highest agreement to lowest agreement. Items one through six in Table 5.1a show near-perfect consensus, since they deal with central evangelical beliefs about the Godhead and Jesus Christ. The slightly lower Canadian percentages on items three through five can be accounted for by less-orthodox respondents in a Baptist church in Ontario and are not indicative of national differences.[5] Table 5.1b presents beliefs that do not receive uniform agreement and show more pronounced national differences. While there is general disagreement with item 22, since most evangelicals believe in a literal hell, Canadians are less likely to disagree with the "hell" item.[6] It deals with the "exclusivity" of conservative Protestant beliefs, since it indicates that those with different religious views are damned. It could be that the emphasis on ecumenism and tolerance in Canada may account for this. For Canadians, intolerance is intolerable, and exclusive truth claims, argues Bibby (1990), are the height of intolerance. Canadians are also more likely to agree that it is good for teenagers to be exposed to a variety of religious beliefs (item 15), since diversity is a Canadian ideal.

Several other differences connect well with national-level influences (and where the data do not implicate regional or institutional uniqueness as an explanation). Considering the comparatively revolutionary and violent history of America, it is not surprising that American evangelicals are more likely to think that taking a life is justifiable (item 12). This difference remains even when the pacifist Mennonites are removed from the Canadian sample. American evangelicals are more likely to feel that present problems are related to

Table 5.1A
Core Beliefs

Item	Overall Percentage	US Percentage	Canadian Percentage
1. Jesus was crucified, died, and was buried but on the third day he rose from the dead. (% agree)	100.0	100.0	100.0
2. Jesus Christ is the divine son of God. (% agree)	100.0	100.0	100.0
3. God exists as Father, Son, and Holy Ghost. (% agree)	99.0	100.0	97.7
4. Jesus was born of a virgin. (% agree)	98.2	99.5	96.6
5. The only way to gain salvation and eternal life is through belief in Jesus Christ. (% agree)	98.1	100.0	96.0
6. God is a personal God. (% agree)	98.4	98.0	98.9

Source: CE sample, 1995.

Table 5.1B
Peripheral Beliefs

Item	Overall Percentage	US Percentage	Canadian Percentage
7. Many problems in our country have occurred because Americans/Canadians have rejected the religious principals this country was founded on. (% agree)	91.9	95.9	87.2
8. Receiving the "baptism of the spirit" after conversion is an important part of the Christian life. (% agree)	74.6	74.5	74.8
9. There will be a literal rapture followed by an 1000 year reign of Christ. (% agree)	70.9	65.3	77.1
10. If enough people are won to Christ, other problems in our society will take care of themselves. (% agree)	69.4	72.9	65.5

HELL
See p. 77

Table 5.1B
Peripheral Beliefs (cont.)

Item	Overall Percentage	us Percentage	Canadian Percentage
11. Speaking in tongues, prophecy, and healing are for the church today. (% agree)	57.7	47.6	69.6
12. Taking a life is justified in some cases, like during wartime. (% agree)	66.6	78.9	52.3
13. Women should be eligible for ordination. (% disagree)	30.0	32.5	27.2
14. A person should be allowed to make a speech in my community against religion and the church. (% disagree)	33.5	32.1	34.9
15. It is good for Christian teenagers to be exposed to a variety of religious beliefs. (% disagree)	48.1	56.8	38.3
16. A person should arrive at his or her beliefs independently of a church. (% disagree)	54.2	54.4	53.9
17. America/Canada is still a Christian nation. (% disagree)	58.3	51.1	66.3
18. Minorities need government assistance to obtain their rightful place in America/Canada. (% disagree)	60.9	68.8	51.5
19. The King James Version of the Bible is more trustworthy than newer versions. (% disagree)	67.6	62.7	73.0
20. People who please God are more likely to receive material blessings than those who don't. (% disagree)	74.8	75.9	73.7
21. One can be a good Christian without attending Church. (% disagree)	75.3	74.1	76.7
22. God would NOT allow people to go to a place of eternal suffering like Hell. (% disagree)	91.9	96.0	87.0

Source: CE sample, 1995.

rejecting the country's religious founding principles (item 7) and that their country is still a Christian nation (item 17).[7] Higher acceptance of these beliefs may be due to American "civil religion," which sees religious significance in political history. The latter item shows that many American (and a surprising number of Canadian) evangelicals feel that their country has rejected its religious roots and thus "broken" its "covenant" with God (Bellah 1975).

Some differences are best explained by institutional factors. Regarding the belief in a literal rapture followed by the millennial reign of Christ (item 9), Timothy Weber has argued that the premillennial eschatology measured by this question has had greatest acceptance among fundamentalists and "pietistic" and holiness evangelicals (including Baptists, Pentecostals, and Presbyterians). However, premillennialism had little support among "classical" evangelicals (like the Lutherans) and "progressive" evangelicals – mostly well-educated neo-evangelicals (1991, 14–15). As a result, it is surprising that premillennialism is more popular in Canada when fundamentalist and pietistic impulses were historically stronger in the US. This difference is explained, however, by the low support for premillennialism in Minnesota, since no Lutherans agreed with the item. Believing in the modern use of charismatic gifts such as tongues, prophecy, and healing (item 11) may be more acceptable in Canada because of the influence and popularity of the previously mentioned "Toronto blessing."[8]

Few beliefs are as symbolically and theologically important to evangelicals as the authority of the Bible. Evangelicals are the "Bible believers" (Ammerman 1987). Core evangelicals hold the Bible in high regard, most being "literalists" (who believe that the Bible should be taken literally) or "inerrantists" (for whom there are no errors in the Bible). To test for a literalist interpretation, respondents were asked if they felt that creation of the world was completed by God in six twenty-four-hour days, as Genesis suggests. Table 5.2 summarizes the findings.

In Table 5.2, we see that nearly ninety percent of the respondents indicated that they believed the Bible was either literal or inerrant. Canadians were less orthodox than Americans on both these biblicism items, and within-country differences are minimal. Stackhouse suggests that, partly because of the relative insignificance of the fundamentalist/modernist debate in Canada, and partly because of the Canadian evangelical emphasis on unity, Canadians through much of their history have not had the "elaborate theological sophistication and precision" of the US (1993b, 394). Such a difference may have a

Table 5.2
Biblicism Views

29. Which of the following items best describes your view of the Bible? (N = 371)	US	CAN	30. Which of the following items best describes your view of creation? (N = 306)	US	CAN
a. It is God's word and should be taken literally, word for word.	51.5	39.3	a. The world was created by God in six 24-hour days.	59.5	41.3
b. It is God's word and has no errors in it, but not everything should be taken literally.	39.4	43.9	b. The world was created by God in six days, but each day was actually an age, much longer than 24 hours.	32.1	46.4
c. It is God's word, though it may contain some minor scientific and historical errors.	8.6	15	c. The Bible's account of the origin of the world is intended to be symbolic and not literal.	8.3	12.3
d. The Bible represents the best human effort to record God's truth but is not inspired by God.	0.5	1.7			

Source: CE sample, 1995.
Note: About .3 percent on item 29 and about 1.6 percent on item 30 responded "don't know," giving a total of 100 percent.

significant effect on views of the Bible, especially when differentiating between literalists, inerrantists, and inspirationists. Precise differences may not be as important or meaningful to Canadians, who may be less concerned about theological minutiae. Hunter's claim that evangelicals are "fixated" on theology may be less true in Canada than in the US.

About the same number of respondents view the creation story literally as those who believe that the Bible should be taken literally. However, nearly thirty percent of those who hold a literal view of the Bible do not hold a literal view of the creation story. This is especially true in Canada, where over forty percent of literalists choose the "age-day" view (30b in Table 5.2) of creation. This indicates that literalists do not always think that everything should be taken literally, as Hunter notes (1987, 29–31; see also Swenson 2000). A Lutheran in Mississippi, a biblical literalist, feels that parts of the Bible should be understood symbolically because they were written symbolically. He gave the example of the "iron hand of God" which "literally means judgment, not that God has a literal iron appendage."

Are Canadians less focused on biblicism, to use Bebbington's term, than Americans? Respondents were asked to choose one of three statements that they considered most important for Christians. The item was an attempt to tap the basic orientation of the person's religiosity, whether primarily towards biblicism, social action, or pietism. The three statements were as follows: 1) The Bible clearly tells us what we should do and should not do, and what is most important is that we do what the Bible says. Christians must obey God's commandments and resist temptation and sin. 2) What is most important for Christians is to care for those around them. We must show God's love to people who are hurting and give of ourselves to help people when we can. 3) What is most important for Christians is to be close to God, to spend time praying, worshiping and experiencing God's great love for us. It was clear from the interviews that the respondents did not like the divisions set up by this question. Some said "they are all important," while many others indicated that if Christians obey the Bible (item one) or love God (item three), they will do all three of these things as a natural result of Christian commitment. Sometimes reluctantly, 34 percent of respondents chose item one, 22 percent item two, 37 percent item three, and the remaining 7 percent volunteered some combination of the three. I expected national differences to be substantial on these items, with the first item on biblicism being prominent in the US, and the second item more often chosen by Canadians. Americans were more likely to choose the first item (37.8 percent US; 29.3 percent CDN) than Canadians, and this difference cannot be explained away by denominational differences between the countries. However, social action (item two) was not a higher priority in Canada than the US. Instead, Canadians chose item three more often than Americans (41.4 percent CDN; 33.2 percent US). Thus, there is some evidence of greater biblicism in the US, and greater pietism in Canada. The greater proportion of pietistic denominations in Canada, along with a stronger fundamentalist movement in the US (among other things), are likely explanations here.

Nationally representative data allow for more detailed geographical analysis. Tables 5.3 through 5.6 present the belief and attitudes from the 1996 God and Society poll. Tables 5.3 and 5.4 compare non-evangelicals, evangelicals, and core evangelicals in both countries. These tables confirm that central tenets of evangelicalism – namely, its crucicentrism, biblicism, conversionism, and activism – are the core beliefs held by evangelicals across North America. One would expect near-perfect consensus on these items among core evangelicals, confirming the findings in Table 5.1. Furthermore, the orthodoxy of the

Table 5.3
Core Beliefs for Non-Evangelicals, Evangelicals, and Active Evangelicals

Item	American Non-Evangelicals (N = 2258)	American Evangelicals (N = 742)	American Active Evangelicals* (N = 440)	Canadian Non-Evangelicals (N = 2697)	Canadian Evangelicals (N = 303)	Canadian Active Evangelicals* (N = 160)
1. The concept of God is an old superstition. (% disagree)	86.2	96.7	98.7	72.1	92.4	96.8
2. Human beings are not made in God's image. (% disagree)	70.1	89.4	96.3	51.8	86.5	97.5
3. The life, death and resurrection of Jesus provide forgiveness of sins. (% agree)	79.9	97.6	99.3	59.4	94.4	100
4. Jesus Christ is not divine. (% disagree)	79.4	95.8	97.7	68.1	93.4	96.5
5. The Bible is the inspired word of God. (% agree)	79.0	96.5	99.3	62.3	91.4	98.2
6. I have committed my life to Christ and am a converted Christian. (% agree)	50.4	88.7	97.5	30.1	81.9	98.1
7. It's very important to encourage non-Christians to become Christians. (% agree)	43.9	82.3	93.9	21.7	69.6	88.1
8. I want to live a spiritual life, more than I want to be rich. (% agree)	78.8	91.8	98.0	60.5	88.5	97.5

Table 5.3
Core Beliefs for Non-Evangelicals, Evangelicals, and Active Evangelicals (cont.)

Item	American Non-Evangelicals (N = 2258)	American Evangelicals (N = 742)	American Active Evangelicals* (N = 440)	Canadian Non-Evangelicals (N = 2697)	Canadian Evangelicals (N = 303)	Canadian Active Evangelicals* (N = 160)
9. Do you consider religion to be an important part of your life? (% yes)	75.5	91.0	97.3	55.1	87.4	97.5
10. Religion provides quite a bit/ great deal of guidance in my day-to-day life. (% agree)	71.8	84.4	94.8	57.8	83.7	94.9
AVERAGE PERCENTAGE	71.5	91.4	97.28	53.9	86.9	96.51

Source: God and Society poll, 1996.
Note: Item wording is simplified.
* Active evangelicals are those who attend church a few times a month or more and pray daily.

region or country should not matter for these items if evangelicals have been successful in maintaining their ideological boundaries.

Table 5.3 contains items that tap the central tenets of evangelicalism (no. 3, crucicentrism; no. 5, biblicism; no. 6, conversionism; no. 7, activism) and other items on which there is near consensus among active evangelicals. All items are coded in an orthodox direction so that the average percentage for each column is comparable to other columns. In keeping with past research, Americans as a whole are far more orthodox than Canadians, as the higher average percentage shows. Canadian evangelicals are slightly less orthodox than their American counterparts but far closer to US evangelicals than to other Canadians on these items. Virtually all committed evangelicals sampled in both countries agreed with the central evangelical beliefs (items one through seven) of evangelicalism, and religion was equally important to all of them (items eight through ten). There is only one notable geographic difference. A lower percentage of Canadian active evangelicals agree with the importance of evangelism. Aggressive proselytizing is less acceptable in the Canadian religious climate where church groups are not to compete but are to service their own (Bibby 1987). As noted in chapter 3, activism is the least clear and salient of the evangelical subcultural boundaries. In spite of this, nearly nine of ten active Canadian evangelicals and seven of ten Canadian evangelicals overall agree that evangelizing non-Christians is very important.

In sum, this table shows little evidence that evangelicals in the less-orthodox Canadian milieu are compromising on the central tenets of evangelicalism. The evangelical subculture evidently speaks clearly on these items, since evangelicals in both countries resemble each other, not the nonevangelicals around them. Even though nonevangelical Canadians are consistently less orthodox than American nonevangelicals (the average difference between the two countries on these items is 17.6 percent), evangelicals in both countries differ only by an average of 4.5 percent in their answers, and core evangelicals differ by a miniscule 1.3 percent. By comparison, American evangelicals differ from other Americans by 20 percent on average, while Canadian evangelicals are 33 percent more conservative than their fellow Canadians. The table makes it clear that the ideological boundaries of evangelicalism are not significantly weakened by a less-orthodox context (except possibly on support for evangelism), but that less-active evangelicals, as expected, show the influence of both the evangelical subculture and the wider national culture.

Table 5.4 presents the same analysis for belief items that receive less support from evangelicals. The first seven items in the table tap attitudes towards churches. In *Continental Divide* (1990), Lipset argues that Americans are more individualistic and more suspicious of established institutions. One might expect this to translate into less support for institutionalized religion in the US, but the data do not support that assumption. While differences are small, Canadians and evangelical Canadians are less supportive of institutional religion than their American counterparts, as Nevitte (1996) and others have found. Notably, roughly three-quarters of evangelicals in North America think that their "private beliefs are more important than what the churches teach," and they are just as likely to privatize their beliefs as nonevangelicals. Evangelicals are not as likely as nonevangelicals to hold privatized views of their religious practice, however, as they are more likely to view church attendance as important for good Christians (item six). The next chapter discusses the issue of privatization in more detail.

It is no surprise that evangelicals disagree that all religions are equally true and good (item eight), since they believe in exclusive truth. The religious relativism that, according to Bibby (1990), plagues Canada because of its overemphasis on "the cultural mosaic" and pluralism does not translate into greater religious relativism among active evangelicals. Agreement with the statement "People who love God and work hard will always have enough money" (item nine) is slightly higher in the US, as expected, where belief in the "American dream" seems to influence evangelicals and nonevangelicals alike. The American meritocracy, which holds that individuals succeed or fail because of their own efforts, is a strong impulse historically in the southern country (cf. Lipset 1990). Finally, higher acceptance for a literal interpretation of the Bible (item ten) and for the statement that "the world will end in the battle of Armageddon" (item eleven) south of the border suggests that evangelicals in the US are more likely to be biblical literalists and premillennialists, as noted above.

Evidently, the evangelical subculture does not speak as clearly to these items. Active American and Canadian evangelicals show far greater differences here than on the items in the previous table. Even on these items, however, evangelical responses more closely match the responses of other evangelicals than their national counterparts. Comparing US-Canada average differences, nonevangelical Canadians and Americans differ the most (averaging 10.6 percent), while evangelicals differ by 8.1 percent, and active evangelicals by 5.3 percent. Evangelicals in the US and Canada show less influence from their national cultures – they differ from nonevangelicals in their countries by 16.8 percent and 20 percent respectively – than from the evangelical subculture on these "non-core" religious items as well.

Table 5.4
Peripheral Beliefs for Non-Evangelicals, Evangelicals, and Active Evangelicals

Item	American Non-Evangelicals (N = 2258)	American Evangelicals (N = 742)	American Active Evangelicals* (N = 440)	Canadian Non-Evangelicals (N = 2697)	Canadian Evangelicals (N = 303)	Canadian Active Evangelicals* (N = 160)
1. Churches should be required to pay taxes. (% disagree)	52.9	73.8	80.0	37.2	59.9	71.1
2. Illegal money given to the church should be returned. (% agree)	78.3	81.9	85.0	81.9	89.0	93.1
3. Churches should spend more helping the poor. (% disagree)	12.4	12.1	13.3	13.7	10.5	11.2
4. Churches put too much emphasis on asking for money. (% disagree)	36.1	49.0	56.7	37.6	46.5	54.7
5. I have quite a bit/a great deal of confidence in the church. (% agree)	64.0	82.5	89.3	48.9	74.4	85.4
6. You don't need to go to church to be a good Christian. (% disagree)	24.9	47.0	64.5	13.6	36.6	52.5
7. My private beliefs are more important than what the churches teach. (% disagree)	26.9	27.7	32.2	23.9	25.7	32.0
8. All religions in the world are equally good and true. (% disagree)	35.4	63.9	73.0	27.2	58.0	78.6

Table 5.4
Peripheral Beliefs for Non-Evangelicals, Evangelicals, and Active Evangelicals (cont.)

Item	American Non-Evangelicals (N = 2258)	American Evangelicals (N = 742)	American Active Evangelicals* (N = 440)	Canadian Non-Evangelicals (N = 2697)	Canadian Evangelicals (N = 303)	Canadian Active Evangelicals* (N = 160)
9. People who love God and work hard will always have money. (% agree)	37.6	47.9	52.2	24.8	40.5	45.9
10. The Bible should be taken literally, word for word. (% agree)	46.7	79.0	87.8	23.9	64.7	84.3
11. The world will end in the battle of Armageddon. (% agree)	33.8	68.1	74.2	12.7	52.6	68.2
AVERAGE PERCENTAGE	40.8	57.5	64.4	31.4	50.8	61.6

Source: God and Society poll, 1996.
Note: Item wording has been simplified.
* Active evangelicals are those who attend church a few times a month or more and pray daily.

Tables 5.5 and 5.6 break down these findings by region. (The columns titled "evan" refer to the evangelicals in that region and "non" refers to the region's nonevangelicals.) As before, the last lines of the tables give the average percentage for the column. Nonevangelicals in British Columbia average 44.8 percent on the ten items in the table, indicating that theirs is the least conservative region in the country on these items, followed by Ontario, Quebec, the Prairies, and – most conservative – the Maritime region. However, evangelicals in Canada do not follow the same pattern, since their averages do not match those of the nonevangelicals in their region.[9] Furthermore, there are few significant regional differences among the evangelical subsample in Canada.[10]

In the US, Table 5.6 indicates that evangelicals are more likely to parallel the conservativeness of their region than are Canadians. The American South is the most conservative region, followed by the Northcentral, Northeast, Mountain, and Western regions, and evangelicals within these regions follow nearly the same order. Nearly all regional differences between American evangelicals are small, however, and very few reach standard levels of significance.[11] I conclude that the orthodoxy of the region has little effect on evangelical orthodoxy on these central tenets.

GEOGRAPHICAL VARIATION
IN MORALS

While Hunter emphasizes the importance of orthopraxy for evangelicals, he argues that the "moral boundaries separating Christian conduct from worldly conduct have been substantially undermined" (1987, 58). Playing pool or cards, dancing, going to movies, smoking, and drinking alcohol are no longer seen as intrinsically wrong by the majority of young evangelicals, unless carried to excess. Prohibitions remain strong, however, against premarital, extramarital, and homosexual sex among those Hunter surveyed (ibid., 63).

In the CE sample, respondents were asked whether they thought certain moral behaviours were always, usually, sometimes, or never wrong. Table 5.7 lists the moral questions and gives the percentage of those in each region that viewed the behaviour as "always wrong." Hunter's results are included for comparison, bearing in mind that the CE sample is not nationally representative, and Hunter's data are limited to evangelical college students (ibid., 61).

In many ways, the results given here are consistent with Hunter's findings. Traditional restrictions on smoking, drinking alcohol, dancing, and movie watching are no longer upheld by the majority, while

Table 5.5
Core Beliefs by Region in Canada

Item	Canadian Non-Evangelicals	Canadian Evangelicals	British Columbia		The Prairies		Ontario		Quebec		Maritimes	
			Non	Evan	Non	Evan	Non	Evan	Non	Evan*	Non	Evan*
1. The concept of God is an old superstition. (% disagree)	72.1	92.4	68.5	95.1	79.8	96.2	73.6	93.9	65.3	74.2	77.9	90.9
2. Human beings are not made in God's image. (% disagree)	51.8	86.5	36.8	83.7	54.6	86.3	53.1	89.9	53.5	80.6	57.0	87.6
3. The life, death, and resurrection of Jesus provide forgiveness of sins. (% agree)	59.4	94.4	43.6	91.8	63.8	91.3	59.7	98.0	58.7	90.3	74.2	96.9
4. Jesus Christ is not divine. (% disagree)	68.1	93.4	56.2	95.1	71.4	93.6	66.0	97.0	71.3	80.7	81.2	90.9
5. The Bible is the inspired word of God. (% agree)	62.3	91.4	47.3	88.5	65.4	90.1	60.7	95.9	66.9	83.9	70.5	93.8
6. I have committed my life to Christ and am a converted Christian. (% agree)	30.1	81.9	20.8	83.9	31.4	83.8	26.5	82.5	36.2	74.2	38.8	79.4
7. It's very important to encourage non-Christians to become Christians. (% agree)	21.7	69.6	13.8	73.7	25.0	72.5	21.7	63.2	20.3	61.3	31.4	72.8

Table 5.5
Core Beliefs by Region in Canada (cont.)

Item	Canadian Non-Evangelicals	Canadian Evangelicals	British Columbia Non	Evan	The Prairies Non	Evan	Ontario Non	Evan	Quebec Non	Evan*	Maritimes Non	Evan*
8. I want to live a spiritual life more than I want to be rich. (% agree)	60.5	88.5	63.5	88.8	59.3	90.1	58.9	93.0	59.9	71.0	67.8	87.9
9. Do you consider religion to be an important part of your life? (% yes)	55.1	87.4	45.6	86.9	57.0	84.8	55.3	88.9	54.7	83.9	66.2	90.9
10. Religion provides quite a bit/ a great deal of guidance in my day-to-day life. (% agree)	57.8	83.7	51.7	87.1	52.6	86.6	58.3	79.5	61.8	76.9	60.6	90.0
AVERAGE PERCENTAGE	53.9	86.9	44.8	87.5	56.0	87.5	53.4	88.2	54.9	77.7	62.6	88.1

Source: God and Society poll, 1996.
* These column percentages are based on small sample sizes (<50) and thus have large margins of error.
Note: Item wording has been simplified.

Table 5.6
Core Beliefs by Region in the United States

Item	American Non-Evangelicals	American Evangelicals	West		Mountain		North Central		South		Northeast	
			Non	Evan	Non	Evan*	Non	Evan	Non	Evan	Non	Evan*
1. The concept of God is an old superstition. (% disagree)	86.2	96.7	80.1	94.2	85.9	97.8	90.0	98.2	87.1	96.5	85.5	98.8
2. Human beings are not made in God's image. (% disagree)	70.1	89.4	58.6	84.5	59.8	86.7	77.2	91.4	74.9	91.4	67.2	83.3
3. The life, death, and resurrection of Jesus provide forgiveness of sins. (% agree)	79.9	97.6	71.6	97.1	68.7	95.6	85.8	98.1	84.6	98.3	77.3	95.1
4. Jesus Christ is not divine. (% disagree)	79.4	95.8	66.8	94.2	73.5	91.1	86.2	98.1	85.2	96.0	75.7	93.0
5. The Bible is the inspired word of God. (% agree)	79.0	96.5	71.6	93.2	70.9	95.6	83.8	96.3	83.6	97.4	76.1	95.2
6. I have committed my life to Christ and am a converted Christian. (% agree)	50.4	88.7	39.1	80.8	41.0	84.1	57.6	90.7	59.1	92.0	43.3	82.9
7. It's very important to encourage non-Christians to become Christians. (% agree)	43.9	82.3	34.8	73.8	40.9	80.0	48.5	85.1	55.8	86.0	34.1	74.7

Table 5.6
Core Beliefs by Region in the United States (cont.)

Item	American Non-Evangelicals	American Evangelicals	West		Mountain		North Central		South		Northeast	
			Non	Evan	Non	Evan*	Non	Evan	Non	Evan	Non	Evan*
8. I want to live a spiritual life, more than I want to be rich. (% agree)	78.8	91.8	78.5	89.4	72.4	88.9	83.2	95.0	79.2	92.3	76.2	89.1
9. Do you consider religion to be an important part of your life. (% yes)	75.5	91.0	69.1	85.4	65.4	86.7	79.8	93.1	80.9	91.7	72.6	92.8
10. Religion provides quite a bit / a great deal of guidance in my day-to-day life. (% agree)	71.8	84.4	72.6	78.4	67.5	76.9	70.5	85.3	75.8	86.3	69.1	84.4
AVERAGE PERCENTAGE	71.5	91.4	64.3	87.1	64.6	88.3	76.3	93.1	76.6	92.8	67.7	88.9

Source: God and Society poll, 1996.
* These column percentages are based on small sample sizes (<50) and thus have high margins of error.
Note: Item wording has been simplified.

Table 5.7
Moral Values

	% saying the activity is "always wrong"					
	Total	Hunter*	Minnesota	Mississippi	Manitoba	New Brunswick
Hitting a spouse	93.6	–	94.4	91.3	96.2	91.5
Homosexual activity	93.5	94	96.2	96.8	87.9	93.1
Sex before marriage	89.1	89	93.5	89.4	85.6	87.5
Buying and looking at pornography	88.8	–	86.9	91.4	87.5	90.3
Not claiming all income on income tax returns	85.3	86	84.8	81.7	85.4	90.3
Littering	72.7	–	76.2	74.2	68.9	70.8
Smoking	66.7	51	54.8	67	71.6	76.8
Gambling	63	–	52.8	64.4	59.8	81.4
Viewing R-rated movies at a theatre	50.3	7	32.1	53.8	53.8	67.6
Working in a bar	42.5	–	43.7	48.3	29	52.9
Overeating	36.5	–	40.4	40.7	27.9	38.2
Drinking alcohol	34.5	17	19.8	48.4	22.1	56.3
Divorce	22.1	–	24.5	22.8	13.7	29.6
Viewing a PG-rated movie at a theatre	14.6	–	4.8	18.9	13.7	25.4
Dancing	14.1	–	7.6	14.6	13	25
Participating in a protest that could lead to arrest	11.2	–	6.9	14.8	10	14.9
Buying a very expensive car	4.9	–	4.9	4.9	1	10.9

* Source: CE sample, 1995, and Hunter's survey of evangelical college students (1987, 61). Based on "percent believing the activity is morally wrong all the time: homosexual relations between consenting adults; premarital sexual intercourse; cheating on your income tax; smoking cigarettes; watching an R-rated movie; drinking alcohol."

sexual mores, such as premarital and homosexual sex, remain always wrong for most. Even though two-thirds of the respondents thought smoking was always wrong, many indicated in the interviews that smoking was wrong for health reasons, not for moral reasons.

The table shows surprisingly few regional differences: not even the perceived moral conservatism of Mississippi stands out. Among core evangelicals, age, not region, is a key factor in moral strictness. Younger evangelicals are less conservative on all items except divorce, hitting a spouse, littering, pornography, premarital sex, and cheating on taxes.[12] To a lesser extent, educated respondents are less conservative.[13] Some of the older evangelical interviewees had never been to a bar or movie theatre. As a result, some older respondents were not familiar with the movie rating system. "What does PG mean?" was a question several of the older respondents asked, including some pastors. One staunch evangelical, an elderly man from New Brunswick, said that he had never been inside a theatre, not even when church members were given free tickets to the Billy Graham film *The Prodigal*. All of the younger respondents were familiar with movie ratings and none of them seemed hesitant to go to a movie theatre.

While cross-national comparisons of morality are limited in nationally representative datasets, what evidence there is suggests that Canadian evangelicals are at least as morally orthodox as their American counterparts, in spite of a more conservative American milieu (compare Tables 5.8 and 5.9 below). Evangelical morality does not seem to mirror the conservativeness of the region in which respondents reside. In light of these findings, I conclude that there is no clear evidence from these data that orthodoxy varies significantly by region among evangelicals, especially on core issues among core evangelicals. The evidence suggests that the evangelical subcultural boundaries are intact and drawn around the same beliefs and morals across the US and Canada. In other words, the boundaries show strength, both in ubiquity and relative impermeability, on certain orthodox beliefs and morals.

Why Minimal Regional Variation?

This finding will surprise many, including some core evangelicals, who assume that evangelical conservativeness increases as one moves south, paralleling regional conservativeness. Why is it that the orthodoxy of the region has little effect on the evangelical orthodoxy in that region? First, evangelicals resist the "outside" influences of the larger culture, since some "worldly" influences are kept out by walls of orthodoxy. Core evangelicals are more likely to succumb to the hidden "inside" influences towards accommodation. Hunter argues that the "coming generation" of evangelical leaders is less conservative than the rank-and-file evangelical partly because of their involvement in higher education and the "debunking" process that it affords. Hunter found that in private evangelical institutions of higher learning, evangelical students were more likely to compromise orthodoxy than evangelicals attending secular institutions (1987, 176–8). Faculty at these Christian institutions are more liberal than students, and students are more liberal when they leave than when they arrive, according to Hunter.

Hunter's argument likely overstates the tendency of evangelical institutions of higher learning to contribute to a weakening of orthodoxy over time, but he is correct that influences come mainly from *inside* the evangelical subculture and from the more educated to the less educated, or from the *top down*. The more educated evangelical leaders may be less orthodox but will generally maintain orthodoxy on those beliefs and morals that are pivotal to evangelical identity and boundary maintenance, since they are evangelicals themselves. Hunter's finding that accommodating influences come from the *inside out* makes sense considering the clear boundaries evangelicals have developed and maintained, as argued in chapter 3. It also fits with the evidence that evangelicalism's central tenets are ubiquitous and exhibit minimal regional variation. Thus, accommodation is limited. Core evangelicals will only tolerate less-orthodox top-down influences within clearly drawn boundaries.

Inside influence seems to stem from the *South up*. American and Canadian evangelicals listen to each other more than they listen to those outside the evangelical fold in areas of orthodoxy, and the loudest voices are coming from the South. Several factors point to this conclusion. First, as Shibley (1996) has demonstrated, it is the southern evangelical denominations that are growing in other regions of the US. Evangelicals migrate to other regions from the US South, and southern church planters and missionaries start churches in northern regions. Many conservative Protestant denominations in Canada originated in the US, and some, like the Lutheran Church – Canada, have only recently separated from their American parent organizations (Bedell 1994). Furthermore, a disproportionate number of the largest evangelical institutions, evangelists and televangelists, magazines and books come from southern US sources. Hunter (1981) notes that the eight largest evangelical publishing houses are in the (southern) Baptist tradition. As a result, Canadian and northern US evangelicals watch and read the opinions of southern evangelicals more than vice versa. Finally, American evangelicals transplant denominations, organizations, leaders, and pastors to Canada more than vice versa (Stackhouse 1993b, 376). Evangelicals and fundamentalists moved freely across the border, but more up than down (Elliot 1993). Of the twenty-two pastors I interviewed in Canada, five were American pastors who had moved north to fill a pulpit, and fifteen of the twenty-two pastors took some or all of their theological training in the US. Based simply on numbers, one assumes that the roughly sixty-two million conservative Protestants in the US – half of whom reside in the southeastern states – have more influence in Canada than the roughly three million Canadian conservative Protestants have on the US.

Interview data suggest the prevalence of south-up influences within evangelicalism.[14] Evangelicals in Minnesota, Manitoba, and New Brunswick referred to the teachings of such southerners as Pat Robertson, Jack Hayford, James Dobson, and Billy Graham, although no one mentioned a Canadian evangelical leader. Grenville reports that when he asked a sample of Canadian evangelicals whom they considered the most influential evangelical leader in Canada, seventy-nine percent said "No one." Only five percent cited David Mainse, host of Canada's evangelical television program "100 Huntley Street," while the same percentage mentioned Southern Baptist evangelist Billy Graham (1995b, 22). The *south-up* and *inside-out* influences in evangelicalism make for less regional variation within the evangelical subculture.

If orthodoxy is influenced from the top-down as Hunter suggests, then one would expect churches to differ according to the orthodoxy of the church leadership, especially the pastor. One might also expect to find pockets of orthodoxy, especially in those areas where evangelicals are relatively immobile and have low education. That is to say, evangelical orthodoxy varies not according to region or nation but according to much smaller units of analysis, such as a congregation or possibly a county. There is ample evidence for within-region variation and congregational variation from the interviews. Pastors who have preached in different locations within the same region reported "pockets" of orthodoxy, like this Pentecostal pastor in Mississippi who had also been a pastor in Florida: "I was raised in Florida, and we did not participate in mixed swimming ... the beach was off limits to the church. We moved to Texas and they have pool parties! [Laughs.] The [church] youth! I pastored a church in West Florida, they were death on anything like that, you couldn't have a pool party or anything like that, very strict. Even within the confines of Florida, I pastored in Pensacola, Florida, they had pool parties there. I pastored in the eastern sector of West Florida and they were very strict again. There is an amalgamation here [in Mississippi]. Some are very strict. We are taking a trip up to Florida this weekend for a beach retreat and some of the parents are not letting their children go because they are going to swim, they are going to the beach."

Other pastoral reports verified smaller pockets of moral strictness within regions. A Missouri Synod Lutheran pastor in Jackson said: "The Missouri Synod Lutherans in the south [part of Mississippi] tend to be a little less conservative particularly in the area of interchurch activities." In Canada, a Maritime Baptist pastor argued that New Brunswick Baptists are more conservative than Nova Scotia

Baptists. This response from a Southern Baptist pastor in Manitoba captures the southern influence, especially in the West: "The conservative right-wing aspect of the Southern Baptists influences the Canadian Convention probably more than any other. Most of the pastors who come here have that [southern] flavour. I would say that about fifty percent of the Canadian pastors would be strongly conservative in all aspects. [Would they be from the US?] Yeah, and from the South. See, Alberta has that [southern flavour], you know with the Reform party, so that is where our headquarters is. Our seminary is in Alberta, the strongest conference is probably the one in Alberta ... Here [the denomination] is so small the tone is set by the pastors." As this pastor and many others suggested, general conservatism and moral strictness varied from church to church, but only with respect to styles of worship and some morals, not the central tenets of the faith. This pastor believed that pastors were the source of church differences, though the church laity had some effect as well, since they control the hiring of the pastor in some evangelical denominations. Variation in orthodoxy, then, seems to have more to do with "inside" influences, influences that can vary by congregation or denomination.

EXAMINING CHANGE OVER TIME

There is little evidence that evangelical orthodoxy parallels the orthodoxy of its regional context. Therefore, it appears that the walls of evangelical orthodoxy are not crumbling under the onslaught of secular forces. Whether they are deteriorating slowly over time is another question. While Hunter claims that orthodoxy is eroding, others disagree. The most notable evidence against Hunter's argument that evangelicalism is being secularized is the work of Penning and Smidt, who replicated Hunter's 1982 survey of evangelical college students in 1996. They concluded: "It is evident that evangelical college students remain highly orthodox in their theological viewpoints. Not only does one find that the theological positions long associated with the evangelical tradition continue to be expressed almost uniformly by evangelical college students today, but one also finds that there has been basically no real change in theological stands among evangelical college students over the past two decades. The same tends to be generally true with regard to moral boundaries as well" (1999, 20). Evidence from the general population of evangelicals supports this claim.

While survey data in the two North American countries may not go back far enough to test longer trends of weakening orthodoxy, we can examine change over time in the last twenty or twenty-five years. The data in Tables 5.8 and 5.9 do not tell us if individuals themselves are becoming more or less orthodox, only whether or not evangelicals as a whole are changing with time. Table 5.8 uses the 1972–98 General Social Survey in the US, and all items in the table run over at least a twenty-year span, except for the Bible item (ten years). Because there are too many years for which to present yearly data, the table gives the overall average and the "slope" – the average yearly percent change. To illustrate how to interpret the table, look at the figures in the first row. Over a twenty-year span, seventy percent of US evangelicals disagree with the proposition that a woman should be able to have a legal abortion for any reason, and there is no significant change in that percentage over time (the slope is not significant). By comparison, just over fifty percent of nonevangelical Americans disagree with this abortion statement, and the percentage is declining by more than six-tenths of a percent per year (–.63). Thus, between the seventies and nineties, the percentage of nonevangelical Americans who disagree with abortion for any reason fell more than twelve percentage points from roughly sixty percent to forty-seven percent (percents vary slightly from year to year), while evangelical disagreement with abortion dipped only slightly. Like their attitude towards abortion, attitudes towards pornography, belief in life after death, belief in the Bible, and practices like church attendance and prayer show no significant change over a twenty-five-year span. On the one hand, evangelicals show weakening orthodoxy relating to premarital sex, legalization of marijuana, opposition to sex education in school, and the viewing of x-rated movies, as the significant and negative slopes indicate. On each of these items, the evangelicals are moving towards the less orthodox views or practices of nonevangelicals, and they are moving in the same direction (of weakening orthodoxy) as the rest of the US population. On the other hand, evangelicals are becoming more orthodox in relation to divorce laws, hitting another man, and smoking. Here again, however, they are moving in the same direction as nonevangelicals, who also are becoming more conservative on these items. In the main, there is evidence that American evangelicals are being influenced by secular society, but there is mixed support for weakening orthodoxy.

Using Reginald Bibby's Project Canada survey series, run every five years from 1975 to 1995, I present the evangelical and nonevangelical percentages for each year. While the evangelical percentages fluctuate somewhat because the number of evangelicals in each sample is relatively small (between seventy-five and one hundred), there is little evidence of increased secularity over time.[15] Canadian

Table 5.8
Change Over Time in American Beliefs, Morals, and Practices

	Evangelicals		Non-Evangelicals	
	Average %	Slope[1]	Average %	Slope[1]
Disagrees that "a woman should be able to get a legal abortion for any reason" (%)	70.7	–0.14ns	53.4	–0.63***
Premarital sex is always wrong (%)	45.9	–0.36***	21.9	–0.39***
Pornography should be outlawed for all (%)	53.4	0.10ns	36.4	–0.26***
Laws should make divorce harder to get (%)	63.8	0.23*	47	0.16*
Marijuana should not be legal (%)	83.5	–0.19**	71.3	–0.04**
Oppose sex education in public schools (%)	22.3	–0.46***	12	–0.31***
Not OK to hit another man (%)	30.6	0.40***	32.9	0.15***
Belief in life after death (%)	83.8	–0.06ns	67.8	0.15***
Belief in literal or inspired Bible (%)	95.4	–0.05ns	80	–0.23**
Doesn't smoke (%)	67.1	0.82***	64.3	0.84***
Doesn't drink (%)	46.8	–0.26ns	23.2	0.39***
Hasn't seen x-rated movie (%)	82.3	–0.25***	76.1	–0.23***
Attend church weekly (%)	38.3	0 ns	25.9	–0.23***
Prays daily or more (%)	64.9	.28ns	51.9	–0.17*

Source: General Social Survey 1972–1998.
Significance: determined by logistic regression. *** .001; ** .01; * .05; ns – not significant.
[1]Slope is determined by average yearly change in percentage, not logistic regression slope.
Item wording has been simplified.

evangelical orthodoxy and orthopraxy is as strong, if not stronger, than it was twenty years ago, even on those items where most Canadians are becoming less conservative (abortion in case of rape, premarital sex, church attendance). While different items, a greater span of years, and larger samples may tell a different story, time does not seem to undermine evangelical orthodoxy, at least in Canada.

Finally, a quick analysis of Tables 5.8 and 5.9 indicates that there are several comparable items between the two tables, with similar or identical wording (those dealing with pornography, divorce, marijuana, smoking, drinking, and church attendance). Comparing the average percentage in the tables indicates that evangelicals in Canada are not less morally orthodox than American evangelicals. One should not take this as conclusive evidence, however, since comparing datasets with different survey strategies is tenuous.[16]

In conclusion, there is some evidence of secular influences on evangelical orthodoxy in the US, but not in Canada. Furthermore, there is little evidence of weakening orthodoxy. Overall, evangelicalism may

Table 5.9
Change Over Time in Canadian Beliefs, Morals, and Practices

Item	Evangelicals					Non-Evangelicals				
	1975	1980	1985	1990	1995	1975	1980	1985	1990	1995
Should not be possible to get an abortion in the case of rape (%)	25.0	23.4	29.1	30.5	47.3	13.7	13.3	12.6	8.0	8.1
Should not be possible to get an abortion if the family can't afford more children (%)	53.1	67.7	74.7	63.2	85.3	40.5	42.7	46.2	42.7	42.2
There should be laws against distributing pornography to all ages (%)	58.6	55.7	62.5	50.0	69.6	32.2	33.5	36.1	32.6	36.1
Premarital sex is always wrong (%)	42.4	42.9	48.7	36.4	53.8	17.7	12.8	12.9	10.6	9.5
Disagree/strongly disagree that marijuana should be legalized (%)	84.1	83.7	83.8	84.7	85.7	73.2	70.0	69.4	74.7	67.3
Disagree/strongly disagree that divorce should be easier to obtain (%)	–	81.3	74.1	73.7	87.9	–	15.2	16.3	12.4	14.8
Believes that Jesus is the divine Son of God (%)*	75.8	79.0	84.1	74.2	88.0	43.4	43.1	51.8	45.0	45.0
Never smoke cigarettes	–	67.4	81.5	–	86.4	–	57.2	60.2	–	69.9
Never drink alcohol	–	44.7	40.0	–	45.7	–	21.5	12.3	–	14.7
Attend church weekly or more	36.0	42.4	44.3	40.8	55.5	17.3	17.9	13.5	13.6	14.3

Source: Project Canada 1975–1995.
*Item wording changes slightly in 1985. Wording has been simplified.

be changing but not consistently towards accommodation. Both the regional analysis and the over-time analysis bear this out. The boundaries of evangelical orthodoxy seem on the whole to be in pretty good shape. Regional similarities in orthodoxy seem to stem from broader influences within North American evangelicalism. These evangelical influences come largely from the south up, since southern evangelicals produce more cultural "stuff" – books, magazines, spokespersons, televangelists, music, pastors, and leaders – that influence the evangelical subculture. In this way, the evangelical subculture regulates certain evangelical beliefs and morals, maintaining (and possibly increasing) international uniformity.

6 Orthopraxy: Evangelical Practice and Commitment

Evangelicals are orthodox, but theirs is an "engaged orthodoxy," argue Emerson and Smith (2000). Evangelicals want to influence the larger culture and society around them. Faith to them is not simply a personal religious preference. Instead, they seek societal transformation, through corporate action, like political-moral campaigning, and through individual action, such as witnessing. Furthermore, evangelical faith has expectations for personal religious behaviour, including church attendance, Bible reading, and prayer.

Evangelicals in Canada and the US distinguish themselves from other religious traditions by their high levels of religious practice (Kellstedt et al. 1993; Bibby 1993). According to the God and Society poll, 73 percent of evangelicals pray at least daily, 36 percent read the Bible at least daily, and 55.5 percent attend church weekly or more, as compared to other religious traditions, which average 48 percent, 12 percent, and 31 percent respectively. Other measures of commitment are higher as well.

On the surface, high levels of evangelical activism do not seem to mesh well with the self-disclosed identities presented in chapter 3. Core evangelicals describe themselves on the basis of certain beliefs and a conversion experience but only rarely on the basis of practice. Even when defining an evangelical or a "Christian," they hardly ever refer to religious practice. No practice, including personal evangelism, seems to be central to evangelical identity and boundaries. Given these findings, one would expect evangelicals to be distinguished by their beliefs but less so by their practices.

Recall from chapter 3 that evangelicals are not comfortable with behavioural requirements as a means of distinguishing evangelicals from nonevangelicals, although interviewees indicated that certain behaviours – including a moral lifestyle, church attendance, and witnessing – demonstrate the authenticity of one's conversion. That is, activism, unlike conversion and orthodox belief, is not a *distinctive* characteristic of the evangelical and is thus not a key part of the evangelical repertoire for distinguishing themselves from other religious groups. However, activism is a demonstration of faith, a *demonstrative* characteristic. It is an indication that one's conversion is authentic. Activism can thus be a central impulse in evangelicalism, without being central to the self-definition of evangelicals.

This chapter examines two types of religious behaviour or practice – public ritual practice and private devotional practice – and levels of commitment.[1] As we shall see, there is little variation in levels of practice and commitment, lending more support to the theme of cross-national similarities within evangelicalism. I also examine the connection between reported beliefs and practices, or how beliefs are translated into action in the world. Do evangelicals carry their faith into the public world of work, or do they have difficulty applying faith to work? Do evangelicals have strategies for influencing their society for the better, and if so, do they implement them? The answers to these questions give us different lenses through which to view the public faith of evangelicals.

PRACTICE

Since the CE sample was limited to regular church attendees, public practice is naturally, even artificially, high. Survey respondents not only attend church regularly but they are frequently involved in other church-related activities.

Table 6.1 shows that the ritual practice of active evangelicals goes well beyond church attendance. These evangelicals give, on average, eleven percent of their income to religious organizations. They frequent prayer meetings and Bible studies at their church and attend interdenominational events such as retreats, prayer walks, or concerts of prayer.[2] The Promise Keepers "stadium" events, in which (mainly) evangelical men gather in sports arenas to worship and listen to motivational speakers, are also popular among those surveyed.[3] In addition, evangelicals claim to witness frequently.[4] On these levels of ritual, there was little difference by region or denomination.

PRIVATIZATION

Do evangelicals limit the relevance of their religious faith to private sectors of their lives? There seems to be agreement among scholars

Table 6.1
Levels of Ritual Practice

Ritual	US	CAN	Total
1. % who attend church weekly or more	90.9	93.8	91.4
2. % who attend prayer meetings or small group Bible studies weekly or more	71.2	50.4*	61.3
3. % who share their faith weekly or more	57.4	50.2	54.2
4. average % of annual income given to church and other religious organizations	10.9	11	10.9
5. % who have gone on a prayer walk or attended a concert of prayer in the last two years	35.7	46.0*	40.5
6. % who attended a retreat or seminar for spiritual growth in the last two years	65.8	68.2	66.9
7. % who have done door-to-door evangelism, street witnessing, or other community outreach in the last two years	38.5	34.9	36.8

Source: CE sample, 1995.
The asterisk (*) indicates that there is a statistically significant difference between the US and
Canadian percentages.

that privatization of religion is widespread (Bellah et al. 1985; Hunter 1983; Roof 1993; Luckmann 1967). However, there is disagreement as to whether privatization would be higher among evangelicals than other religious groups, or whether it would be higher in Canada or in the US. Hart suggests that the relative individualism, voluntarism, sectarianism, and antinomianism of evangelicals, as compared to other Protestants, may mean higher levels of privatization (1987). However, research by Regnerus and Smith (1998) and Hunter (1981) found that evangelicals were less privatized in their faith than other religious traditions in the US. This might be expected of core evangelicals who are actively involved in the institutional church. Even among the most active evangelicals, however, we may find evidence of privatization if we look for public faith in the workplace. Does the tendency towards privatization in North America mean that evangelicals no longer apply religious symbols and meanings in their occupations?

The question is particularly important because of the historical significance of work to the conservative Protestant. Weber (1958) argued that through the influences of Luther, all vocations became viewed as equally valuable in God's eyes, and that as a result the ultimate demonstration of devotion to God was diligence in one's "calling," or profession. Since salvation was based on God's elective process and not on human effort, success in work was an indication of God's favour, the best assurance of salvation one could hope for on earth. This belief, according to Weber, in conjunction with the anxiety of not knowing one's eternal destiny, led many generations of Protestants to strive for economic achievement. Hunter finds (1987, 54) that the spiritual meaning of work has waned significantly in the minds of Protestants in modern times, as Weber predicted it would (1958, 181–2).

Of the core evangelicals who work full time outside the home, 67 percent consider their work a calling, and nearly all respondents (94 percent) said that their faith had "a great deal" (72 percent) or "quite a bit" (22 percent) of an effect on them at work. Respondents were then asked: "Can you tell me how your faith affects you at work?" Since the answers were often vague (e.g., "love others"), respondents were prompted to give specific answers relating to whether or not they attempted to evangelize co-workers; whether they implemented or recommended policy or structural changes that reflected their religious principles; whether their faith affected their choice of job; whether they had refused contracts for ethical reasons; or other such indications that they applied their faith at work. About one-third of the respondents (35 percent) gave only private answers (to do with honesty, for example, or a positive attitude, patience with others, hard work, etc.), in spite of the probing follow-up questions. Forty-five percent were public with their faith (witnessing, counselling work friends on spiritual and other matters, speaking out against "sinful" behaviours at work). About 30 percent of respondents recalled incidents that I considered potentially detrimental to their careers (confronting a superior, refusing a contract, taking a lesser job, etc.). The percentage of those who were public about their faith at work was not substantively affected by region. The following response from a bank manager in Manitoba discloses private and public applications of his faith at work:

Well, I want to live my life in a way that is pleasing to the Lord ... In other words, when people see me will they see that Christ has made a change in my life? If they don't something is wrong. In the things that I say, my language, and sharing with people when the opportunity arises as to who I belong to. Telling people about Christ, I would say ... (How does it influence relationships with employees, customers?) Well, integrity, honest in what I tell them ... I have gone through a situation in another [bank] branch I was in where people needed to be disciplined and I tried to guard against my own prejudice ... My boss knows who I belong to ... I've been talked to about [saying] God stuff too much at work. My bosses' boss told me "At work, the work is first." I said, "No, the Lord Jesus Christ is first, want my resignation?" and the conversation just went someplace else ... So I would like to touch some lives through the process, and just being a good guy doesn't cut it. If I don't tell people about Christ I'm really not doing a lot.

One of the commonly reported ways evangelical faith influences behaviour at work is the degree to which respondents separate themselves from what they perceive to be immoral behaviour. At one extreme, two older respondents mentioned that they refused to interact with certain people at work who did not, in their view, live morally. One retired Minnesotan woman gave this answer when I asked whether her faith affected relationships at work: "Yes it did. I had people that I worked with that I shared the gospel with, and ... if I see someone who is not living my lifestyle, I am pleasant to them but I don't seek out a relationship." Others would not steer away from certain people but would refuse to participate in events that featured immoral behaviour (drinking, dancing, etc.). A younger Minnesotan said: "Well, many people at work are devout non-Christians, so that prevents me from socializing with them in a manner that they might expect me to ... That's not to say I wouldn't socialize with them, but that when I did I would not necessarily engage in the activities that they were engaging in." Still others would attend the events but would not participate in the behaviour they considered immoral. A New Brunswick teacher who had just hosted a teacher's party at her house, said: "If you take a stand and they know who you are it cuts back on the [bad] language, the dirty jokes, and that cuts back on what they expect of you. For instance, they know when they came to my house that there would be lots of pop but no beer." Overall, evangelicals suggested they were friendly and personable at work, although they separate themselves from people, events, or certain behaviours at an event, to maintain orthopraxy.

One way to contextualize this discussion is to compare the interview data with what evangelical authors say about work.[5] A review of five books from evangelical authors and publishers showed at least two weaknesses in the link between faith and work among core evangelicals.[6] First, both the content of the responses and the lack of religious language used to articulate the work-faith relationship indicate a separation between work and religion. While respondents were able to articulate how their faith affected them personally at work, many responses were limited to character, guidance, moral prohibitions, and a sense of higher purpose. All of the responses indicated an orientation of the heart, such that if the heart was right, the actual labour performed was not important. Four authors decry this chasm between work and faith as stemming from a "Christian dualism" between the sacred and secular realms (e.g., Bernbaum and Steer 1986, 81). Having no religious language to apply to their work, evangelical respondents imported private religious language and applied it to themselves while at work, not to work itself. Note the response of this Canadian, who was part of a racial minority. At work he was treated unjustly, but his faith helped him deal positively, though personally, with the situation.

In spite of me training younger people to be supervisors, I was never asked to be a supervisor ... That disturbed me for awhile, but because of my faith in God, I looked beyond human indiscretion and human discrimination. Although I was disappointed I was not embittered by those who failed to recognize me for who I was. I nevertheless gave my all ... I knew I had a greater mission than selling stock in the store. Young people flocked to me for advice and council in marital problems. They found that I was a person that believed in prayer and they asked me to pray for them. My personal involvement helped me look beyond the drudgery of everyday living. If my life had been centred around the getting of things and money, I would have been very disappointed, perhaps embittered. But God allowed me to see beyond that ... That gave me a sense of purpose that I would do again if I had opportunity.

Second, no respondent gave evidence that their faith affected the work structure, their choice of job, or other corporate issues. Only informal relational influences were mentioned, such as witnessing or resisting immoral pressures. After stating that his honesty was one way his faith affected him at work, this Minnesota contractor, like several other evangelical business owners, refused contracts with some clients in less-honourable professions. There is no suggestion that his faith has structural implications for his business. "I feel I need to share my faith with [clients and employees], not necessarily taking out my Bible and preaching at them, but sometimes they might just need a lifestyle sharing of my faith." After several prompts, he added: "I used to be in the sign business for awhile ... and this guy [client] owns some commercial property but he also owns a chain of liquor stores, and I chose not to bid on any signs for those stores. Two general contractors this spring wanted me to do work for them. I've done a little work for them already, but because of their dishonesty and lack of integrity in the kind of work they do, I told them both that I would no longer bid on any work for them."

While sometimes affecting contracts, the faith of the respondents did not seem to affect hours of work, profit sharing, preferential treatment of the poor, minorities, or women, company hierarchy, promotions, hiring practices, use of technology, the physical work environment, etc., even though several respondents were in management positions and could effect change in these areas. Comparatively, the authors made a clear connection between faith and structural-level work issues. The personal faith of core evangelicals is not easily transferable to the corporate/structural level issues at work.

In *God and Mammon in America* (1994), Robert Wuthnow discusses the effect of religious faith on ethics in the workplace. Wuthnow found that the religious faith of weekly church attenders did not affect their career choice or their work hours. Furthermore, they are only slightly less likely to engage in "ethically dubious" behaviour at work. Religiously active people differed from others in their work satisfaction, not in their work behaviour (1994, 73). Wuthnow states: "We have come to think of religion ... as a way of making ourselves feel better and have largely abandoned the idea that religion can guide our behaviour" (ibid., 39). Wuthnow's findings suggest that other religious people struggle to apply their faith to their work as well.

COMMUNITY TRANSFORMATION

Public religiosity is important for evangelicals, not only at work but in the community as well. CE respondents thought it was very important (eighty-five percent) or somewhat important (fifteen percent) to try to change the world around them for better. Historically, the evangelical modus operandi for world transformation is evangelism. The fundamentalist-modernist split at the turn of the century bifurcated evangelism and social action along conservative and liberal lines respectively (Marsden 1980; Hunter 1987). This split was not nearly as significant in Canada, with the result that social action was never rejected by Canadian evangelicals to the same extent (Stackhouse 1993a). One might predict that Canadians would be less likely than Americans to think that "winning the world," a typical phrase for evangelism, was their first priority (cf. Kellstedt 1989). Table 6.2 shows that the evangelistic choice was the top priority among core evangelicals in both countries, but it did not receive fifty percent support, and the "spiritual growth" item received the highest total responses. Furthermore, there are no important substantive differences between the two countries. This less-than-overwhelming support for evangelism suggests that it is not as central to evangelical identity as orthodox beliefs and conversion, as indicated in chapter 3.

While evangelism is a priority, the link between priority and practice is weak. Evangelicals who chose the priority of evangelism were not more likely to evangelize. When asked how Christians could best influence the world around them, only thirteen percent gave answers that clearly related to evangelism, while another six percent focused on philanthropy or social action. Most, however, gave general answers like "Emulate Christ," or "Love people" (45 percent), or

Table 6.2
First and Second Priorities

"Here is a list of items that some think should be priorities for Christians. Which one do you think should be the top priority for Christians? Which one should Christians make the second highest priority?"	% who chose item as no. 1 priority		% who chose item as no. 2 priority	
	Canada	US	Canada	US
1. Help win the world for Christ	48.5	48	28.2	28.7
2. Concentrate on the spiritual growth of self and family	41.2	45.9	37.8	39.8
3. Work to improve the moral fibre and values of the community and country	1.2	3.1	7.1	8.8
4. Strive to eliminate poverty and injustice in the world	0.6	0	5.1	1.7
5. Strengthen the local church by investing time and money in the people and programs there	3	2.6	21.2	21
6. Other	5.5	0.5	0.6	0

Source: CE sample, 1995.

"Getting involved with people and helping them" (20 percent). A handful focused on prayer (3 percent) or private spirituality (4 percent). These vague responses were equally prominent in all regions. Even among those who felt that evangelism was the best means to world betterment, there is no agreement on how evangelism is best conducted, whether by direct techniques such as door-to-door or street witnessing, social action (feeding the poor, visiting the sick) that might provide opportunities to witness, making non-Christian friends and trying to witness to them, or simply living a godly life and hoping that people will ask questions. A Baptist woman in New Brunswick gave this answer when asked how one might best change the world: "I think a lot is by example, the way you live your life. I think if you live your life accordingly that people will see that there is something different about you and I think that is probably the best way, just by example ... Like last year I had a little boy in my class who was 'special needs' and he comes from a real abusive home and now they are going to our church. Its not always the goal to get them to come to your church, yes, you want them to become a Christian and everything but just to get some of the [abusive] behaviour to stop." In this example and many others, it was implicit that bringing others to salvation was important, though the theme was often hidden in disjointed prose about how it might be accomplished.

For most evangelicals, real change comes from inside a person, that is, through conversion, not through removing external constraints. Nonetheless, evangelicals are involved in political and social action, even though political or social action does not mesh well with an emphasis on changing society by changing the heart of an individual through conversion. Core evangelicals engage in evangelism for individual transformation and in sociopolitical action to promote change on the societal level. At least in areas of practice, then, the historical bifurcation between evangelism and social action is weak today. However, verbal consent to the primacy of evangelism is of symbolic importance to evangelicals as a demonstration of their evangelicalism. For instance, one Pentecostal man in Minnesota explained in some detail his inclination towards starting a petition to control liquor sales in his area, and he had researched the process. Yet his answer to how Christians might best bring change was decidedly individualistic and evangelistic: "[People need] a genuine born-again experience. That's where I think the key is. Changing society per se is not the answer, but if they experience the born-again experience, yeah, then you will change society, a long-term effect ... Change the heart."

Some interviews indicated that the lack of consensus on these issues stemmed from God's directing people to get involved in the world in different ways, each specific to the situation or the individual. For a young Baptist in Minnesota, "We pray and God tells us what to do ... I mean, its not a clear-cut thing. [There is no] recipe to save America." Others, like this Pentecostal in Manitoba, suggest that world transformation happens naturally through Christlike living: "[We don't need] an agenda to change the world, I think an effective Christian will change the world just because of Christ who lives in them. [Its] just the effect of Christian life."

When concrete examples of ways to "change the world" were given, they were often justified in light of past excesses on the part of zealous evangelicals who encouraged negative stereotyping. Evangelicals, particularly in Mississippi, wanted to distance themselves from proselytizing that is extreme, too political, overly aggressive, or hypocritical. Evangelicals in all regions preferred more holistic or civil approaches to evangelism and societal betterment (cf. Smith 2000). As one Southern Baptist woman from Minnesota put it:

I think the best way to making a change around you is to change yourself inside, change what's in you, take the log out of your eye before you start looking for the specks in other people's [eyes] ... I also put a lot of weight in caring for others, and doing everything in love, and really a lot of community outreach – not just putting people out there knocking on doors asking, "Are you a Christian?" but doing things in love where you expect nothing in return – going out to the mall and handing out free pop, not taking any money ... I know people who go around to businesses cleaning rest rooms for absolutely no charge ... anything that can be seen. I think that we as Christians get so much popularity for things that are bad in us instead of what is good, you know, just like being part of the pro-life movement, and someone goes out and shoots doctors and then "this is what pro-lifers do," its sad.

With this emphasis on civility (Hunter 1984), old obtrusive methods have become outdated, and the respondents advocate new gentler approaches. Aggressive evangelism, they seem to say, has fallen into disrepute, and in order to regain a positive corporate image, some revamping of methods is necessary. As a result, there seems to be some ambiguity about how to maintain an emphasis on evangelism without appearing too "evangelistic."

In sum, evangelicals find it difficult to articulate how their faith applies in the public world in each of the four locales where interviews took place. Evangelicals generally agree that evangelism is important, but their distaste for aggressive evangelistic methods leaves them without a clear strategy. They have only a vague idea of what to do (evangelize), and there is even less clarity on how to go about it. Smith (2000) found the same ambiguity in responses from the American evangelicals he interviewed. Evangelicals found it difficult to mesh their commitment to evangelism as a principle with their support for political lobbying, their distaste for aggressive large-scale evangelistic methods, and their dedication to civility. Smith concludes that "ambivalence" best describes the strategies for world betterment among evangelicals (ibid., 195). Once again, regional differences are minimal. Canadian and American evangelicals seem to find it equally difficult to articulate a strategy for world transformation and share a distaste for aggressive evangelism.

DEVOTIONALISM

Moving now from ritual practice to devotionalism, high levels of private religious practice were the norm in the CE sample. Nearly all evangelicals I surveyed prayed, read the Bible, and said grace (before meals) frequently. There were other common devotional practices, as shown in Table 6.3. As with ritual practice, regional and denominational differences in levels of devotionalism are minimal.

The uniformity in levels of private and public practice can be supported with the God and Society poll, as shown in table 6.4.

Table 6.3
Devotional Practices

	US	CAN	Total
% who pray privately daily or more	90	85.3	87.8
% who say grace daily or more	84.5	86.4	85.4
% who read the Bible daily or more	53.3	57.4	55.2
% who memorize Scripture weekly or more	18.8	14	16.6
% who listen to Christian music weekly or more	79.4	85.8	82.4
% who watch religious TV weekly or more	48.5	48.5	48.5
% who speak in tongues weekly or more	18.5	16.8	17.4
% who have fasted from food/drink for religious reasons in the last two years	38.1	34.7	36.3

Source: CE sample, 1995.

Nonevangelical Americans report higher levels of orthopraxy than Canadians, which is similar to our findings for orthodoxy in chapter 5. Canadian evangelicals have slightly lower levels of orthopraxy according to the table, but the difference can nearly be accounted for by the low orthodoxy of the Quebec evangelicals. (Since Quebec evangelicals are known to be conservative, sampling problems likely account for this unexpected finding.)[7] Significant within-country differences, like the lower levels of practice in the US Mountain region or Quebec, are based on sample sizes that are small and unstable. Evangelical orthopraxy has little to do with the orthopraxy of the region, and evangelicals on both sides of the border are more closely matched on these practices than the general population. This uniformity is noteworthy in its own right. It suggests, again, that evangelicals do not take their cues for religious practice from their social context.

COMMITMENT

In Table 6.5, we look at commitment, measured by a combination of orthodox beliefs, church attendance, devotionalism, and the importance of one's faith (salience).[8] Predictably, we once again find the pattern of much-lower commitment among nonevangelicals in Canada than in the US but similar levels of commitment across the regions for evangelicals (except in Quebec). If the Quebec evangelicals are removed from the sample, regional differences in commitment among evangelicals are not statistically significant. Consistent with other findings in the book, evangelicals in regions where religious commitment is lower do not have matching levels of low commitment.

Table 6.4
Practices by Region in the United States and Canada

Item	American Non-Evangelicals	American Evangelicals	West		Mountain		North Central		South		Northeast	
			Non	Evan	Non	Evan*	Non	Evan	Non	Evan	Non	Evan*
I attend religious services once a week or more.	33.7	57.3	27.2	46.6	26.3	40.9	38.6	59.4	37.2	61.0	31.5	60.9
I pray outside of formal religious services once a day or more.	51.4	75.0	47.4	68.0	50.4	73.3	49.5	78.1	59.4	76.0	48.6	77.1
I read the Bible or other religious material once a day or more.	14.4	35.6	14.7	34.6	12.4	28.9	12.9	32.3	18.0	38.7	12.8	34.9
AVERAGE PERCENTAGE	33.17	55.97	29.8	49.7	29.7	47.7	33.7	56.6	38.2	58.57	31.0	57.6

Table 6.4
Practices by Region in the United States and Canada (cont.)

Item	Canadian Non-Evangelicals	Canadian Evangelicals	British Columbia		The Prairies		Ontario		Quebec		Maritimes	
			Non	Evan	Non	Evan	Non	Evan	Non	Evan*	Non	Evan*
I attend religious services once a week or more.	17.3	50.3	12.0	51.6	13.4	59.2	20.4	45.5	15.3	18.8	25.1	66.6
I pray outside of formal religious services once a day or more.	30.5	68.5	26.9	74.2	26.6	75.3	30.7	65.3	31.5	45.2	38.0	71.0
I read the Bible or other religious material once a day or more.	5.6	36.3	6.1	40.3	5.2	41.8	6.3	33.3	3.9	9.4	7.0	48.5
AVERAGE PERCENTAGE	17.8	51.7	15	55.4	15.1	58.8	19.1	48.0	16.9	24.5	23.4	62.0

Source: God and Society poll, 1996.

* These column percentages are based on small sample sizes (<50) and thus have large margins of error.

Note: Item wording has been simplified.

Table 6.5
Average Commitment Scores

| | Canada | | | United States | |
	Non-Evangelicals	Evangelicals		Non-Evangelicals	Evangelicals
British Columbia	12.28	23.10	West	17.25	22.62
Prairies	13.47	23.73	Mountain	17.00	22.14
Ontario	14.15	23.57	North Central	19.66	24.66
Quebec	13.66	18.25	South	20.48	24.95
Maritimes	15.63	24.10	Northeast	17.94	24.27
Total	13.81	23.05	Total	18.86	24.29
	All Canadians 14.77			All Americans 20.24	

Source: God and Society poll, 1996.

Table 6.6
Measures of Commitment for Evangelicals,
Mainline Protestants, and Catholics

	Evangelicals	Mainline Protestants	Catholics
% weekly church attenders	55.3	29.0	34.5
% attending church more than once a week	34.5	8.7	8.7
% who read the Bible daily	35.9	12.3	7.4
% who pray daily	73.7	47.2	48.0
% who say their faith provides a great deal of guidance to their lives.	62.0	39.9	32.1

Source: God and Society poll, 1996.

Commitment, then, does not vary regionally within evangelicalism in the US and Canada. It does, however, distinguish evangelicals from other Christian traditions. In Table 6.6, I present measures of religious participation and include mainline Protestants and Catholics for comparison. About two-thirds of Canadians and roughly three-quarters of Americans claim to be Christian, and evangelicals are the most religiously active Christian tradition. They make up roughly ten percent of the Canadian population, and about twenty-five percent of the American population.

Evangelicals are far more likely to attend church (particularly more than once a week), pray, and read the Bible more frequently, and they are far more likely to feel that their faith provides guidance in their lives.

In sum, evanglicals in their devotional lives and in ritual practice in the church, are active and show minimal variation across borders. Evangelicals give money, attend church, pray, read the Bible, and say grace frequently. Regarding life "in the world," like work and community transformation, faith is not easily translated into action. With unclear strategies of action for world betterment and limited application of faith in the workplace, it appears that evangelicals have "blindspots" that limit their impact on society (Smith 1998).

Examining regional variation, evangelicals in the US and Canada show little tendency to follow the orthodoxy/orthopraxy of their regional milieus. I find only minor regional differences in beliefs, morals, practice, and commitment among evangelicals. The maintenance of boundaries and subcultural distinctiveness once again seem to resist regional effects and support high levels of practice and commitment.

7 The Forty-Ninth Parallel and Evangelical Differences

To this point, the evidence I have presented suggests that there is minimal variation in the religiosity of evangelicals in different regions of North America. However, the core evangelicals I interviewed disagree with this conclusion. Their perception was that evangelicals vary from region to region. Those in the southern US are more legalistic, more conservative, and possibly less committed, according to some evangelicals in the northern US and in Canada. To them, the Mason-Dixon line is a significant boundary. Some Canadian evangelicals view their American counterparts as more fundamentalist and legalistic, more extreme politically and morally, more expressive in worship, and more aggressive in evangelism. Like most Canadians, evangelicals feel that the forty-ninth parallel is not only a geographical boundary but a boundary with cultural relevance as well. West Coast Evangelicals in both countries are sometimes perceived to be more liberal. Some Canadian evangelicals think that Maritime and Prairie evangelicals are more conservative than those in other Canadian regions. Ontario evangelicals are more conservative than those in British Columbia but more liberal than those in the Prairies or Maritimes. In general, the differences articulated by respondents were predictable, since they match broader national and regional perceptions. Even the well-travelled interviewee, however, may simply be reiterating stereotypical differences that may have existed in the past but have since disappeared except in cultural myth. An older Canadian Nazarene pastor recalled his seminary days in Kansas:

I had the sense that they [southern evangelicals] were much more strict, they were more concerned about morals and standards and things like that in the southeastern part of the [United] States ... People would come up from the southeast and they were more emotional. You could almost identify which part of the country they were from by just seeing their religious practice for a while. The way they worshipped and everything, they were much more emotional, almost charismatic, [in] the southeast. Those from California, Oregon, Washington, and so forth, they were much more liberal and you could pick them right out by the way they worshipped and the way they dressed, it was quite interesting to us. They referred to us as the "formal Canadians" ... We found it easier to identify with those from California and the New England area. We just felt like we were in a different church when we were around the guys from the southeast.

Like this pastor, respondents apply broad stereotypical labels to their general impressions. Furthermore, distancing themselves from those who have been labelled with negative stereotypes is natural, even if it means separating themselves from their own brethren. For example, Canadian evangelicals will distinguish themselves from American evangelicals, who are associated with people who shoot abortionists, or with a televangelist caught in moral failure. In light of the similarities demonstrated above, do these perceptions of difference find any empirical support?

In chapters 3 through 6 I have emphasized similarities between evangelicals in Canada and the US, and between regions within both countries. Evangelicals across North America share a similar religious identity and sociocultural boundaries; they exhibit similarities in religious experiences and similar levels of orthodoxy and orthopraxy. The evangelical subculture is distinct as well as transnational and transdenominational. But this is not the whole story. This chapter tells the rest of the story the story of differences within similarities.

Research supports the notion that American and Canadian evangelicals differ in significant ways. Based on the hundreds of items from the core evangelical sample, the God and Society poll, and other national surveys, I found four significant differences between evangelicals in the Canada and the US. In comparison, other differences appear inconsistently. These differences – incongruity, national perceptions, political alignment, and what might best be called irenicism, which I define below, – match national differences. Political alignment and irenicism are likely more significant than incongruity and national perceptions because they appear to have far-reaching implications and show sharper contrasts. To begin, let us look at the minor differences.

INCONGRUITY

In recent years, the media have publicized the downfall of various prominent religious personalities, such as American evangelical tel-evangelists Jim Bakker and Jimmy Swaggart. Scandalous behaviour by prominent Canadian evangelicals has received less publicity, pos-sibly because moral failure is less common north of the border, more probably because there are fewer prominent Canadian evangelicals. The moral failure of evangelical leader Ralph Rutledge of Toronto's Queensway Cathedral is one case. The cumulative effect of these litigations and allegations, along with many directed toward none-vangelical religious representatives,[1] have led to a "dramatic drop in public confidence in religious leaders in the past decade," notes Reginald Bibby (1993, 73). Public scandals call into question the pri-vate and public practices of those who claim religious motivations for their behaviour. Do committed evangelicals, who decry moral degradation and theological liberalism in society, practice what they preach? Do they walk the walk, or just talk the talk?

These questions deal with the congruity between what one says and does. The morals and orthodox beliefs of evangelicals are strict and clear, leaving plenty of room for incongruity between the stan-dards they adhere to and their actual practice. There is some sombre evidence of incongruity. Political scientist Lyman Kellstedt has found that some Americans who claim to be "born again" do not believe that Jesus was God, do not pray, are not committed to Christ, and are not sure of the resurrection. In fact, one-third of the white "born again" respondents in a 1984 survey considered themselves to be agnostics or atheists (1989, 5; see also Smidt and Kellstedt 1987). Such findings call into question the congruity of responses, and most of the evidence of incongruity seems to be in the US. Is there a difference between American and Canadian evangelicals in behaviour that is consistent with beliefs?

Incongruity is lower among the core evangelical interviewees, as one might expect. Most respondents reported practices that matched their beliefs and moral convictions. Furthermore, most reported doing the sort of things that they considered important priorities for Christians. To check for incongruity, I compared moral prohibitions and actual practice. As Hunter notes, moral orthodoxy among evan-gelicals has to do with practice (orthopraxy) as an external measure of internal commitment (1987, 56–64). Nonetheless, about fifteen per-cent of CE respondents who said that a certain behaviour was always wrong had in fact indulged in it during the last two years.[2] Table 7.1 indicates that even the core evangelicals show inconsistencies,

Table 7.1
Inconsistencies Between Moral Attitudes and Practices

% who say drinking alcohol is always wrong	34.5	% who say viewing a R-rated movie in a theatre is always wrong	50.3	% who say gambling is always wrong	63.0
% who have drunk alcohol in the last two years	39.9	% who have seen an R-rated movie in the last 2 years	44.4	% who have bought a lottery ticket in the last two years	17.4
% who say drinking alcohol is always wrong but have drunk alcohol	6.3	% who say viewing R-rated movies is always wrong but have seen an R-rated movie	16.0	% who say gambling is always wrong but have bought a lottery ticket	11.7

Source: CE sample, 1995.

particularly with respect to R-rated movies, which about half of all core evangelicals consider it always wrong to view.

To put these findings in perspective, one can compare evangelicals with nonevangelicals on several measures of consistency that are available in the 1988 General Social Survey in the US and in Project Can90 data in Canada. The items and the percentage of those who gave incongruent answers are given in Table 7.2.

Note that evangelicals have somewhat lower levels of incongruent answers when compared to their national samples. In spite of the public evangelical scandals, the rank-and-file evangelical seems to walk the talk better than most. (While US and Canadian evangelicals have similar levels of incongruity in this table, cross-country comparisons are risky because the datasets are not strictly comparable.) Of course, one could argue that survey data cannot verify the behaviour of evangelicals. Surveys and interviews only record people's responses ("talk"), or *reports* of behaviour; *actual* behaviour ("walk") has not been observed. The point is well taken. There is evidence that survey respondents overreport certain socially desirable behaviours, such as church attendance.[3] Researchers have compared church attendance as reported on surveys to actual in-church counts. Their findings indicate that overreporting church attendance seems to be more common among Americans than Canadians, and less common among conservative Protestants than other Christian traditions. It may be that Americans overreport more than just their church attendance because it is conventional to do so. It has been argued that it is more desirable to understand oneself as religious in the US than in Canada (Reimer 1995),[4] increasing the tendency to report higher

Table 7.2
Comparing Evangelicals and Non-Evangelicals on Incongruent Responses

	US total (N = 1481)	US Evangelicals (N = 342)	Canada total (N = 1249)	Canada Evangelicals (N = 98)
Individuals who attend church at least monthly but have "hardly any" (GSS) or "little/none" (Can90) confidence in the church	6.5	2	8.4	1
Individuals who believe that it is possible to communicate with the dead but do not believe in life after death	6.6	5.8	1.2	3.1
Individuals who do not believe "God exists" (Can90) or who do not think one can know if God exists (GSS) but pray at least weekly	4.9	0.6	2.7	2
Individuals who do not believe in God (as above) but say grace	0.8	0	1.5	2
Individuals who do not believe in God (as above) but "feel close to God" at least some of the time (GSS) or have felt "God's presence" (Can90)	0.7	0	0.6	2

Source: 1988 General Social Survey (GSS) and Project Can90.

orthopraxy than is actually practised. This may mean that there is a weaker connection between religious "walk and talk" among Americans and American evangelicals than among Canadians and Canadian evangelicals, as the tendency to exaggerate church attendance suggests. One way to test this is to see how strongly correlated, or how tightly coupled, beliefs and practice are among evangelicals in the two countries. Table 7.3 does so using the God and Society poll. The correlation table below requires some explanation. A correlation of zero indicates no relation between two items, and a correlation of one means a perfect relation (i.e., a correlation of one between orthodox beliefs and church attendance would mean that everyone who reports orthodox beliefs also attends church regularly). Since the Canadian correlations in Table 7.3 are closer to one, they indicate that these measures of commitment are more strongly coupled in Canada than in the US. In other words, importance of religion, orthodox beliefs, church attendance, and devotionalism are more strongly correlated in Canada than in the US among evangelicals. It is also true

Table 7.3
Correlations between Measures of Evangelical Commitment

	Salience	Orthodox Beliefs	Devotionalism	Church Attendance
CANADIAN CORRELATIONS (N = 303)				
Salience	1.0			
Orthodox beliefs	.643**	1.0		
Devotion	.622**	.736**	1.0	
Church attendance	.520**	.613**	.677**	1.0
AMERICAN CORRELATIONS (N = 742)				
Salience	1.0			
Orthodox beliefs	.521**	1.0		
Devotion	.535**	.510**	1.0	
Church attendance	.446**	.458**	.604**	1.0

Source: God and Society poll, 1996.
Significance: *** .001; ** .01; * .05; ns – not significant.
Salience: religion provides guidance to my life.
Orthodox beliefs: salvation through Jesus, Jesus is divine, Bible is inspired.
Devotion: Bible reading and prayer.

that correlations between commitment measures are also higher for all Canadians than for all Americans. The table indicates that the linkages between different aspects of commitment are tighter among Canadian evangelicals, which suggests that there may be more of a tendency to inflate one's religiosity in surveys in the US. Evidence from the US General Social Survey, the Project Can90 poll, and the World Values Survey support this conclusion (Reimer 1995).

NATIONAL PERCEPTIONS

As previously mentioned, Americans have historically had the tendency to interpret their national history as religiously significant. Bellah (1975) refers to this tendency as "civil religion," a term he borrows from Rousseau (1966). America's sense that it has a national calling to be a light to the world, a defender of freedom and democracy, is at least as evident in the writings of the founding fathers as it is in today's political rhetoric. Failure to measure up to divine standards will lead to a "broken covenant" between God and the nation. Research suggests that civil religious views are still widespread in America.[5] Lipset calls this national ideology "us utopian moralism." The American sense of divine national calling means that moral and political dramas are seen as "morality plays, as battles between God and the devil, so that compromise is virtually unthinkable" (1990, 77).

Recently, Hunter (1991) has argued that conservatives and progressives in the US have formed battle lines in a "war" to define America. In the "culture wars," both sides seek to legitimate their views by applying the myths of national ideology to their side and are energized to do so by a sense of national purpose. Evangelicals, Hunter suggests, have largely defined the conservative side, where traditional morality and religious and economic freedom are key issues in the debate. By contrast, Canadians have been largely unable to sustain national myths of any kind, much less ones that are seen as religiously significant.[6] Issues that divide Canadians do not tend to fall along moral or religious lines but along ethnic and geographic lines.

Differences in the national ideology of Canadian and American evangelicals are evident in questions about national problems. But there are similarities as well. It is no surprise that the first and greatest evangelical concern is related to the disintegration of the moral and spiritual foundations of the community or country. Evangelicals in both countries see a wide variety of problems related to a general moral decline, including the breakdown of the traditional family, abortion, crime and violence, political corruption, "value-neutral" education, the rise of special interest groups that are antagonistic to their world view, and so on. For evangelicals, both institutional problems (e.g., media corruption) and individual problems (e.g., people rejecting God) are related to a general moral malaise, and moral and spiritual disintegration are inseparable. This reply by a fifty-year-old Canadian Pentecostal is typical of many core evangelical interviewees: "I think [the greatest problem is] a lack of any basis for what we are ... I think at one point in time this country, like the US, had some biblical values: the decisions that were made [and] the laws that were put in place had some biblical foundation. An example might be this whole area of abortion, [or] the whole welfare system. I think these laws are gone because we no longer see Scripture as the basis for what we do, there are no absolutes ... It's like the end of [the Old Testament book of] Judges, 'everyone does what's right in his own eyes'".

The second most common concern relates to general economic problems, as described by a pastor in New Brunswick: "I would say [the greatest problem is] the economic problem ... The deficit, well, its all tied together. The disparity in society, the rich are getting richer and the poor poorer. It actually is the triumph of ... capitalism." Third, evangelicals raise concerns about social or institutional problems, such as the government or health care. One Mississippi Pentecostal suggested that the main problem was "the government's inability to manage its affairs, [like the] inability to balance the budget. [They are] unable to faithfully administrate some areas, [like the] inability to stay out of areas they shouldn't be in, [making] more complicated administrative situations that they put on the citizens like cumbersome tax codes. ... There is no one answer to that, just a general level of incompetence. That may be something that is not ever going to go away."

While evangelical national concerns follow these themes, the themes were not equally voiced in each region, as Table 7.4 shows.

Americans are more likely to emphasize moral problems while Canadians are more likely to raise economic problems. Americans are more concerned about crime, violence, and drug/alcohol abuse than Canadians, not surprisingly since these problems are more common in the US. Canadians are more concerned about the national debt, which is somewhat higher on a per capita basis in Canada, though both countries face serious debt. Note, however, that no Canadian raised concerns about the government's being too big, although the Canadian national government has historically exercised greater control. This difference points to the American tendency to emphasize individual freedom and reject "big" government, while Canadians are more group-oriented and accept more government intervention (Lipset 1990). These national and regional differences in perceived problems point to important sources of variation.

National polls suggest that the difference is best explained as a national difference. The 1996 God and Society poll found that the top five issues facing Canadians are jobs, national unity, the economy, the deficit, and healthcare. In the US, international peace and defence, crime/violence, education, and drugs all rank ahead of economic issues. In both countries, regional differences are not nearly as significant as the national differences. Evangelicals, moreover, do not differ significantly from other religious groups on these issues. Similarly, Bibby's Project Can90 (1990) poll reveals that evangelicals in Canada follow the tendency of Canadians to put more weight on economic problems, in that the Goods and Services Tax (GST) and the economy were more likely to be considered "very serious" problems than drugs, crime, and violence.

POLITICAL ALIGNMENT
AND EXTREMISM

The biggest and most consistent differences between evangelicals north and south of the border show up in the realm of politics. Canadian evangelicals who had travelled south of the border were

Table 7.4
National Concerns

% who named this response as the greatest national concern	Minnesota (N = 100)	Mississippi (N = 85)	Manitoba (N = 94)	New Brunswick (N = 71)
1. MORAL/SPIRITUAL DECLINE	97	94	72	70
Values decline	30	25	15	18
Family breakdown	7	10.6	3.2	2.8
Crime and violence	7	10.6	5.3	1.4
Drug/alcohol abuse	0	5.9	0	0
Corrupt government officials and policies	1	1.2	7.4	4.2
People/nation reject God	12	15	14	9.9
Sin	4	4.7	2.1	5.6
Materialism/greed	6	4.7	0	1.4
Relativism	3	0	3.2	1.4
Self-centred/lack respect	9	0	2.1	0
People lack salvation or commitment to God	8	5.9	4.3	9.9
Other moral/spiritual concerns	10	10.6	16	15.5
2. ECONOMIC CONCERNS	2	1.2	21	18
National debt	0	0	5.3	8.4
Poverty	1	1.2	4.3	2.8
Unemployment	1	0	11	5.6
Other economic	0	0	1.1	1.4
3. SOCIAL/INSTITUTIONAL CONCERNS	1	4.7	6.4	11.3
Health care	1	0	0	1.4
Quebec separation	0	0	4.3	5.6
Other social/institutional concerns	0	4.7	2.1	4.2

Source: CE sample, 1995.

quick to notice this difference. As one Mennonite pastor from Manitoba found during his time in the northern US: "My experience in the churches and the Christian community down there was [that] patriotism was much more closely married to faith than it is in Canada. That was striking. Politics is also much more closely connected with faith."

The tendency for evangelicals in the US to align themselves with (conservative) politics can be linked to national ideology as well. Moral debate becomes politicized partly because of a national tendency to see divine consequences for moral failure. There is ample evidence from the interviews that conservative politics and conservative morals are connected in the minds of American evangelicals. Unsolicited comments indicated that some evangelicals in the US voted republican because of the candidate's stand on moral issues.

Regnerus, Sikkink, and Smith (1999) found that those listening to conservative Protestant political organizations are motivated to vote based on the party's stance on moral issues. But morality is not the only issue. American evangelicals gave more conservative answers to political questions, as indicated in Table 7.5.

Regarding political party choice, 72 percent of Americans in the CE sample vote Republican, while Canadians are more diverse in party affiliation: 36 percent Progressive Conservative (PC), 16 percent Liberal, 4 percent New Democratic Party (NDP), and 20 percent Reform. Not even the combined Canadian support for the conservative PC and Reform parties matches US levels of support for the Republican party.

National samples substantiate the stronger connection between conservative religion and conservative politics in US. The God and Society poll is the best poll ever on religion and politics in Canada and the United States and gives a wealth of data to compare evangelicals politically on both sides of the border. Tables 7.6 through 7.8 use this poll to show the greater political conservatism of American evangelicals.

Table 7.6 lists six political attitudes, where in each case the higher percentage indicates greater political conservatism. American evangelicals give consistently more conservative responses than nonevangelical Americans, and conservatism increases for core evangelicals. The numbers in the penultimate row of the table indicate the average percentage difference between evangelicals (or core evangelicals) and their corresponding national population. For example, the 6.0 percent in the column for American evangelicals indicates that they give more conservative responses on average than most Americans, and the difference is even greater when we compare core American evangelicals with all Americans. Comparatively, Canadian evangelicals show minimal differences in political conservatism from other Canadians. In the last row of the table, Canadian evangelicals are compared with their American counterparts. Here, the minus 10.7 percent in the column for Canadian evangelicals means that, on average, they are more than ten percentage points *less* conservative than American evangelicals. The gap between core Canadian and American evangelicals is even greater, at 12.5 percent. In sum, the table supports two conclusions. First, Canadian evangelicalism fails to promote the particular political alignments of American evangelicalism. Canadian evangelicals seem to take their political cues from their national context, not from the evangelical subculture. Second, Canadian and American evangelical political attitudes show significant national differences, and those differences increase the closer one gets to the core.

Table 7.5
Political Attitudes – CE Sample

Question	Canada (N = 184)	United States (N = 201)
Political identification		
% strongly conservative	2.9	28.3
% (moderately) conservative	51.2	53.5
America/Canada is still a Christian nation. (% agreeing)	27.6	38.3
Many problems in our country have occurred because Americans/Canadians have rejected the religious principles this country was founded on. (% agreeing)	87.2	95.9
Strict laws to protect the environment are necessary even if they cost jobs. (% agreeing)	64.6	39.0
The national government should do more to fight hunger and poverty even if it means higher taxes. (% agreeing)	50.9	30.7
Minorities need government assistance to obtain their rightful place in America/Canada. (% agreeing)	27.2	17.4

Source: CE sample, 1995.
All between-country differences are significant at the .01 except the % of those who are (moderately) conservative.

Evangelicals in both countries are more likely to support the conservative Reform and Republican parties than nonevangelicals in their countries as Table 7.7 shows.[7] However, the notable difference is that American evangelicals support their conservative party at twice the rate of Canadian evangelicals.

Table 7.8 shows the stronger connection between politics and religion in the American mind. Americans are twice as likely as Canadians to consider religion very important to their political thinking, and American evangelicals follow this tendency as well. Americans and American evangelicals are also slightly more likely to think traditional values should inform politics and more likely to hear political messages from the pulpit. Again, we find support for the closer coupling of religion and politics in the US.

Regarding political activism, Americans claim slightly more political activity than Canadians, and evangelicals are only marginally more active than nonevangelicals. The evidence clearly does not support perceptions of unusually high political mobilization among evangelicals, who are the strength of the Christian Right. Furthermore, not even half of the core evangelicals in the US feel very close to the Christian Right, and the percentage is predictably lower in Canada.

While all North American evangelicals say that religion informs their political views, Canadian evangelical faith does not seem to say

Table 7.6
Political Attitudes

Item	All Canadians (N = 3000)	Canadian Evangelicals (N = 303)	Core CN Evangelicals (N = 139)	All Americans (N = 3000)	American Evangelicals (N = 743)	Core US Evangelicals (N = 395)
The less government the better. (% agree)	45.4	46.7	49.6	52.4	63.2	67.0
The free market can handle economic problems. (% agree)	31.0	30.4	30.9	39.6	44.5	47.0
Social problems are best addressed locally. (% agree)	76.8	79.5	79.0	80.5	83.7	85.5
The number of legal immigrants should be reduced. (% agree)	56.6	56.1	54.0	68.5	73.3	73.4
Government should spend more on fighting poverty. (% disagree)	39.4	38.7	43.2	41.3	49.0	55.1
The gap between the rich and poor is significant problem. (% disagree)	22.6	26.9	25.8	24.2	29.0	29.7
Average % difference from national population	0	1.1	1.8	0	6.0	8.5
Average % difference from counterparts in other country	−5.8	−10.7	−12.5	5.8	10.7	12.5

Source: God and Society poll, 1996.

Table 7.7
Political Party Support

CANADA	PC	Liberal	NPD	Reform	Other	None/DK
Most likely to support in federal election						
All Canadians (N = 3000)	11.3	41.2	6.4	9.0	7.3	24.8
Canadian evangelicals (N = 303)	11.6	33.7	5.0	24.4	5.3	20.1
Core CN evangelicals (N = 139)*	14.4	29.5	2.9	25.9	7.2	20.2

UNITED STATES	Clinton/ Demo.	Dole/ Repub.	Perot/ Indep.	Other	None/ DK
Most likely to support in federal election					
All Americans (N = 3000)	49.9	30.1	6.8	5.8	7.4
American evangelicals (N = 743)	37.1	44.1	5.8	5.5	7.4
Core US evangelicals (N = 395)	30.2	53.8	3.8	4.3	7.8

Source: God and Society poll, 1996.

* These percentages are based on small sample size and thus have large margins of error.

as much about political alignment. Whence the difference? The answer is partly given in the last line of Table 7.8, which shows that Americans are about twice as likely to hear about candidates and elections from the pulpit (cf. Guth 1996; Welch et al. 1993). Furthermore, the weight of social issues (abortion, gay rights, etc.) on political outcomes and the successful mobilization efforts of American groups like the Christian Coalition have pushed evangelical voters to align with the Republican party.[8] In Canada, where evangelicals are comparatively active in proportion to their size, politically motivated Canadian evangelical organizations are not predominantly conservative. In fact, one of Canada's evangelical political organizations is a labour union (Hoover 1997a). Using the God and Society poll, Hoover, Martinez, Reimer, and Wald (2002) found that evangelicals in both sides of the border are morally conservative, but economic conservatism seems to be distinctively American.

Hoover suggests two other mechanisms that moderate evangelical political activity and alignment. First, the configurations of religious traditions represented within evangelicalism differ between the two countries. Proportionally, Canadian evangelicals are much more likely to come from Anabaptist and Reform traditions, which historically are liberal on social justice issues. There are proportionally fewer fundamentalists and Baptists in Canada, who tend to support both economic and moral conservatism. Evidence suggests that self-identified fundamentalists in the US promote economically conservative

Table 7.8
Religion and Politics

Item	All Canadians	Canadian Evangelicals	Core CN Evangelicals	All Americans	American Evangelicals	Core US Evangelicals
Religion is very important to political thinking.	11.4	32.8	49.6	27.5	44.4	62.5
Traditional Christian values should play a role in politics.	45.0	75.4	87.8	57.2	74.9	86.9
Christians should get involved in politics to protect values.	45.9	69.0	78.5	64.3	79.0	86.8
Political activism score*	21.3	23.2	24.3	27.0	27.6	31.9
Very close to Christian right	7.5	23.4	35.3	16.8	32.5	43.1
Clergy speaks about candidates and elections	13.6	20.9	26.6	26.1	30.8	34.8

Source: God and Society poll, 1996.
* The score is the average percentage of those claimed to 1) work for a candidate/party, 2) give money to a candidate/party, 3) contact political office, 4) attend community meeting, 5) be a member of political group.

evangelical politics south of the border (Hoover et al. 2002). Second, Hoover points to the differences in the "political/regulatory structure" in the two countries. In Canada the "political opportunity structure" is not conducive to the mobilization of special interest groups because the concentration of power in the hands of government élites limits the influence of such groups. The aggressive populist "outsider" tactics of interest groups are often met with indifference by political leaders, whereas the discrete and respectful development of government allies may be necessary for "inside" influence. In addition, government controls on religious broadcasting mean that Canadian evangelicalism lacks an important "consciousness-raising and fundraising" tool available south of the border (1997b, 207). Hoover suggests that such moderating effects give Canadian evangelical politics an irenic tone, as noted below. The cumulative result of these influences is that Canadian evangelicalism does not support clear political alignment and moderates political extremism.

Historically, in fact, evangelically motivated political action in Canada has sometimes been decidedly left-wing, especially in the Prairies. In Saskatchewan, evangelicals were influential in the formation of a socialist party, the Cooperative Commonwealth Federation, that later became the secular New Democratic Party. One wonders, however, whether evangelical Canadian politics is changing. Hoover notes the increased mobilization of "Christian Right" organizations in Canada to an extent that equals American levels of mobilization in proportion to the size of the evangelical community. The blend of fiscal conservatism, populism, and evangelical religious convictions visible in Stockwell Day and his Canadian Alliance party suggests to some that American-style politics is taking root in Canada. What has yet to be determined is the degree to which the Alliance garnered the long-term support of Canadian evangelicals. Regardless of voting alignment, it is unlikely that Canadian evangelical politics will lose its comparatively moderate tone in the near future (Hoover 1997b).

IRENICISM

Irenicism, for our purposes, can be defined as attitudes towards other individuals or groups that are not sectarian, partisan, prejudiced, or patriarchal, which captures the essence of the definition given by Webster: "conducive to or operating toward peace, moderation, harmony, and conciliation, and away from contention and partisanship." The former definition suggests four dimensions: religious, political, social, and moral irenicism.

Based on this definition, irenicism is used broadly to include notions of tolerance and comfort zones. Hoge, Johnson, and Luidens (1994) provide a helpful distinction between tolerance and comfort zones in their study of mainline Protestants in the US. The former refers to boundaries directed towards what is acceptable for *others*, and the latter reflect choices the subjects would consider for *themselves*. For example, evangelicals are likely to tolerate a broad scope of religious groups in their country or city but the set of religious groups that they would be comfortable attending is much smaller.[9]

Civility, or the tendency to communicate in a polite and noncombative way, is also part of irenicism as I define it. Surprisingly few Canadian respondents suggested that Americans lacked civility (which may relate to their desire to be civil towards Americans). A few thought that Americans were "more vocal in their faith" and "more aggressive," as one Pentecostal pastor in New Brunswick put it. A few respondents stated that American evangelicals were more fundamentalist. Other pastors, who were more likely to have lived in other locations,[10] spoke of a more reserved Canadian-style evangelicalism. An American Lutheran pastor in Manitoba noticed the Canadian tendency to towards moderation: "Canadians are much more apathetic ... towards things in general, but they are much more even keel. You get an American right winger who is really a right winger and you will get an American left winger who is really a left winger and you will get a Canadian who will just sit there and go, '[Oh] well' [laughs]. You get the same in the spiritual realm as well, the Canadians in my opinion do not embrace the Lord with the same fervour nor do they object to the Lord with the same fervour as Americans do." Still another American pastor in Canada noticed the greater cooperative spirit. After remarking that Pentecostals in Canada were less exuberant in worship, he said that he thought most denominations in Canada were more ecumenical. "It amazes me here in Winnipeg that Pentecostal churches will work in conjunction with Mennonite churches, Alliance churches, Evangelical Free churches, you see that in other places in the world. That's probably why I call myself an evangelical [instead of a Pentecostal] ... because I realize that we are working alongside other churches."

Such anecdotal evidence is of questionable validity, although respondents tended to perceive a more irenic Canadian evangelicalism. Others, however, stated that their perception was that evangelicals were similar in other parts of Canada and the US, or that differences were limited to minor stylistic differences. The research presented below supports a difference in irenicism between the two countries.[11] Eight items in the God and Society data measure irenicism as defined. Table 7.9 gives the results.

Table 7.9
Irenicism Measures

Item	All Canadians (N = 3000)	Canadian Evangelicals (N = 303)	All Americans (N = 3000)	American Evangelicals (N = 742)
RACIAL/ETHNIC IRENICISM				
1. If I had my choice, I would rather have next-door neighbours who are my own colour. (% disagree)	85.8	82.5	78.3	75.3
MORAL IRENICISM				
2. How close do you feel to abortion rights and pro-choice groups? (% close)	31.7	32.3	35.2	27.8
3. Homosexuals should have the same rights as other Canadians/Americans. (% agree)	66.1	47.9	64	47.2
RELIGIOUS IRENICISM				
4. How close do you feel to Roman Catholics? (% close)	28.2	13.5	28.5	13.2
5. How close do you feel to the Christian Right? (% close)	17.7	46.8	33.5	56.2
6. Would you vote for an evangelical political leader?* (% yes)	79.5	89.4	78.2	84.7
7. Would you vote for a political leader who is an atheist?* (% yes)	71.9	55.1	42.7	23.4
8. Would you vote for a Muslim political leader?* (% yes)	73.6	65.2	62.2	45.1

Source: God and Society poll, 1996.
* Wording simplified on these items.
Significance:
1. Between Canadian/American differences (first and third columns): All differences are significant at the .01 level except for items 3, 4, and 7 (not significant).
2. Between Canadian/American evangelical differences (second and fourth columns): All differences are significant at the .01 level except items 3, 4, 5, and 7 (not significant).
3. Between Canadian/Canadian evangelical differences (first and second columns): All differences are significant at the .01 level except items 1 (not significant), 2 (not significant), and 3 (.05).
4.3. Between American/American evangelical differences (third and fourth columns): All differences are significant at the .01 level.

According to the table, Canadian evangelicals are more irenic than American evangelicals overall, although the percentages for moral irenicism are not significantly different, nor are attitudes towards Catholics and evangelical political leaders. To determine which group is most irenic, I computed the average percent for each column in the table. Canadian nonevangelicals averaged 55.3 percent indicating that they are the most irenic (albeit only slightly), Canadian evangelicals averaged 52.9 percent, American nonevangelicals average 50.4 percent, and American evangelicals are the least irenic, averaging 44.3 percent.

The CE sample included social-distance measures, which are appropriate measures of irenicism as defined above. They also give evidence of significant similarities and were used previously in chapter 3 to demonstrate shared group boundaries for evangelicals. Here I emphasize the differences within the similarities. To review, the measures ask "how close or far" the respondents feel towards people in certain groups, measured on a five-point scale from very close (1) to very far (5). The percentage of those who feel close or very close to the group is given in Table 7.10. The last column gives the country that is more irenic, based on the differences between the national means (arithmetic averages).

Focusing on the differences in these data, the most prominent finding in the table is that Canadian evangelicals rank most groups closer than American evangelicals, supporting the Canadian irenicism hypothesis. When US evangelicals come out more irenic, it is either because it is a US group (US evangelicals, Southern Baptists) or because Canadians view the group as intolerant (Right to Life, fundamentalists). Some evangelicals I interviewed, particularly Canadians, distance themselves from Right to Life because their demonstrations and other actions are too "political" or "radical," even though they are strongly against abortion.

In Canada, not only is tolerance a virtue but it is fundamental to what it means to be Canadian, according to former prime minister Pierre Elliott Trudeau (cited in Bibby 1990, 7). The emphasis on tolerance and respect for diversity in Canada likely encourages Canadians to report that they feel close to most groups. Canadian tolerance also indicates that there is higher emphasis on being civil, or irenic. Irenicism is symbolically important to Canadians as an indication of their "Canadian-ness," particularly in distinguishing themselves from their American counterparts. Thus, pushy religious and political groups can easily overstep proper levels of decorum in the minds of Canadians (cf. Bibby 1990, 141–55). Canadians are less tolerant of intolerance but more tolerant of diversity. Americans, however, with their historical tendency towards revolution and dissent, are more tolerant of less-than-irenic political and religious behaviour. For these reasons, Canadians distance themselves from fundamentalists, who are viewed as far from irenic. One Manitoba Pentecostal said that she hated the word "fundamentalist" because it carried the connotation of being extreme. Brian Stiller, former president of the Evangelical Fellowship of Canada, reacted against the

Table 7.10
Social Distance Measures

Item: How close do you feel to:	Canadian % Close/Very Close	US % Close/Very Close	US/Canada Difference[2]
Right to Life (N = 346)	70.9	80.6	US
US evangelicals (N = 348)	66.5	81.6	US
Canadian evangelicals (N = 271)	78.9	43.8	CN
National Assoc. of Evangelicals (NAE)/Evangelical Fellowship of Canada (EFC) (N = 272)	66.7	53.8	CN
Southern Baptists in the US (N = 332)	46.2	71.6	US
Pentecostal (N = 349)	66.1	49.8	CN
Fundamentalists (N = 302)	42.2	49.0	US
Catholics (N = 351)	33.6	25.2	
Episcopalians/Anglicans (N = 326)	33.5	15.4	CN
Jews (N = 341)	32.5	19.0	CN
Environmentalists (N = 351)	28.0	15.5	CN
National Council of Churches in Christ (NCCC)/ Canadian Council of Churches (CCC) (N = 264)	18.9	7.7	CN
Clinton/Chrétien government (N = 307)	9.6	1.6	CN
Feminists (N = 353)	11.5	3.7	CN
Homosexuals (N = 358)	5.5	1.0	
American Civil Liberties Union (ACLU) (N = 243)	1.3	0.6	
Secular humanists (N = 305)	2.8	1.2	CN
New Age movement (N = 344)	0	0	CN
Movie producers (N = 347)	0	0	

Source: CE sample, 1995.
[1] Groups are ranked from closest to farthest in the table based on means.
[2] The country listed is (significantly) closer to the group based on means.

media's use of the term "fundamentalist" in referring to Canadian evangelicals, since such "pejorative language" conveys "contempt and ridicule" (*Faith Today* [January/February 1994]: 56). Surprisingly, several Canadians reacted negatively to the "evangelical" label for the same reason. One Manitoba pastor qualified his identity as an "evangelical" by stating that the term was caricatured as "judgmental, narrow, critical, dogmatic," a view that is common among English Canadians, according to historian Michael Gauvreau (1990, 50–1). The differences in Table 7.10 imply a culturally significant national boundary.[12]

Among Canadian evangelicals, the tolerance of difference, coupled with low tolerance for intolerance, likely influences several related national differences, including ecumenism, the occurrence of fewer

denominational schisms, the greater number of evangelicals in mainline churches, less fundamentalism, and a relatively minor funda-
mentalist/modernist split in Canada compared to the US. In addition,
the fact that they are more tolerant of the least popular groups, such
as feminists, secular humanists, and New Agers, gives them a less
militant or fundamentalist tone than American evangelicals. This
may be one of the main sources of perceived differences between US
and Canadian evangelicals.[13]

Table 7.11 shows results of seven social-distance items in the
Bogardus tradition (1928; 1958). Core evangelical respondents were
asked if they would "approve, have reservations about, or would
disapprove if someone in your immediate family were to marry the
following types of people." The emphasis evangelicals place on the
protection of the traditional family makes intermarriage a particularly salient issue and is likely to bring out less-irenic responses.

The key similarity across locations is that evangelicals are least
supportive of intermarriage with nonevangelicals; much less supportive, in fact, than any other group mentioned. As argued in chapter 3, this is a key evangelical boundary. Evangelicals note that the
Bible teaches that Christians are not to be "unequally yoked," meaning that they are not to marry non-Christians. However, there is
geographic variation in the responses in this table.

I suspected that the historical presence of racial tension between
whites and African Americans in Mississippi and, to a lesser extent,
between whites and native people in Minnesota and Manitoba, and
ethnic tension with regard to the Acadian French in New Brunswick
would cause white evangelicals to be less willing to intermarry with
these groups. Mississippians show less support for intermarriage
with African Americans that evangelicals elsewehere but are the least
supportive of intermarriage with other ethnic groups as well. Thus,
my assumptions were not supported. The level of irenicism is lower
in Mississippi than in Minnesota on a few items, suggesting that the
Mason-Dixon line might be a significant cultural marker for ethnic
irenicism. However, the differences are even greater between the two
countries. Overall, Table 7.11 suggests that the forty-ninth parallel
seems to be the important cultural boundary for irenicism. In the
main, all this evidence supports a more irenic brand of evangelicalism north of the border.[14]

Table 7.12 presents ecumenical attitudes using the CE sample. The
items tap religious irenicism, or how accommodating evangelicals
feel towards members of other denominations.

Evangelicals in Canada are unlikely to limit themselves to one
denomination when looking for a new church. This could indicate

Table 7.11
Marriage Approval

Would you approve if someone in your immediate family was to marry a ... (% approving)	Minnesota (N = 107)	Mississippi (N = 97)	Manitoba (N = 103)	New Brunswick (N = 81)
Catholic	17.0	17.4	24.3	20.0
black American/Canadian	25.5*	5.4*	44.2	41.4
non-practising Christian	5.7	2.2	5.8	7.1
practising member of a non-Christian religion	0.9	1.1	3.8	2.8
native Indian	32.4	26.1	46.1	48.6
Hispanic American (US)/French Canadian (CN)	35.8	25.6	65.4	72.5
Presbyterian	44.8*	69.9	62.5	65.7

Source: CE sample, 1995.
* indicates a significant difference from other locations.

restricted comfort zones in the US, but it might also relate to the fact that there is less need for evangelicals in the US to look outside their denomination, as noted below. Canadians are also more supportive of church cooperation and less supportive of church competition than their American counterparts. While there is some within-country variation, the most striking difference is that Canadian evangelicals are more ecumenical, which suggests they are more irenic.

Why might this be so? One possible reason is differentially drawn evangelical subcultural boundaries. That is, American evangelicals create tighter boundaries or perhaps, have more ways of drawing boundaries than Canadians do. All evangelicals distinguish themselves from nonevangelicals on the basis of orthodoxy and orthopraxy (Hunter 1987), but American evangelicals are quicker to apply additional boundaries based on political issues and attitudes towards various groups. Second, American evangelical spokespeople create tension with some groups through heated public rhetoric with little negative backlash. Such rhetoric is tolerated partly because less-irenic public rhetoric is acceptable in the US, whether from the pulpit, town hall, or election platform. Third, historical racial tensions have been difficult for American evangelicals to shake (Emerson and Smith 2000), while the emphasis on ethnic and racial tolerance in Canada makes it more socially desirable to appear ethnically tolerant, which may affect responses. Fourth, civil religious sentiment in the US creates tension between liberal and conservative groups, which probably undermines irenicism. Finally, the relatively small evangelical population in Canada supports cooperation and ecumenism. To use a specific example, church-seeking Canadians may find it necessary

Table 7.12
Ecumenism Measures

	Minnesota (N = 106)	Mississippi (N = 89)	Manitoba (N = 102)	New Brunswick (N = 73)
1) If the respondent moved, he/she would look for a church:				
a) within his/her present denomination only (%)	25.8	35.7	11.1	10.9
b) within his/her present denomination first, but would consider other denominations (%)	51.5	47.6	66.7	56.3
c) among certain denominations only (%)	10.3	10.7	12.2	14.1
d) from a wide variety of denominations (%)	9.3	2.4	8.9	17.2
2) OK to proselytize from other Christian churches (% agreeing)*	21.3	16.3	10.9	9.6
3) Christian churches should cooperate in evangelism (% agreeing)*	75.4	89.9	91.2	90.4

Source: CE sample, 1995.
* The "strongly agree" and "agree" categories were combined.

to consider a broader range of denominations because there may be fewer churches to choose from.

From this evidence, I conclude that Canadian evangelicals are more irenic than American evangelicals. In fact, Canadian evangelicals appear more irenic than nonevangelical Americans, who are in turn more irenic than American evangelicals. It is also clear that evangelicals do parallel their national cultures in irenicism, which suggests that the larger national influences have a limited, though significant, effect on the evangelical subculture. Regression analyses reveal that national differences could not be accounted for by demographic, denominational, or regional differences, and differences in irenicism remain even for committed evangelicals.[15]

While the differences discussed in this chapter follow national boundaries, one should not assume that there is no within-country variation. That is, political alignment and irenicism vary to some degree by region. As a case in point, interview data indicate regional differences in irenicism, particularly in the area of racial-ethnic irenicism. Historically recent racial injustices are manifest in lingering racial tensions in Mississippi, and those tensions are qualitatively different there than elsewhere in North America. Most evangelicals I spoke to in Mississippi were eager to heal racial tensions, and several churches were working to increase racial harmony. When they voiced concerns about their local community, however, their responses reflected the legacy of racial tension.

The greatest local concern for evangelicals in Mississippi was crime and violence. Several pastors reported that the relatively peaceful neighbourhoods in which their church was located had been recently transformed by criminal activity. One pastor said that his church was relocating outside the city since churchgoers were afraid to come to so violent an area. He reported that cars had been stolen out of the parking lot during broad daylight. Mississippi respondents attributed increases in crime to dispersion of blacks from the inner city and the corresponding white flight. Several respondents mentioned the problem of racism in the city. A Mississippi pastor said:

What's happening now is what is labelled "white flight," where basically now so many whites have left; our community now is one of these transition communities. Its very interesting, the parsonage was sold to a black couple in their forties, both of them working white-collar jobs, their incomes probably higher than all but two-three families in our church, and yet there will be fear from whites around here, just because there is a black family around them, the value of their home will go down. And it's true, it will. So that's an issue for the church, the blacks are coming in, so the value of the church is going down, but its an imaginary [problem] ... See, we have been here eight months, and our next door neighbours are black, and when we got here there were no [houses up for sale]. Now there are ten [houses for sale] all around us, all those are whites ... The value [of the homes] does come down, and blacks say, "Well, I want to live in that nice neighbourhood," and why not? It's almost funny to me because for me it's not a big deal at all ... I watch and I see that whites are creating the opportunities themselves [for neighbourhood decline] by selling cheaper ... It just doesn't make any sense whatsoever but that's the way prejudice is.

Like this pastor, the US evangelicals interviewed by Emerson and Smith (2000) saw the black-white race problem related to prejudiced individuals or poor interaction between the races. More broadly, they argue, white evangelicals embrace explanations that hold individuals responsible for social problems, problems they think are best addressed through the conversion of nonChristians and the need for individuals to stop sinning by harbouring bigoted attitudes and hatred towards people of other races. Evangelicals tend to reduce macro social problems to individual-level problems because of the dominance of what Emerson and Smith call "accountable free-will individualism" (ibid., 76), a tendency to view humans being as relatively unfettered by social structural constraints such that they are free to make individual choices and are accountable (before God) for those choices. Evangelicals in Mississippi wished that people of all races would get over their racist past and embrace a more tolerant future.

Evangelicals from Minnesota and Manitoba connect crime with First Nation people instead of African Americans, but their concerns are different in tone. Minnesotan and Manitoban respondents are not so much concerned about racism as about the well-being of native people. One Manitoban pastor said that the greatest local problem was substance abuse and other problems among the First Nation people:

I think we have to start with the [native] kids. I am not sure; quite frankly, [the problem] is enormous. Just a little history ... [when we opened up a soup kitchen in our church] we were getting two hundred people a day, and a number of them were substance abusers whose brains were fried ... I have come to the point of realizing that there are some people who cannot be helped, quite literally because they don't have enough brain cells left in their head to make a choice ... that was a horrible thing to realize. I even got to the point of thinking that maybe what you could do is take someone home for maybe five years, "adopt a native" kind of thing ... [but] the odds are that in six months they would be right back because there will be people who come and influence them or because they just don't have the capacity to respond. So quite frankly I don't know how to solve the problem.

To conclude, both qualitative and quantitative evidence suggest within-country and between-country differences in racial-ethnic irenicism, although the national boundary is the more significant boundary for irenicism.

The differences found in these data sets are peripheral to the orthodoxy and orthopraxy that has traditionally distinguished evangelicals from nonevangelicals. In chapter 2, I noted that Hexham and Poewe expect religious movements to show international uniformity on their central tenets, while other elements "take on local colour" (1997, 43). The evangelical subculture does not seem to promote uniformity in areas of incongruity, national concerns, political attitudes, or irenicism. As a result, national differences seem to influence these areas, for which subcultural boundaries are not clearly and uniformly drawn.

Is the presence of national cultural influences an indication that the inroads made by secular society will dissolve boundaries and secularize evangelicalism? Not necessarily.[16] As Smith argues (1998), religious subcultural boundaries are constantly in a state of flux. Religious traditions negotiate boundaries by which they distinguish themselves from other religious and social groupings in

their environment. In Smith's model, evangelicals will fortify boundaries and retrench on issues that are salient and perceived to be
threatening at the time, while other fronts may be unguarded and
thus somewhat permeable to societal influences. At present, evangelicals in both countries are fortifying walls around the salient areas of
sexual mores and religious freedoms. Particular beliefs about Jesus
and the Bible have remained salient over much of the twentieth century since they distinguish evangelicals from "liberal" Christians. In
the southern country, fortification includes political alignment for
many. In the North, it does not. On unguarded fronts, evangelicals
resemble their countrymen to varying degrees. Canadians are more
concerned about economic issues than Americans. American evangelicals, like most Americans, seem more concerned about individual
freedoms like freedom of speech, while Canadians are quicker to
denounce public tirades because they are not irenic. Furthermore,
there is some evidence that in the US, the religious talk and walk are
not as tightly coupled.

DIFFERENCES WITHIN SIMILARITIES

One should not assume that the four differences discussed here are
the only differences among evangelicals in North America. Future
polls with different questions will probably uncover other areas of
difference. These four differences, however, particularly irenicism
and political alignment, appear consistently in the qualitative and
quantitative data available. They exist within widespread similarities.
In areas of religious experience, belief, morals, practice, and commitment, differences are minimal. I have argued that a distinctive subculture, with a shared identity and subcultural boundaries, helps
explain similarities. In political alignment and irenicism, variation is
significant, since these attitudinal areas are not explicitly religious
and thus less central to what it means to be an evangelical. Differences indicate that subcultural boundaries are not clearly drawn in
these areas.

This does not mean, of course, that there is nothing distinctive
about evangelical political attitudes or irenicism. Moral issues moti-
vate evangelical political action on both sides of the border, and even
Canadian evangelical voters show some tendency towards conservative politics. As noted above, evangelicals generally agree on which
groups they feel close to and which groups they feel far from, even
though Canadian evangelicals rate as close many more groups than
American evangelicals do. Measures of irenicism indicated that evangelicals are least supportive of marriages between Christians and non-
Christians, indicating general agreement on the symbolic importance

of this boundary. The fact that differences exist within similarities is further evidence of an influential and international subculture.

However, religious traditions do not inform, with equal clarity, all areas of life. Some areas are left undetermined or underdetermined, and evangelicals vary without implication to their religious devotion. If this argument is correct – that evangelicalism is a distinctive subculture that promotes similarities and that differences exist where evangelicals do not speak with one voice – then areas of difference should be evident even among the most devoted evangelical. That is, involvement in the subculture should not significantly minimize differences, if indeed the subculture does not inform these choices in a consistent manner.

Table 7.13 shows in summary form the similarities and differences presented in chapters 3 and 7. Most of the beliefs, attitudes, and practices available in the 1996 God and Society poll are used in the table, placing the items into the categories of orthodox doctrinal beliefs (those doctrines typically accepted by evangelicals), other beliefs (on which evangelicals vary), conservative political attitudes, religion and politics (the influence of religion on politics), irenicism, and also measures of practice and commitment. Besides evangelicals, mainline Protestants and Catholics are included for comparative purposes, as well as those with high commitment in each tradition.

The numbers in the table give the average percent difference between American and Canadian evangelicals. For example, the typical difference between Americans and Canadians on available doctrinal belief items is 5.5 percent, as indicated in the first column. The plus sign indicates that American evangelicals consistently gave more conservative answers to these doctrinal items. Looking across the row, the "varies" in the next column indicates that on some items, committed evangelicals in Canada are more conservative, while on others American committed evangelicals are more conservative. In fact, the belief responses of committed evangelicals on both sides of the border were nearly identical, giving an average difference of a miniscule one percent. Committed evangelicals are equally doctrinally orthodox on both sides of the border, as noted in chapter 5. In comparison to evangelicals, mainline Protestants and Catholics show much larger average differences in doctrinal scores, indicating that there is for less international similarity between them.[17] In keeping with the argument of this book, minimal doctrinal differences among evangelicals may indicate that the evangelical subculture has more distinctive doctrinal subcultural boundaries, and that evangelical boundaries protect them from regional variation in orthodoxy. Canadian and American evangelicals show greater differences in other beliefs, although the average percent difference is still smaller than

Tableau 7.13
Average Percent Difference between US and Canada

Item	All Evangelicals (N = 1035)	Committed Evangelicals (N = 533)	All Mainline Protestants (N = 1190)	Committed Mainline Protestants (N = 278)	All Catholics (N = 1594)	Committed Catholics (N = 376)
Orthodox Doctrinal Beliefs (7 items)	+5.5	varies	+18.1	+7.9	+12.6	+2.2
Other Beliefs (6 items)	+7.4	varies	+12.1	+7.1	+10.8	+9.6
Conservative Political Attitudes (5 items)	+11.8	+13.7	+9.3	+7.5	+6.6	+6.0
Religion and Politics (3 items)	+7.5	+7.4	+12.0	varies	+10.2	varies
Irenicism (4 items)	−16.1	−13.8	varies	varies	−8.6	−4.3
Devotionalism (2 items)	varies	−4.0	+18.7	+6.0	+10.1	+1.2
Church Attendance	+7.0	+1.5	+16.9	+4.1	+18.1	+8.7
Salience	+1.9	+1.0	+12.7	+7.9	+16.1	+8.2
Commitment (% high)	+7.2	0	+19.2	0	+15.1	0

Source: God and Society poll, 1996.

Plus sign (+) means consistently more conservative in the US. The minus sign (−) means more irenic or higher devotionalism in Canada.

"Varies" means roughly an equal number of more conservative/irenic responses in the US and Canada.

Orthodox Doctrinal Beliefs – God is not superstition, humans are made in God's image, Jesus is divine, Jesus forgives sins, Bible is inspired, committed life to Christ, evangelism important.

Other Beliefs – world will end in battle of Armageddon, don't need to go to church to be good Christian, all religions are equally true, spiritual life better than riches, private beliefs more important than what is taught by the church, those who love God and work hard will have enough money.

Conservative Political Attitudes – government is too big, free market better, reduce number of immigrants, rich-poor gap not a problem, government should not spend more reducing poverty.

Religion and Politics – religion is very important to my political thinking, Christian values should play major role in politics, Christians should be involved in politics to protect values.

Irenicism – rather have neighbour of my own race, would vote for evangelical political leader, vote for atheist political leader, vote for Muslim political leader.

Devotionalism – frequency of prayer and Bible reading.

Church attendance – frequency of church attendance.

Salience – faith provides great deal of guidance in day to day life.

Commitment – combination of devotionalism, church attendance, salience, and some evangelical beliefs.

for other Christians. This tendency towards similarity does not hold true for political attitudes, as shown in the next two rows of the table. Conservative political attitudes diverge more among evangelicals than among Catholics and mainline Protestants. Furthermore, there is no convergence for committed evangelicals. Again, "religion and politics" items show no convergence for committed evangelicals. Not surprisingly, Americans are consistently more conservative politically for all religious traditions.

Canadian evangelicals are for more irenic than their American counterparts (as the negative sign indicates). Among the traditions, the gap between evangelical Canadians and Americans is the largest. However, mainline Protestants in Canada are not more irenic according to these measures. This finding is surprising considering that Canadians are on the whole more irenic. I am not sure how to interpret this, except by saying that mainline Protestants in the US tend to be irenic, and that the irenicism items available on the 1996 God and Society poll are somewhat limited in scope. For devotionalism, church attendance, and salience, we see minimal differences between evangelicals in the two countries, in comparison to other Christians. Committed evangelicals on both sides of the border show minimal differences in attendance and salience measures. Regarding commitment, evangelicals again show a smaller US-Canada gap than the other Christian traditions do, partly because they tend towards higher levels of commitment. Of course, committed religionists in all traditions show no differences, since they are all committed by definition.

Overall, committed evangelicals show less cross-national variation than committed mainline Protestants and Catholics. In sum, the table supports the arguments of this book: evangelicals show similarity in beliefs and levels of practice and commitment but differ in political attitudes and irenicism. These differences exist even among the most committed evangelicals. In beliefs and practices (and probably moral orthodoxy too), evangelicals do not follow the conservatism or religiosity levels of their geographic environments.

INTRANATIONAL VARIATION?

To this point, the data have indicated areas of similarity and difference among evangelicals, comparing Americans and Canadians. Within-country differences, or differences between regions within a country, have been given less attention. However, the historic differences between the American South and the rest of the country (or continent) likely have some influence on evangelicals today, particularly since this is an area of evangelical concentration. Regional differences within English Canada cannot be ignored either. It is particularly important to examine the sources of difference because international differences may actually stem from intranational differences. Then too, as mentioned in chapter 1, a distinctive region within either country could account for the international differences I found.

Based on evidence from previous chapters, I have concluded that national boundaries are more significant than local boundaries in influencing beliefs, practices, and attitudes. There is no reason to conclude that the source of perceived national differences is in reality regional differences, the sum of which account for national differences. Table 7.14 substantiates this conclusion. In the table, analysis of variance is used to determine whether there is statistically significant variation between countries and between regions within each country. With this statistical technique, one can check to see whether significant variation exists between countries or regions within each country. I examine differences among the wider population and among evangelicals in devotionalism, beliefs, commitment, church attendance, conservative political attitudes, and irenicism (as measured in Table 7.13). The "between-country" comparisons simply look for significant variation between Canada and the US. "Within-country" variation tests the significance of differences between five regions in each country. In Canada, the regions are British Columbia, the Prairies, Ontario, Quebec, and the Maritimes. In the US, regions include the Western, Mountain, Southern, North Central, and Northeastern states.

In the first three rows of the table, we find significant variation between the countries and within each country for the total sample. This was expected, given the findings discussed in previous chapters. Americans are more religious, more orthodox, and more politically conservative than Canadians, and these traits vary within each country. The only exception is the low variation within Canada in the area of irenicism. Evidently, Canadian influences push Canadians in all regions towards similar levels of irenicism, at least to respond in irenic ways. The next three lines repeat the analysis for evangelicals. Variation between American and Canadian evangelicals remains significant for beliefs, political attitudes, and irenicism (once the anomalous small sample of Quebec evangelicals is removed; see note 7, chapter 6). Here, the difference in beliefs is a surprise, although it is not as significant as differences in the areas of politics and irenicism. As noted above, American evangelicals tend to be slightly more consistent in giving conservative responses to belief

Table 7.14
Significance Levels of Regional and National Variation for Evangelicals

	Devotion	Beliefs	Commitment	Church Attendance	Political Attitudes	Irenicism
Between-country variation Total sample (N = 6000)	***	***	***	***	***	***
Within-country variation All Canadians (N = 3000)	***	***	***	***	***	Ns
Within-country variation All Americans (N = 3000)	***	***	***	***	***	***
Between-country variation[1] All Evangelicals (N = 1004)	Ns	**	Ns	Ns	***	***
Within-country variation Canadian Evangelicals (N = 272)	Ns	Ns	Ns	Ns	Ns	*
Within-country variation American Evangelicals (N = 742)	Ns	***	***	**	Ns	***
Between-country variation All Core Evangelicals (N = 533)	Ns	Ns	Ns	Ns	***	***
Within-country variation Canadian Core Evangelicals (N = 139)	Ns	Ns	Ns	Ns	Ns	Ns
Within-country variation American Core Evangelicals (N = 394)	Ns	**	Ns	Ns	Ns	***

Source: God and Society poll, 1996.

Significance: *** .001; ** .01; * .05; ns – not significant.

[1] Quebec evangelicals removed.

[2] Quebec evangelicals removed.

items than Canadians, but these differences are not substantive. As expected, evangelicals in both countries show similar levels of devotionalism, commitment, and attendance since they do not reach standard levels of significance (ns). One can conclude that American and Canadian evangelicals have matching levels of religiosity. There is no significant variation among Canadian evangelicals, save minor variation in irenicism. Thus regional differences among evangelicals in

(English) Canada are minimal. In the US, evangelicals differ on beliefs, commitment, church attendance, and irenicism. American evangelicals are more conservative in the South and more liberal in the West, showing some tendency to follow their regional milieus. Finally, the last three lines show analysis for committed (core) evangelicals. The only between-country variation that remains significant is in the area of political attitudes and irenicism, supporting the arguments made in this book. Canadian core evangelicals show no regional variation, and American core evangelicals show moderate variation only in beliefs and, as noted above, in irenicism.

EXPLAINING COMPETING PERCEPTIONS

Interviewer: In the Southeast where you have travelled, are the Southern Baptist churches all the same?
Pastor: All the same.
Interviewer: What do you hear about other areas?
Pastor: I think they are similar all over. I think that you could go all over the US and Southern Baptists would be almost a norm, which are good conservative, Bible-believing, God-fearing people.
Interviewer: Are there variations among SBC churches in this area?
Pastor: [They are] all the same.
Interviewer: Is the worship style the same?
Pastor: We are all pretty traditional.

Interviewer: Are there variations among the Southern Baptist churches where you have travelled?
Pastor: All the churches are different even across this town. You get some churches that are "high church" like the Episcopal Church. Here we are kind of in the middle; [we] try to fit everyone's tastes. Some churches are like the Grand 'Ol Opry. We [the Southern Baptists] are not a church, we are just a mission organization of 40,000 churches that got together ...
Interviewer: Do some churches in this area have contemporary worship?
Pastor: Some churches are going into a Saturday night contemporary worship, and all last summer our evening services were straight contemporary ...

These two Southern Baptist pastors, both from Mississippi, were interviewed during the same week at churches in the same city. Like these pastors, some respondents report striking regional differences while others felt they were minimal. From the evidence given in this book, one might expect that people would perceive few significant regional differences among evangelicals in the US and Canada, particularly at the core. As previously noted, this does not fit the conclusions drawn by the respondents themselves. If many of them reported regional differences, why is it that I found so few? Let me suggest four reasons for the perceived differences between evangelicals.

The first explanation is that evangelicals take on more local differences the further one moves from the core. Obviously, less-committed evangelicals would be less devoted to subcultural beliefs, norms, and practices and would thus exhibit regional variation. Second, it is likely that regional *stereotypes* are ascribed to evangelicals in a region, which are sometimes inaccurate. As social psychologists know, people see what they expect to see. One perceptive pastor in Mississippi said that even Mississippians share the stereotypical view that they have economic and racial problems and joke about their backwardness, a stereotype he thought was more fiction than fact. Evangelicals in a region are perceived to fit regional stereotypes as well. Third, general perceptions stem from differences in *emphasis*. Evangelicals with similar beliefs and practices will emphasize different scripts, rules, and myths in their subculture depending on which aspects are salient to them. The salience of a certain script or norm is no doubt related to environment. For example, we would expect evangelicals in Mississippi – who share with nonevangelicals in their (local, regional, and national) environment fears about the rapid increase in crime and violence – to be more concerned about moral and spiritual decline than people in low-crime areas where these issues are not as salient. As a result, Mississippians who emphasize the moral/spiritual decline appear more "legalistic" than those who emphasize economic reform, partly because they have seen lawlessness escalate. Canadian evangelicals, who share with most Canadians a desire to distinguish themselves from Americans, will emphasize national differences.

Fourth, general perceptions are affected by a "loose coupling" between stated attitudes (in a survey or interview) and actual practice. As previously stated, new institutionalists emphasize that regulations are not always adhered to in actual organizational practice (Meyer and Rowan 1991, 55–60). The same seems to be true in evangelical churches and denominations, where moral prohibitions do not always match practices. This incongruity is related to the tendency of evangelicals and other religious conservatives to prohibit practices that become associated with certain taboo behaviours. Prohibiting these behaviours is thought to protect against temptation that could lead to sin, thus allowing for a margin of safety. For example, several respondents mentioned that mixed swimming is (or at least was) taboo in congregations in certain locales but not in others. Mixed swimming, some conservatives reason, while not prohibited by the Bible, could arouse lustful thoughts or, worse, lead to inappropriate sexual behaviour. Thus, mixed swimming becomes associated with lustful thoughts, or even premarital/extramarital sex, which nearly all evangelicals agree is wrong. Listen to this Baptist pastor in Mississippi, who described himself as a fundamentalist:[18] "If you say mixed swimming [is okay], well, eventually the young people are going to wear next to nothing. I've had that happen too. So rather than put yourself in a position where you have to say, 'Now, this is enough' … you just don't do it." I asked him if, to keep it from progressing, one should draw the line on the strict side. "Yes. If this were something that you have to do that would be different. Where in the word of God does it say you have to take young people swimming? That's an issue you don't have to deal with and that's a battle you don't have to fight." Conservative evangelicals like this pastor may not think mixed swimming is "always wrong" and may answer survey items based on biblical fiat, just like other evangelicals. The difference is that the conservativeness of the area allows him the luxury of a safety margin. Such prohibitions seem overly strict to evangelicals elsewhere, and pastors would have trouble persuading others of the value of their strictness. Thus, evangelicals may be more similar on reported moral attitudes than they are in practice, which gives the observer a sense that evangelicals in the area are "legalistic," but this difference does not appear on the survey. It appears that moral attitudes are institutionalized, and that verbal adherence to them is an important aspect of evangelical identity. Practice, however, is loosely coupled with attitudes and varies by region.

I am suggesting that the quantitative survey items may not completely capture regional differences in religiosity. The quantitative data have brought out differences in ecumenism, ethnic tolerance, political alignment, civil religion, and a few beliefs and attitudes. Some differences, however, are difficult to measure quantitatively, because certain regional differences within North American evangelicalism amount to differences in *tone*, which do not appear in standard measures of belief, practice, and attitudes. Observers pick up these differences and apply labels ("legalistic," "strict," etc.) on subjective impressions based on their "sense" of the area. Thus, an observer's impression of the regional differences may be correct but difficult to quantify. These differences are accentuated by differences in emphasis and loose coupling between attitudes and practice, and possibly for other reasons as well.

North American evangelicalism shows differences within similarities. These differences, which are limited to peripheral issues, do not indicate subcultural weakness but natural diversity housed within widespread homogeneity. Diversity should be seen as natural because of the complex web of influences that shape beliefs, attitudes and practices. In light of this complexity, *either/or* conclusions are unlikely, while *both/and* conclusions are expected. Predictably, then, there are both differences and similarities to be found in a comparison of American and Canadian evangelicals. In this case, however, differences are bounded by a distinctive and international religious subculture.

8 Conclusions

This book is not the first analysis of evangelicalism in the US or in Canada, but it is the first sociological comparison of the two. Furthermore, it employs new strategies. What is new about this book is the approach used to develop the themes of *subculture* and *geographic variation*, introduced in chapter 1 and interwoven throughout. The *subculture* theme focused on core evangelicals, who are best suited to reveal the inner workings of the evangelical subculture. The question of subculture delves into the characteristics of North American evangelicalism. *Geographic variation* is comparative in nature. Comparing evangelicals in similar but not identical cultural and religious contexts allows one to discern the contributions of national and regional distinctions to the evangelical subculture. Much of what we know about evangelicalism in general is based on a unique American brand of evangelicalism. The comparative approach presented in this book allows us to look at evangelicalism in another national context. Previous students of evangelicalism have examined the relationship between evangelicals and their environment on the basis of changes over time. Geographical variation is another way to examine the effect of broader culture on the evangelical subculture. Geographic variation presents two questions: What differences or similarities do evangelicals exhibit across national and regional lines, and what is the effect of broader secular culture on evangelicals? Based on the evidence in the proceeding chapters, it is time to suggest tentative answers.

SUBCULTURE:
CHARACTERISTICS OF EVANGELICALISM

What characterizes evangelicalism at its core? Core evangelicals share a distinctive identity and maintain clear boundaries and norms, all of which are supported by an evangelical subculture that spans regions and national boundaries. Their religious experiences, tension with the larger society, and friendships with other evangelicals mutually enhance commitment, which in turn gives vitality to the evangelical subculture.

Evangelical identity rotates around four historic emphases of evangelicalism. Evangelicals describe themselves as those who have experienced salvation (conversionism), and as those who embrace the historic doctrines of the Christian faith, including the authority of Scripture (biblicism) and the redemptive work of Christ on the cross (crucicentrism). In the US and Canada, it appears that the fourth historic emphasis, activism, forms the weakest part of evangelical identity. Evangelicals rarely identified themselves on the basis of practice, nor did they feel comfortable identifying other evangelicals by such criteria. The considerable ambiguity that shrouds the area of activism has at least three sources: the doctrine that entrance into the evangelical fold is based not on works but solely on God's grace, the discomfort evangelicals feel with their reputation for aggressive proselytizing, and the difficulty they have articulating how faith leads to action in the world. Because of this ambiguity, evangelicals seem less willing to use activism as a distinguishing characteristic of evangelicals. Evangelicals in Canada, moreover, show less support for evangelism than US evangelicals.

Evangelicals have clear boundaries around their subculture. These boundaries allow them to determine who is within the evangelical camp – those who are truly "Christians" – and who is not. On the individual level, boundaries are drawn on the basis of whether or not one has experienced salvation, or been "born again." In addition, true Christians accept the authority of the Bible and the redemptive work of Christ as the only means to salvation. These boundaries of conversion, crucicentrism, and biblicism cut across denominational lines. Evangelicals feel that true Christians can and do affiliate with a broad spectrum of Protestant denominations, and within Catholicism as well. Finally, there is the expectation that true Christians will meet certain behavioural standards. While works do not bring salvation, doing certain things while avoiding others is evidence of salvation. Attending church, Bible reading, and prayer are expected and widely practised by evangelicals. Moral issues of sexuality that are perceived to threaten the traditional family remain taboo, like the hot topics of premarital sex, homosexuality, and abortion. Adopting pro-choice or pro-homosexual stances or involving oneself in sexual impropriety (without remorse) are serious enough offences to call into question one's position as an evangelical. Other moral issues are less salient, and evangelicals are no longer overwhelmingly against smoking, dancing, drinking, and the like. At the institutional/group level, evangelicals distinguish between those who are "for us" and those who are "against us" based on their perception of that groups' allegiance to their goals. Core evangelicals seem to share boundaries on this level as well, both in Canada and the US.

Probing past the subcultural boundaries into the inner workings of evangelical faith, religious experience is central. The majority of evangelicals consider their salvation to be their most important religious experience, for it ushers them into an ongoing relationship with the divine. This relationship is experienced through a sense of God's presence, divine guidance, miraculous healings, and other answers to prayer. Religious experience reinforces the reality of their faith and enhances commitment. The distinctiveness – the clear identities, norms, and subcultural boundaries – of the evangelical subculture supports its vitality (Smith 1998). Evangelicals see themselves as different from others in society, and that difference is important enough to them to encourage devotion. Among evangelicals, religious commitment and participation is high.

GEOGRAPHIC VARIATION: SIMILARITIES AND DIFFERENCES

Do North American evangelicals differ significantly by country or region? The data suggest that core evangelicals show surprising uniformity across regions in North America. First, all the North American evangelicals I interviewed share a common understanding of their central identity as evangelicals and agree on the boundaries that separate evangelicals from nonevangelicals. The scope of their identity as a subculture is uniform, as respondents in all regions are more likely to refer to themselves as Christians than to identify themselves by denomination or as evangelicals. Core evangelicals are also equally likely to choose an "evangelical" label in each region. The tendency to identify themselves on the basis of orthodox beliefs and conversion is equally true of all the evangelicals I interviewed. Further, evangelicals are in agreement on which groups they consider to be "ingroups" and which they consider to be "outgroups." The majority of evangelicals in all regions are most concerned about the moral disintegration of society and all indicate some tension with the "world." They are more likely to associate with other evangelicals. All evangelicals feel that Catholics could be Christians (according to their definition of Christian), and there are no regional differences in the percent that feel that homosexuals or racists could be Christians. I conclude that these similarities point to a distinctive widespread evangelical subculture.

Second, core evangelical religious experience shows few regional differences. As previously stated, the majority of evangelicals in all regions choose conversion as their most significant religious experience. There are no regional differences in how often they experience God's presence or receive answers to their prayers. Third, they do not differ substantively on levels of private devotional or public ritual practice. In addition, there is evidence of privatization in all regions. Evangelicals in each region demonstrate a lack of clarity when it comes to applying one's faith in the "world." Fourth, regional differences in moral orthodoxy are minimal, and variation is better explained by age than by region. Most evangelicals in all locations base their moral views on biblical fiat. Evangelicals that I talked to were not consistently more conservative in Mississippi and New Brunswick than in Manitoba and Minnesota.

Explaining Similarities

It is impossible to point to one cause for all these similarities, but a combination of reasons can be given. In chapter 3 I said that similarities could be explained in terms of historical similarities, globalization, new institutionalism, and subcultural distinctiveness. These approaches are interrelated, not competing, and they provide different pieces to a complex puzzle of influences. Matching what globalization theorists say about religion in our globalizing world, significant similarities across regions suggests the diminishing significance of geographic boundaries, shrinking the effects of space. Evangelicalism is shaped by influences that are international in scope. Inglehart's thesis, for example, sees Canada and the United States as part of an international movement away from materialist towards post-materialist values. Globalization suggests substantial cross-border influences from within the evangelical subculture. It is likely that the increased transience of the population, the growth of international markets, and the media, among other factors, lessen differences between evangelicals in the two countries.

This globalization argument intersects with the cultural production of evangelicals and their embrace of modern technology and media.

I have already noted the plethora of marketable products produced by evangelicals, including distinctively evangelical music, books, clothing, videos, computer and board games, television programs, and much more. Historically, evangelicals have also led the way in using media technology for evangelism and discipleship, whether radio, television, and now the Internet (Schultze 1990). Besides propagating the evangelical message in North America and worldwide, evangelical media provide a way to market evangelical products. As a result, the evangelical has both the technological means and the marketable goods to globalize. Put another way, the globalization of evangelicalism operates, at least in part, through evangelical subcultural production.

It has been argued that for evangelicalism to embrace modern technology and consumer culture is to sell out to a corrupt "worldly" system (see, for example, Guinness 1993). In fact, the relationship between evangelicalism and technology is double-edged. On the one hand, technology and consumerism may weaken the prophetic role of evangelicalism in the West. Instead of critiquing the culture, evangelicals blend into it. The medium of television and radio spawn a "pop" brand of the gospel, where preachers must "sell" their religious wares in packages that entice consumers, giving them what they want, not necessarily what they need. Detractors fear that the individualistic nature of media consumption will undercut community and accountability within the church. Churches and parachurch organizations trust marketing schemes to provide funds and survey research to illuminate the means to reaching their target consumer, replacing trust in God and reliance on God's Spirit (Schultze 1991). On the other hand, the embrace of technology and consumerism provides the tools that build subcultural strength. Media spokespeople publicize evangelicalism and give it a public "image," an important ingredient of modern identity. Consumer products and institutions strengthen religious identity and boundaries, since the uniqueness of "being evangelical" is bolstered by consumer choice. Furthermore, market-driven churches, which provide the modern consumer with multiple programs and "seeker-sensitive" styles of worship, attract the unchurched and lead to church growth and vitality (Cimino and Lattin 1998).

Some observers speculate that evangelicals in Canada and the US may show few differences because the broader Canadian and American cultures are converging, while regional differences are diminishing. However, this study suggests that any such conclusions would be premature. Subcultural similarities may simply mean that evangelicals insulate themselves from their surrounding cultures by creating alternative institutions, which provide the basis for a distinct subculture. If evangelicals deflect external secular influences and absorb internal evangelical influences, as argued in chapter 5, then similarities in national culture become less relevant. In fact, the evidence presented in chapters 6 and 7 suggests that while Canadians and Americans in general differ substantially in their levels of support for certain religious beliefs, morals, and practices, evangelicals in these countries show minimal differences. Evangelicals, the evidence suggests, are not similar because they live in matching cultural environments but because they have created a distinctive subculture of their own.

This subculture, I argued earlier, is endowed with a clear set of boundaries that separate it from other religious and special interest groups. Evangelicals take their cues from other evangelicals within the subculture. Evangelicalism is shaped by influences that are international in scope, and evangelicals produce the cultural "stuff" and have the institutional base required to maintain themselves as a viable subculture. These claims resemble what proponents of the "new institutionalism" have been observing in other institutional spheres.[1] Organizations that form a recognized area of organizational life tend towards similarity, since they adapt or orient themselves to the norms and practices of the "organizational field." New institutionalists focus their attention on the environments that shape the organization. They emphasize that the norms and scripts that shape organizations are superorganizational, and that organizational fields are often international in scope. In the same vein, I have focused on the environments in which evangelicals find themselves and emphasized the effect of supra-organizational influences, which can outweigh the influence of the local church or denomination. Faced with this evidence, it is reasonable to suggest that evangelicalism (at least in Canada and the US, and possibly in the West overall) has become an "organizational field," that is, it has formed an area of recognized institutional life.

To connect "New Instititutionalism" to the "distinctive subculture" argument, one need only note that "supply-side" institutions (churches and parachurch organizations) and the cultural products they produce (sermons, evangelical television, radio, music, books, videos, etc.) make for an increasingly homogeneous evangelical "product." That is, the increasing spread and volume of evangelical "cultural stuff" leads to similarities among the participants in the subculture. It is reasonable to assume, in other words, that similarities among evangelicals indicate similarities in the organizations that support them.

Another possible indication is similarity in "demand." In other words, evangelicals who are embedded in the evangelical subculture seek a "structured" evangelical product. Just as conformity to the norms of to the organizational field gives a secular organization added legitimacy and stability (Meyer and Rowan 1991, 53), so following the norms of evangelical religiosity gives a church added legitimacy and stability and increases its chances of growth. To be legitimately evangelical, a church must emphasize the core beliefs and experiences of evangelicals, including biblicism, crucicentrism, conversionism, and activism.[2] Similarly, evangelically "structured" churches emphasize traditional family values (anti-abortion, anti-pornography, anti-extramarital sex, etc.) and must support evangelism. Some support for the notion that evangelicals seek out generically evangelical churches can be given from the interviews. Recall that the majority of evangelicals I surveyed were against competition between "Christian" (evangelical) churches and supported cooperation between them and would consider attending other Christian churches if one in their denomination was not available. Recall also that evangelical identity centred around a "Christian" identity, not one based on denomination. Several core evangelicals indicated that they seek a standard evangelical content, not a certain "brand" of evangelicalism, as this Southern Baptist pastor in Mississippi said: "[When I was called into ministry], I was attracted to a nondenominational type church ... but if you want to get anything done, you have to choose a brand, just like you need to choose a type of car if you are going to go anywhere. I chose SBC because it has autonomous congregations, because of its commitment to the Bible." Pastors in all four regions were also actively involved in ecumenical efforts, including attending regular interdenominational meetings, swapping pulpits with other (conservative Protestant) denominations, conducting joint services, and sharing costs and personnel across denominational boundaries. Furthermore, some researchers in Canada and the US have observed that denominational boundaries are losing significance (Wuthnow 1988; Roof and McKinney 1987; Hammond 1992). When Posterski and Baker asked active church members in Canada the importance of different factors in choosing a church to attend, seventy-eight percent of conservative Protestant respondents gave "local evangelism" a high priority rating, while only fifty percent gave denomination a high priority rating (1993, 259).

In sum, the evidence suggests that evangelical Christians both seek and are influenced by a "structured" evangelical "organizational field" that is supraregional and international in scope. As a result, core evangelicals show surprising similarity throughout North America. Further, because core evangelicals are group conscious, they are influenced more from inside the institutional sphere than from outside in areas of religiosity.

DIFFERENCES

Of course, there are limits to the arguments given above. The evangelical subcultural boundaries are permeable to larger societal influences in many areas that are less central and salient to evangelical identity. Besides variation in political attitudes and irenicism, evangelicals vary in their degree of separation from modernity, denominational loyalty, attitudes towards women in leadership, desire for contemporary versus traditional or liturgical worship styles, and of course on doctrinal specifics. (This research, however, indicates that denominational loyalties seem less salient than broader evangelical loyalties and identities.) While evangelicals show similarities across regions, they still differ in important ways from denomination to denomination, church to church, and person to person. These differences should not be underemphasized, for the evangelical subculture remains multivocal, internally disjointed, and even in conflict. In fact, some core evangelicals resisted being lumped together with evangelicals in other regions. Differences, though fewer than originally anticipated, are an important part of this story.

These differences are consequential. Important regional differences are not reducible to congregational, denominational, demographic, or local contextual factors. The most prominent difference is in the political attitudes of evangelicals in the two countries. Americans are more conservative politically, and they are predominately Republican. They believe that government is too big and they blame it for societal problems more often than Canadians do. American evangelicals list moral issues as the source of national and local problems more often than Canadians, who are more concerned about economic issues. There is some evidence, though limited, of national differences in belief. Canadian evangelicals are less likely than Americans to believe that taking a life is justified but more likely to accept certain characteristic gifts (tongues, healing, prophecy) as appropriate for the church today (as they were at Pentecost), and they are more likely to criticize the institutionalized (evangelical) church than Americans. Finally, there are weaker linkages between beliefs and practices among US evangelicals, suggesting that some American evangelicals verbalize orthodoxy because it is conventional to do so, while other aspects of commitment are not as strong.

There are some regional differences, but fewer than expected. I assumed, for instance, that New Brunswick and Mississippi evangelicals would demonstrate greater racial intolerance (towards Acadian

French and African Americans) than evangelicals from other regions, but this hypothesis found limited support. New Brunswick evangelicals are quite tolerant towards the French (at least on survey responses). Mississippians, however, are considerably less tolerant towards blacks than Minnesotans are. In this case, there appears to be an American regional difference but not a Canadian one.

In chapters 6 and 7, I noted that evangelicals in the US are more likely to vary slightly from region to region in much the same way that the regions themselves differ, whereas Canadian evangelicals show no significant variation. Why do American evangelicals show some tendency to parallel the orthodox religiosity of the region in which they find themselves, whereas Canadian evangelicals do not? Two possible explanations come to mind. First, the average American is more orthodox and religious than the average Canadian; hence differences between American evangelicals and nonevangelicals are less extreme in the southern country. Evangelicals in Canada seem to perceive themselves as more distinct from nonevangelicals than evangelicals in the US. This difference may open American evangelicals to external regional influences, which they perceive as less antagonistic, resulting in more regional variation among them. A better explanation may be that evangelicals in the US vary from region to region because of their relative size. In the US, where evangelicals number over sixty million, significant evangelical populations in each region allow for a substantial local institutional base that can serve a local constituency. In Canada, where roughly three million evangelicals are sparsely spread across a vast land mass, evangelical institutions have a greater need to serve a wider geographic area, bringing less variation. Put another way, evangelicals in the US are more likely to create regional organizations (or regional offices of national organizations) that can take on local colour, because there are enough evangelicals in the region to warrant regional institutions. It must be remembered, however, that regional differences among US evangelicals are slight, and that evangelicals in all regions more closely resemble other evangelicals than they resemble nonevangelicals in their respective regions.

In this chapter, I have suggested that evangelicalism can claim sufficient cultural production and distinctiveness to be defined as an "organizational field," to borrow a term from organizational theorists. Also, evangelicalism is globalized, and national and regional boundaries lose their significance. It is a subculture that is international in scope, and influences internal to evangelicalism have shaped the religiosity of core members more than external cultural influences, minimizing regional differences. Intranational and international differences in national perceptions, political attitudes, and irenicism distinguish between evangelicals in the two countries, and these differences substantiate the remaining (though possibly weakening) significance of the forty-ninth parallel.

APPENDICES

APPENDIX ONE

Core Evangelical Sample

The Core Evangelical (CE) sample involved in-depth face-to-face interviews and self-administered surveys of active evangelicals, including pastors and church adherents. The sample was not intended to be representative of all evangelicals in Canada and the US but to delve deeply into the evangelical subculture in both countries. The purpose was to probe the beliefs, practices, and attitudes of those most active in the evangelical subculture, in order to understand its inner workings and to detect more subtle regional variation that could not be captured by the "broad, but not deep" data from national surveys. Locations, denominations, churches, and individuals were determined by the following criteria.

As noted in chapter 1, the closely matched pair of locations – Winnipeg, Manitoba, and Minneapolis, Minnesota – was chosen in order to study the significance of national context in each country. The second pair of locations – Saint John, New Brunswick, and Jackson, Mississippi – was chosen because they are the largest cities in the most evangelical province/state in their respective countries.

The first two cities were carefully matched according to several criteria: historical, political, and economic similarities; racial composition and a history of racial tension; percentage of conservative Protestants; size of other denominations in the area; rural/urban distribution; and the existence of a suburban area that contains a wide variety of conservative Protestant denominations where interviews could take place. Mississippi and New Brunswick were chosen because they are quintessential evangelical locations, as described in chapter 1.

After selecting the states and provinces, I chose the largest urban centre in each. (In New Brunswick, I used the two largest urban centres since one did not provide the necessary range of churches and denominations.) Studying suburban churches in each city minimized the inner-city differences between the two countries and provided a variety of conservative Protestant churches in close proximity, a convenience that a rural location could not offer.

Table 1.1 in chapter 1 presents the denominations I selected. In each location, I chose the largest church within the selected denominations. The denominations included the largest denomination in the area, denominations (if possible) that existed in all four locations, and denominations that represented the three largest streams within evangelicalism – Baptist, Holiness, and Pentecostal. This strategy provided some control over variation that could be attributed to denominational differences.

The same research protocol was followed in the four locations. Upon arrival, I contacted the local denominational headquarters of each of the four denominations and, after explaining my study, acquired from the regional director the number and size of churches in the city. I also inquired about variations among churches (based on style of worship, pastor and parishioner characteristics, where they sat in the liberal-conservative spectrum of churches within that denomination in that area, etc.) and got a sense of the demographics of the city. Since all churches have some idiosyncrasies, it is impossible to find churches that matched perfectly across the regions. Conversations with denominational leaders, however, made me aware of the unique aspects of the church. I then contacted the senior pastor of the largest church as well as several other pastors in each denomination by phone, and after explaining my study I informally discussed with them their churches, as well as other churches in their denomination and the local area. I then set up interviews where appropriate. I often interviewed more than two pastors within a denomination if another church was recommended to me as an interesting case or if there was significant variation between churches. After the pastoral interview, I asked the pastor to recommend five active parishioners – at least two male and two female – from his congregation for interviews, one from each of four age categories (twenties, thirties, forty to fifty-five, and fifty-five plus) and one parishioner in leadership at the church. I then asked the pastor's permission to hand out survey forms in the adult Sunday school class or classes. If there were several large classes or no classes, I asked the pastor to recommend the best way to hand out at least thirty surveys to active adult parishioners covering a full range of ages. Because it was summertime, evening services substituted for Sunday school classes on two occasions.

The cooperation rate among both pastors and parishioners was very high; only a few refused interviews during the course of the project. All open-ended responses in the interviews were recorded on tape and transcribed. All those I interviewed or surveyed consented in writing to be involved in the study. Adult Sunday school class members were instructed to take the forms home, fill them out, and return them to the church office during the next week. The return rate on the surveys was about sixty-seven percent. In this way I obtained comparable samples of the most active evangelicals in four locales. This design also allowed me to control for variation that could be attributed to denomination, urban/rural differences, and race. Only evangelicals from white suburban churches of matching denominations were surveyed.

In sum, pastors from thirty-eight churches and five parishioners from each of sixteen churches were interviewed in four separate regions of North America for a total of 118 interviews. Interviews varied from fifty minutes to one hundred and thirty minutes, with an average length of eighty-three minutes. In addition, 268 survey forms were completed in the Sunday schools and returned in usable form, giving me a total sample of 386.

INTERVIEW AND SURVEY FORMS

Below, I combine all three of the forms used in this study: a pastor interview form, a parishioner interview form and a self-administered survey form for parishioners. Most of the questions below are on all three forms. There is a (p) before the items asked only of pastors, an (i) before items asked on parishioner interviews, and a (s) in front of items listed on self-administered forms. Items that have no letters before them appeared on all three forms.

1. ID number:
2. type of interview
   1 pastor interview
   2 parishioner interview
   3 parishioner – Sunday school survey
   4 interview with scholar or denominational leader.

CHURCH

3. How long have you been attending your church?
(pi) 4. Starting from when you were growing up, have you ever attended a church for six months or more that is not part of your present denomination?
   1 Yes Which ones (list)? About how long did you attend that church? What about after that?
   2 No
   8 DK [Don't know]
(pi) 5. (If yes) Why did you change denominations?
(is) 6. So what denomination do you consider yourself a part of now?
(p) 7. Which is the most influential congregation in your denomination in this area?
(is) 8. Suppose you were to move and needed to find a new church. Which of the following four items best describes how you would select a church to attend?

1 I would ONLY look for a church that is part of my present denomination.
2 I would start by looking for a church within my denomination, but I would consider churches of other denominations.
3 I would start looking at churches that belonged to CERTAIN denominations ONLY and attend the one that best fit my beliefs and needs. (**If 3 is chosen, ask which denominations**)
4 I would consider a wide variety of Christian churches with little concern for denomination.
5 Other (describe)
8 DK, refused

(is) 9. As you know, it is common for people to attend a church without becoming a member of that church. Do you happen to be an actual member of your church, or do you participate without being an official member?

1 Yes, member
2 No, participant
8 DK

(is) 10. Do you hold a position or are you part of any committees in your church or denomination? (**Circle all that apply**)

1 Deacon/ess, elder, or trustee for congregation
2 SS teacher
3 Small group leader
4 Usher
5 Member of missions, music, Christian Education, etc., board, or committee
6 Denominational position
7 Other
8 None

11. Here are four statements indicating different views about churches. Please tell me if you strongly agree, agree, have no opinion (neither agree or disagree), disagree or strongly disagree with them. Here is a card listing the possible answers. (**Card A**)

	SA	A	NO	D	SD	DK
a. One can be a good Christian without attending church.	1	2	3	4	5	9
b. A person should arrive at his or her beliefs independent of a church.	1	2	3	4	5	9
c. Christians should encourage other people to come to their church even if those people already attend other Christian churches nearby.	1	2	3	4	5	9
d. Christian churches from different denominations should cooperate in evangelistic outreach even if they disagree on some beliefs.	1	2	3	4	5	9

VIEWS

Now let me ask you a few questions about your religious views.

12. Suppose for a moment that you were discussing religion with an acquaintance who knew nothing about your faith. If this acquaintance were to ask you to identify yourself religiously, how would you place yourself, or how would you identify your religious views? **(If tradition given, skip to 15)**

13. **(If tradition is NOT given)** Sometimes Christians use more general terms to identify themselves religiously. Which of the following terms, if any, would you use to describe your religious views? evangelical, fundamentalist, pentecostal, charismatic, mainline, or none of these?

1   Evangelical
2   Fundamentalist
3   Pentecostal
4   Charismatic
5   Mainline
6   None of these, other tradition
8   Not familiar with terms

(p) 14. How would you define a(n) [ANSWER to 13]? In other words, are there particular beliefs or behaviours that you think are absolutely essential in order for someone to be a(n) [ANSWER to 13]?

(pi) 15. Would you be most likely to identify yourself as a(n) [ANSWER to 13], a Protestant, or a Christian?

_____ [ANSWER to 13)

11 Protestant
12 Christian
13 DK

(pi) 16. How you would define a Christian? What would you say distinguishes a Christian from a non-Christian?

(Probe if necessary: Are there particular beliefs or behaviours that you think are absolutely essential for someone to be a Christian?)

(pi) 17a). Could a Catholic be a Christian in your view? **(Do not read responses. Check accuracy of response 2, after R answers, i.e.: So would you say that a Catholic could be saved but is not living in obedience to Christ?)**

1   Yes
2   Yes, could be saved but are not living in obedience to Christ
3   Yes, if (**respondent qualifies**)
4   No, unless (**respondent qualifies**)
5   No
8   Don't know

17b) A racist or prejudiced person?

1 Yes

2 Yes, could be saved but are not living in obedience to Christ

3 Yes, if (**respondent qualifies**)

4 No, unless (**respondent qualifies**)

5 No

8 Don't know

17c) A homosexual?

1 Yes

2 Yes, could be saved but are not living in obedience to Christ

3 Yes, if (**respondent qualifies**)

4 No, unless (**respondent qualifies**)

5 No

8 Don't know

18. Here is a list of items that some think should be priorities for Christians. Which one do you think should be the top priority for Christians? Which one should Christians make the second highest priority? (**Write "1" for first choice and "2" for second choice.**)

a. ____ Help win the world for Christ

b. ____ Concentrate on the spiritual growth of self and family

c. ____ Work to improve the moral fiber and values of the community and country

d. ____ Strive to eliminate poverty and injustice in the world

e. ____ Strengthening the local church by investing time and money in the people and programs there

f. ____ Other

8 DK, refuse

19. I will now read you a list of groups in North America. Please tell me how close you feel or how much in common you have with the following groups. Here is a card that lists the possible responses. (**Card B**) Do you feel very close, close, neither close nor far, far, or very far from them? You may not be familiar with all the groups. If you are not familiar with the group, just answer "I don't know."

	V. close	Close	Neither	Far	V. far	DK
a. Jews	1	2	3	4	5	8
b. Evangelicals in the US	1	2	3	4	5	8
c. Hollywood movie producers	1	2	3	4	5	8
d. (US) The Clinton Administration (CN) The Chrétien government	1	2	3	4	5	8
e. Right to Life	1	2	3	4	5	8
f. (US) National Council of Churches (CN) Canadian Council of Churches	1	2	3	4	5	8
g. Catholics	1	2	3	4	5	8

	V. close	Close	Neither	Far	V. far	DK
h. ACLU (American Civil Liberties Union)	1	2	3	4	5	8
i. Fundamentalists	1	2	3	4	5	8
j. New Age Movement	1	2	3	4	5	8
k. (US) Episcopalians/ (CN) Anglicans	1	2	3	4	5	8
l. (US) National Association of Evangelicals/ (CN) Evangelical Fellowship of Canada	1	2	3	4	5	8
m. feminists	1	2	3	4	5	8
n. environmentalists	1	2	3	4	5	8
o. evangelicals in Canada	1	2	3	4	5	8
p. secular humanists	1	2	3	4	5	8
q. Pentecostals	1	2	3	4	5	8
r. Southern Baptists in the US	1	2	3	4	5	8
s. homosexuals	1	2	3	4	5	8

20. Christians have different ideas about what is most important to the Christian faith. I will read you three statements. Please tell me which one of the three best represents your view about what is most important for Christians.

　　1　The Bible clearly tells us what we should do and should not do, and what is most important is that we obey what the Bible says. Christians must obey all of God's commandments and resist all temptations and sin.

　　2　What is most important for Christians is to care for those around them. We must show God's love to people who are hurting and give of ourselves to help people when we can.

　　3　What is most important for Christians is to be close to God, to spend time praying, worshipping, and experiencing God's great love for them.

　　(**Volunteered combinations**)

　　4　one and two

　　5　one and three

　　6　two and three

　　7　all three

　　8　DK

Now I have some questions about your religious experience.

21. What would you consider the most significant religious experience of your life?

22. Have there been times in your life when you have felt the presence of God or felt very close to God?

　　1　Yes (Can you describe a situation where you felt God's presence in a special way?)

　　2　No (**skip to 25**)

23. How often would you say you feel the presence of God, or feel very close to God? Would you say

   1 Once or twice in my life

   2 Several times in my life

   3 A few times in a year

   4 Once a month or so

   5 Every week or nearly every week

   6 Daily or nearly every day

   8 DK

24. Under what conditions are you most likely to experience God's presence or feel very close to God?

   1 In a church service or in a large group of believers

   2 In a small group or Bible study

   3 At times of private prayer or Bible reading

   4 Throughout my day

   5 All of these / at any time

   6 Other

   8 DK

(pi) 25a. Can you point to occasions where you have had specific answers to your prayers?

   1 Yes

   2 No (skip to 26)

   8 DK (skip to 26)

(pi) 25b. (If yes) Can you recall an example?

   1 Yes (Please describe it)

   2 No

26. Do you consider yourself a "born-again" Christian?

   1 Yes

   2 Yes, born again at infant baptism

   3 No, conversion at infant baptism

   4 No (skip to 28)

   8 DK (skip to 28)

27. (If yes) By "born-again" do you mean a specific, one-time conversion or a gradual change over time?

   1 One-time conversion

   2 Gradual change

   8 DK

BELIEFS

28. As you know, committed Christians agree on some beliefs but disagree on others. We will use the same set of responses as on **Card** A, that's the first card I gave you. Please tell me if *you personally* strongly agree, agree, have no opinion, disagree, or strongly disagree with the following statements.

	SA	A	NO	D	SD	DK
a. Jesus Christ is the divine Son of God.	1	2	3	4	5	8
b. The only way to gain salvation and eternal life is through belief in Jesus Christ.	1	2	3	4	5	8
c. God would NOT allow people to go to a place of eternal suffering like hell.	1	2	3	4	5	8
d. Jesus was crucified, died, and was buried but on the third day he arose from the dead.	1	2	3	4	5	8
e. Many problems in our country have occurred because Americans/Canadians have rejected the religious principles this country was founded on.	1	2	3	4	5	8
f. Jesus was born of a virgin.	1	2	3	4	5	8
g. God exists as Father, Son, and Holy Ghost.	1	2	3	4	5	8
h. Taking a life is justified in some cases, like during wartime.	1	2	3	4	5	8
i. There will be a literal rapture followed by a 1,000-year reign of Christ.	1	2	3	4	5	8
j. Receiving the "baptism of the Spirit" after conversion is an important part of the Christian life.	1	2	3	4	5	8
k. America/Canada is still a Christian nation.	1	2	3	4	5	8
l. Speaking in tongues, prophecy, and healing are for the church today.	1	2	3	4	5	8
m. It is good for Christian teenagers to be exposed to a variety of religious beliefs.	1	2	3	4	5	8
n. God is a personal God.	1	2	3	4	5	8
o. A person should be allowed to make a speech in my community against religion and the church.	1	2	3	4	5	8
p. People who please God are more likely to receive material blessings than those who don't.	1	2	3	4	5	8
q. Women should be eligible for ordination.	1	2	3	4	5	8
r. The King James Version of the Bible is more trustworthy than newer versions.	1	2	3	4	5	8
s. If enough people are won to Christ, other problems in our society will take care of themselves.	1	2	3	4	5	8

29. Which of the following items best describes your view about the Bible?
    1 It is God's Word and should be taken literally, word for word.
    2 It is God's Word and has no errors in it, but not everything should be taken literally.
    3 It is God's Word, though it may contain some minor scientific or historical errors.
    4 The Bible represents the best human effort to record God's truth, but is not inspired by God.
    8 I am not sure how I feel on this issue.
30. Which of the following items best describes your view of Creation?
    1 The world was created by God in six twenty-four-hour days.

2 The world was created by God in six days, but each day was actually an age, much longer than twenty-four hours.

3 The Bible's account of the origin of the world is intended to be symbolic and not literal.

8 I am not sure how I feel on this issue.

31. Would you say that your faith provides you with (1) some, (2) quite a bit, or (3) a great deal of guidance in your daily life?

1 Some

2 Quite a bit

3 A great deal

8 DK, refused

(pi) 32a. Have your religious beliefs changed significantly over your lifetime or have they remained fairly stable?

1 Changed

2 Stable **(skip to 33)**

(pi) 32b. **(If changed)** In what ways have they changed?

WORK AND POLITICS

Now I would like to ask a few general questions about your work and political views. Let's start with your work.

(is) 33. Are you currently employed full time, employed part time, presently unemployed, retired, keeping house, going to school, or what?

1 Full time

2 Part time

3 Unemployed

4 Retired

5 Keeping house **(skip to 38)**

6 Going to school **(skip to 38)**

7 Other

8 Refused

(is) 34. **(If employed, unemployed, or retired)** What is (was) your occupation?

(is) 35. Do you view your work as a calling from God?

1 Yes

2 No

8 DK

(i) 36. Would you say your faith has (1) a great deal of, (2) quite a bit of, (3) some, or (4) hardly any influence on you at work?

1 A great deal

2 Quite a bit

3 Some

4   Hardly any (**skip to 38**)

8   DK

(i) 37. (**If 1, 2, 3 above**) Can you tell me how your faith affects you at work? How else? (**Press to get beyond character or ethical responses to issues like evangelism, policy/structural differences, job choice, refusing some contracts, i.e.:** In what ways does your faith affect your relationship with other employees? Are there some tasks at work that you will do that others will not, or are there tasks at work that you will not do that others will because of your faith? Have you ever refused a contract, confronted a superior or client on an issue, changed jobs, etc., because of your faith?)

38 People sometimes refer to their political views (CN: not their party) as conservative or liberal. Would you consider yourself strongly liberal, liberal, moderate (neither liberal nor conservative), conservative, or strongly conservative?

1   Strongly liberal

2   Liberal

3   Moderate, neither liberal or conservative

4   Conservative

5   Strongly conservative

8   Don't know

39a. Now regarding your political party preference (CN: not their political views), do you generally consider yourself a Republican, a Democrat, an independent, or something else? (CN: a Progressive Conservative, Liberal, NDP, Reform, or something else)?

1   Republican (**ask b**)

2   Democrat (**ask b**)

3   Independent (**ask c**)

5   Other

1   PC (**ask b**)

2   Liberal (**ask b**)

3   NDP (**ask b**)

4   Reform (**ask b**)

5   Other

(pi) b) Would you consider yourself a strong ***** or a not very strong *****?

1   Strong

2   Not very strong

(pi) c) Do you think of yourself as closer to the Republican or Democratic party?

1   Lean republican

2   Lean democrat

40. Using **Card** A again, please tell me if you strongly agree, agree, have no opinion, disagree, or strongly disagree with the following items.

	SA	A	NO	D	SD	DK
a. The national government should do more to fight hunger and poverty even if it means higher taxes.	1	2	3	4	5	8
b. Strict laws to protect the environment are necessary even if they cost jobs.	1	2	3	4	5	8
c. Minorities need government assistance to obtain their rightful place in America/Canada.	1	2	3	4	5	8

SETTING

Now I would like to move to some questions about the people around you, your friends, neighbours, and others that you come in contact with. To start, I would like you to take a minute to bring to mind the names of your five closest friends in this area. **(Pause)** Have you got five names in mind? For the next few questions, I would like you to think of those five friends each time you answer.

41. How many of them, if any, are part of your congregation?

    0   1   2   3   4   5

42. How many of them, if any, would you consider non-Christians?

    0   1   2   3   4   5

43. With how many of your five friends, if any, would you feel comfortable starting discussions about your religious views?

    0   1   2   3   4   5

(pi) 44. Possibly you have heard some or all of your five friends raise concerns about problems in this local area? What problems are they concerned about, if any?

    1   Raise concerns, list below
    2   No concerns raised/can't recall

(pi) 45. How about national concerns?

    1   Raise concerns, list below
    2   No concerns raised/can't recall

I am finished with the questions regarding your five closest friends. I now have a few questions about problems that concern YOU.

46. What would you say is the greatest problem facing America/Canada today?

(pi) 47. There may be some problems in this community that particularly concern you.

    a) If you have such concerns, can you tell me which problems concern you the most?
    b) Which of these would you consider the greatest problem in your community? **(Put a "1" beside the problem above)**
    1   Yes, has concerns **(list below)**

2 No concerns

8 DK, refused

(pi) 48. What do you feel can be done about this problem, if anything?

(pi) 49. As a dedicated Christian, you may have concerns about the actions or attitudes of Christians from your church or other churches around here. Without mentioning names, can you tell me about problems you see with certain Christians in this area, if there are any?

1 Yes, has concerns (**list below**)

2 No concerns

8 DK, refused

50. When it comes to instilling values in our youth, I suspect that parents and other adults around here would agree on some of the values and beliefs that we need to teach our children and would disagree on others. I will read you a list of values and beliefs that some adults try to instill in young people. (**Card** c) As I read each one please tell me 1) whether or not you think it is important to teach our children these values or beliefs, and 2) please tell me if you think *most of* the parents and adults in your community would think that it is an important value. That is, would other adults that you come in contact with in this area think these values and beliefs are important to teach our children? The first item is the value of helping those who are less fortunate. Do you think this is an important value to instill in our children? Do you think parents around here feel this is an important value to teach our children?

		Important?				*Other adults important?*		
		Yes	No	DK		Yes	No	DK
The value of helping those who are less fortunate	a)	1	2	8	b)	1	2	8
The belief that God exists	c)	1	2	8	d)	1	2	8
The belief that those who work hard will get ahead	e)	1	2	8	f)	1	2	8
The belief that non-Christians will go to hell	g)	1	2	8	h)	1	2	8
The value of learning about other cultures	i)	1	2	8	j)	1	2	8
The belief that sex outside of marriage is wrong	k)	1	2	8	l)	1	2	8

51. As you know, there is a lot of talk about values these days. Thinking of the values that exist in America/Canada today, would you say:

1 In general, values in society today make it possible to follow Christ.

2 There are lots of different values in our society, and only some of them make it possible to follow Christ.

3 The dominant values in our society make it difficult to follow Christ, and Christians need to work to change these dominant values.

4 We should promote Christianity in our society without being concerned about changing the dominant values.

8 DK

(pi) 52a. How important do you feel it is for Christians to try to change the world around them for good? Would you say very important, somewhat important, or not very important?

1 Very important (ask b)

2 Somewhat important (ask b)

3 not very important (ask c)

(pi) b) How can Christians best bring change around here?

(pi) c) Why do you feel it is not very important for Christians to try and change the world around them?

53a. Have you ever been put down or ridiculed because of your Christian faith?

1 Yes

2 No (skip to 54)

8 DK, refused

(pi) b. Can you think of an example?

1 Yes (please describe it)

2 No

54. In general, would you say values in this country are becoming better, remaining about the same, or becoming worse?

1 Becoming better

2 About the same

3 Becoming worse

8 DK, refused

55a. Have you ever felt pressure from people around you to do things you feel are wrong?

1 Yes

2 No

8 DK, refused

(pi) 55b. Can you recall such a situation?

1 Yes, please describe it

2 No

MORALS

56. As you know, Christians do not all agree on moral issues, like smoking or drinking, appropriate sexual behaviour, or what type of movies to watch. I would like to ask you about morals and where you draw the line on some of these issues. (Card C2) Tell me if you think it is always wrong, usually wrong, sometimes or never wrong for people *in general* to do the following things. If you are not sure how you feel about the issue, you may answer "don't know." The first item is sex before marriage; do you think sex before marriage is always, usually, sometimes, or never wrong?

	Always	Usually	Some	Never	DK
a. Sex before marriage	1	2	3	4	8
b. Participating in a protest that could lead to arrest	1	2	3	4	8
c. Viewing R-rated movies at a theatre	1	2	3	4	8
d. Drinking alcohol	1	2	3	4	8
e. Smoking	1	2	3	4	8
f. Dancing	1	2	3	4	8
g. Gambling	1	2	3	4	8
h. Divorce	1	2	3	4	8
i. Homosexual activity	1	2	3	4	8
j. Littering	1	2	3	4	8
k. Viewing PG-rated movies at a theater	1	2	3	4	8
l. Not claiming all income on income tax returns	1	2	3	4	8
m. Buying and looking at pornography	1	2	3	4	8
n. Working in a bar	1	2	3	4	8
o. Hitting a spouse	1	2	3	4	8
p. Overeating	1	2	3	4	8
q. Buying a very expensive car	1	2	3	4	8

57. Please tell me if you would approve, have reservations about, or disapprove if someone in your immediate family were to marry the following types of people. The first is a Catholic. Would you 1) approve of, 2) have reservations about, or 3) disapprove of someone in your immediate family marrying a Catholic?

	Ap	Res	Dis	DK
a. A Catholic	1	2	3	8
b. A Black American/Canadian	1	2	3	8
c. A non-practising Christian	1	2	3	8
d. A practising member of a non-Christian religion	1	2	3	8
e. A native Indian	1	2	3	8
f. (US) A Hispanic American/(CN) A French Canadian	1	2	3	8
g. A Presbyterian	1	2	3	8

58. As you know, in most places in the US/Canada, women can get a legal abortion, at least in the earlier stages of pregnancy. Would you say you are strongly for, moderately for, neither for nor against, moderately against, or strongly against the legal availability of abortion?

1   Strongly for
2   Moderately for
3   Neither for nor against
4   Moderately against
5   Strongly against
8   Refused

59. Consider now more specific cases. Do you think it should be possible for a pregnant woman to obtain a legal abortion if:

	Yes	No	DK
a. there is a strong chance of a serious defect in the baby	1	2	8
b. she is married and does not want to have any more children	1	2	8
c. her own health is seriously endangered by the pregnancy	1	2	8
d. the family has a very low income and cannot afford more children	1	2	8
e. she became pregnant as a result of rape	1	2	8
f. she is not married and does not want to marry the man	1	2	8

(pi) 60a. Now that I know some of your moral views, I am interested to know what guides you in deciding what is right or wrong. In general, what helps you determine right from wrong, or what guides you in your moral decisions? (**Don't read list, check item after R answers**)

   1 Bible .
   2 R sense of values or principles
   3 Christian friends
   4 Pastor
   5 Radio or TV speaker
   6 Magazines or books
   7 Other
   8 DK

(pi) b) Let's specifically take your views on abortion now. What guides you in that decision? (**Probe for clarity**, i.e.: The Bible doesn't specifically say that abortion is wrong. Do you know where your values come from?)

PRACTICES

61. Here is a card that lists the possible answers to some questions about religious practice (**give Card D**). Which of the options on the card indicates about how often you do the following: would you say more than once a day, daily, several times a week, about once a week, two to three times a month, about once a month, hardly ever, or never?

	>day	daily	sev/wk	1/wk	2–3/mo	1/mo	nev
a. Pray privately	1	2	3	4	5	6	7
b. Read the Bible outside church services	1	2	3	4	5	6	7
c. Say table grace	1	2	3	4	5	6	7
d. Watch religious TV	1	2	3	4	5	6	7

	>day	daily	sev/wk	1/wk	2–3/mo	1/mo	nev
e. Share your faith with others	1	2	3	4	5	6	7
f. Speak in tongues	1	2	3	4	5	6	7
g. Attend prayer meetings or small group Bible studies	1	2	3	4	5	6	7
h. Spend time memorizing Scripture	1	2	3	4	5	6	7
i. Listen to Christian music	1	2	3	4	5	6	7

62. In the last two years, have you ever:

	Yes	No	Refuse
a. done door-to-door evangelism, street witnessing, or other community outreach	1	2	8
b. seen an R-rated movie	1	2	8
c. gone on a prayer walk or attended a concert of prayer	1	2	8
d. fasted from food and/or drink	1	2	8
e. drunk beer, wine, or other alcoholic beverages	1	2	8
f. attended a retreat or seminar for spiritual growth	1	2	8
g. bought a lottery ticket	1	2	8

(is) 63a. About how often do you attend church these days? Would you say:
63b. About how often did you attend church when you were growing up?
(Reread list or age 12 if necessary)

a) now	b) then	
1	1	Once a year or less
2	2	Several times a year
3	3	About once a month
4	4	2–3 times a month
5	5	Nearly every week
6	6	Every week
7	7	Several times a week
8	8	DK, refused

(pi) 64a. Has your church attendance been fairly stable through your lifetime or was there a time when it decreased or increased significantly?
  1 Stable (**skip to 67)**
  2 Decreased
  3 Increased
  8 DK, refused (**skip to 67)**

(pi) 64b. **(If increase or decrease)** Can you tell me what caused the increase/decrease?

(p) 65. I would now like to ask you a few questions about subjects you preach about. Before I do that I need to ask you about how many times a week do you speak?

| 1 | 2 | 3 | 4 | 5 | 6 | 7 | 8 |

(p) 66. Here is a card listing the possible answers on how often you speak on each item, that is, how often you bring up each subject when you speak **(Card D2)**. Would you say you speak on these items: nearly every week, two to three times a month, about once a month, a several times a year, two to three times a year, about once a year, once every two to three years, or never?

	wkly	2–3mo	1mo	sev/yr	2–3yr	1yr	1/2–3yr	never
a. Abortion	1	2	3	4	5	6	7	8
b. Hunger and poverty	1	2	3	4	5	6	7	8
c. Patriotism	1	2	3	4	5	6	7	8
d. Homosexuality	1	2	3	4	5	6	7	8
e. The authority of the Bible	1	2	3	4	5	6	7	8
f. Drugs and violence	1	2	3	4	5	6	7	8
g. Cults and false religions	1	2	3	4	5	6	7	8
h. Candidates and elections	1	2	3	4	5	6	7	8
i. Heterosexual morality	1	2	3	4	5	6	7	8
j. The media	1	2	3	4	5	6	7	8
k. Public school education	1	2	3	4	5	6	7	8
l. Family breakdown	1	2	3	4	5	6	7	8
m. The environment	1	2	3	4	5	6	7	8

DEMOGRAPHICS

Now I would like to ask you a few quick questions about yourself before we conclude.

67. What year were you born?

(p) 68. Is your salary based on pastoring full time, part time, or did you not receive any salary for your pastoral work?

  1 Full time **(skip to 59)**
  2 Part time
  3 No salary
  8 Refused **(skip to 59)**

(p) 69. **(If part time or no salary)** What other work, if any, do you do to supplement your income?

  1 Full-time outside salaried work, give occupation:
  2 Part-time outside salaried work, give occupation:
  3 Volunteer outside work, give type:

4 No outside work

8 Refused

70. Which category on this card does your TOTAL FAMILY income for 1994 (before taxes) fall into? Just tell me the number. (**Show card** E).

   0 Less than $5,000 (CN $ LT 7,500)

   1 $5–9,999 (CN$7,500–12,499)

   2 $10–19,999 (CN$12,500–24,999)

   3 $20–29,999 (CN$25–34,999)

   4 $30–39,999 (CN$35–47,999)

   5 $40–49,999 (CN$48–62,999)

   6 $50–59,999 (CN$63–74,999)

   7 $60–75,000 (CN$75–100,000)

   8 >$75,000 (CN>$100,000)

   9 DK, refused

71. Approximately what percentage of your income do you give to churches and other religious organizations in an average year?

   _____ %

72. Are you presently single, married, or remarried, divorced, separated, or widowed?

   1 Single (**ask**: so you have never married?)

   2 Married (**ask:** You've never been divorced, right?)

   3 Remarried

   4 Divorced

   5 Separated

   6 Widowed

   8 Refused

73. How many children do you have?

   1   2   3   4   5   6   7   8+

74. What are their ages? (**Write number of children in each blank**)

   _____ Preschool

   _____ 6–12

   _____ 13–18

   _____ 19+

75. What is the highest level of formal education you have COMPLETED?

   1 Grade school

   2 High school

   3 Junior college or some degree less than a four-year degree

   4 Bachelor degree or similar four-year degree

   5 Graduate or professional degree

   8 DK, refused

76. Was some of your education in a private school, college, or seminary?

   1 Yes

2 No (**skip to 78**)

8 DK, refused

77. (**If yes**) At what level did you attend a private school? (**Ask name of school if college or seminary**)

1 Grade school

2 High school

3 Junior college or some degree less than four-year degree

4 Bachelor degree or similar four-year degree

Name of school:

5 Graduate or professional degree

Name of school:

8 DK, refused

(pi) 78. Have you lived in other regions of the US (Canada) or in Canada (US) for more than two years?

1 Yes

2 No (**skip to 81 or end**)

8 DK, refused

(pi) 79. What state(s)/province(s)?

(pi) 80. Did you feel there were differences between the Christians you came in contact with there and the Christians here?

1 Yes (In what ways?)

2 No

8 DK

81. (**If person is not white, ask**) What race are you?

0 White

1 Black

2 Hispanic

3 Oriental

4 Other

Thank you so much for your time. Your answers will be extremely helpful in this study.

82. Gender   1 Female   2 Male

(pi) 83. Time of interview: start: _____ end: _____

length: _____ minutes

84. Location: 1 church   2 home   3 work   4 other

85. Region: 1 MINN   2 MISS   3 MAN   4 NB

86. Denomination

0 Southern Baptist

1 Lutheran – Missouri Synod

2 Nazarene

3 Assemblies of God

4 Canadian Convention of Southern Baptists (CCSB)

5 Canadian Baptist Federation/ Federation Baptist (CBF)

6   Lutheran Church – Canada
7   Nazarene (Canada)
8   Mennonite Brethren
9   Pentecostal Assemblies of Canada

The 1996 God and Society Poll

The God and Society poll, officially called "God and Society in North America: A Survey of Religion, Politics and Social Involvement in Canada and the United States," contains data from 6,023 phone interviews in Canada (3,000) and the United States (3,023). Interviews were conducted between 19 September and 10 October 1996 by the Angus Reid Group using Computer Assisted Telephone Interviewing (CATI). This project was funded by a grant from the Pew Charitable Trusts. The survey samples were stratified by region disproportionately to provide larger samples in less-populous regions. Seven hundred interviews were performed in each of Ontario and Quebec, and four hundred in each of British Columbia, Alberta, Manitoba-Saskatchewan, and the Atlantic region. In the United States, four hundred interviews were performed in each of the following regions: East North Central, Middle Atlantic, Pacific, South Atlantic, and West South Central. Two hundred and fifty interviews were conducted in each of the East South Central, Mountain, New England, and West North Central Census regions. The sample was then weighted using the 1995 Census data projections in the US and 1995 Statistics Canada projection in Canada to ensure representativeness. The weighted sample size of three thousand in Canada and three thousand in the US resulted. The data were made available by Andrew Grenville, senior vice-president of Angus Reid. According to a press release made available by Dr Smidt, the primary investigators were the Angus Reid Group with Queen's University's George Rawlyk Research Unit on Religion and Society; Institute for the Study of American Evangelicals; Dr John Green, University of Akron; Dr Jim Guth, Furman University; Dr Lyman Kellstedt, Wheaton College; and Dr Corwin Smidt, Calvin College. More information about these data, including a complete list of questions used in the poll, is available on the American Religion Data Archive Web site at http://www.arda.tm/archive/QUEEN's.html.

This website offers a slightly different version of these data than I originally received from Angus Reid. Since the primary authors were not able to tell me which version was best, I used the data originally sent to me. The differences in the versions are minor, and my research shows that the major findings presented here are supported by both versions.

DEFINING EVANGELICALS IN THE 1996 GOD AND SOCIETY POLL

An empirical definition of evangelicalism is always a challenge for survey researchers, because there is little agreement on how this religious tradition is best defined. Evangelicalism has been defined in survey research doctrinally (those who give credence to certain conservative religious beliefs) and denominationally (those who affiliate with conservative, usually Protestant, denominations). In this book, I focus on evangelicalism as a *subculture*. I make an argument for a clearly defined evangelical subculture in chapter 3. Looking at evangelicalism as a subculture necessitates a denominational definition, since churches in conservative Protestant denominations are the organizational base for the evangelical subculture. A belief-based definition, which may define an evangelical as one who believes in a personal God, in the divinity and unique saving work of Jesus, and in the unique authority and inspiration of Scripture (Ammerman 1982; Kellstedt 1989; Hunter 1981, 1983), would find evangelicals in Catholic and mainline Protestant churches, but these "belief" evangelicals would not be part of the evangelical subculture, at least not to the same degree. For these reasons, a denominationally based definition is used.

While all the evangelicals in the CE sample meet criteria for any definitional strategy, the 1996 God and Society poll presents a variety of definitional dilemmas. For one thing, the denominational data are not strong. For another, evangelicals in Canada are more likely to remain in mainline denominations. In light of these problems, a denominational strategy developed by Kellstedt, Green, Guth, and Smidt seemed like the best strategy. The definitional strategy used denominational affiliation as a base and included the following groups: Adventist, Alliance, Baptist, Brethren, charismatic, Church of Christ, Church of God, evangelical, fundamentalist, Mennonite, nondenominational, Pentecostal, and Quaker (provided they agree that Jesus provides forgiveness of sins). In addition, those who gave their denominational affiliation as "Christian," "Protestant," or "Other" could make the evangelical category if they considered themselves charismatic, Pentecostal, evangelical, or fundamentalist. African Americans and African Canadians were not part of the evangelical category, since historically, black conservative Protestant-ism represents a separate tradition from white conservative Protestantism. I also use the measure of high commitment developed by these four political scientists. Christians have high commitment if they pray weekly, attend church a few times a month or more, and say that faith provides "a lot" or "a great deal" of guidance in their lives. (For a defence of these measures, see Kellstedt et al. 1996, 174–92.)

While this denominational measure has weaknesses, it fits well with exist-ing research and other measures of evangelicalism. It places 25 percent of Americans and 10 percent of Canadians into the evangelical category, figures that match previous research (Kellstedt et al. 1993; Moerman and Hunter 1998). Furthermore, nearly all those in the evangelical sample fit evangelical belief criteria: 97 percent believe that Jesus provides forgiveness of sins, 96 percent disagree that Jesus is not the divine son of God, 95 percent believe the Bible is the inspired word of God, and 87 percent consider themselves con-verted Christians, and among committed evangelicals support for these beliefs is nearly unanimous – 99.5 percent, 98.5 percent, 99.7 percent, and 98.6 percent respectively. In sum, the measure used here matches both criteria well.

Alternative Causes of Variation

The national differences emphasized in this book are not the only important source of variation. There is a complex array of interacting forces that influence any religious or social group, whether national, regional, institutional, or individual. That is, differences or similarities may stem from microlevel (individual), mezolevel (institutional), or macrolevel (regional or national) influences. Table A1 attempts to categorize possible combinations of influences and predicted results.

Table A1
Relationship of Macro-, Mezo-, and Microlevel Variables
in Explaining International Similarities and Differences

		Similar Institutions – Church and Parachurch	Different Institutions – Church and Parachurch
Similar Cultural Environments –	Networking evangelicals	Convergence	Similar
National and Regional	Isolated evangelicals	Similar	Different
Different Cultural Environments –	Networking evangelicals	Similar	Different
National and Regional	Isolated evangelicals	Different	Unrelated

Adapted from Michael Howlett, "The Judicialization of Canadian Environmental Policy, 1980–1990: A Test of the Canada-United States Convergence Thesis." *Canadian Journal of Political Science* 27, no. 1 (March 1994): 99–127.

Since national similarities and differences have a variety of sources, to assume that differences stem from national differences is not necessarily correct. In fact, the complex interaction of these factors means that any attempt at causal connections between national influences and individual beliefs and behaviours is risky. For this reason, I tested for a variety of alternative explanations whenever data allowed. Second, if evangelicals across geographical boundaries show many similarities or differences, one should not assume convergence (increasing similarities) or divergence (increasing differences). Evidence of convergence or divergence requires evidence of trends over time. Third, in reality the possible combinations of outcomes do not fit neatly into boxes as the table suggests. Instead, countries, regions, institutions, and people differ by degree, on a "similarity-differences" continuum. Furthermore, cultures or subcultures are not stagnant; they are constantly changing and adapting to their environment. Evangelicals in Canada and the US will show some differences and some similarities, and they may be becoming more distinctive in some ways while becoming more alike in others. In this book, explanations of similarities and differences will be examined at all three levels, although national differences are emphasized. The reader must decide if the evidence is convincing enough to warrant the conclusions.

Just as national differences are only one of several levels of influence, so also are historical and cultural differences only one source of national difference. Demographic variation is another possible source. Income, education, gender, age, and other demographic variables have often been shown to affect religious and attitudinal variation (e.g., Lenski 1961). According to Hunter, American evangelicals tend to be disproportionately female, rural, poor, elderly, and poorly educated (1983, 49–50; 1987, 10–13). Similarly in Canada, Rawlyk finds that Canadian evangelicals are more likely to be older, less well educated, rural, and female but with about the same levels of education as non-evangelicals (1996, 142–3). However, the demographic attributes typically associated with evangelicals may vary by region.

Table A2 compares evangelical demographics by region with the nonevangelical population in that region. This table allows for several important comparisons using the 1996 God and Society poll. First, it allows us to determine whether evangelicals differ demographically from nonevangelicals. If we compare all Americans with American evangelicals, we find that evangelicals in the southern country are more likely to be married and have low levels of education; they are slightly less likely to be employed, they are more rural, and they have lower incomes. Most of Hunter's demographic characterization still fits American evangelicals. However, Canadian evangelicals differ significantly from nonevangelical Canadians only in that they are more likely to be married. The table indicates that there are some significant regional differences between evangelicals and nonevangelicals in the US but few in Canada. These differences all tend towards the expected direction of more married, less education, and more rural. Since regional differences

Table A2
Demographic Comparisons by Region

	% Married	% High-school education or less	% Employed full time	% Rural[1]	% Age 55+	% Income less than $40,000	% Female
ALL AMERICANS							
(N = 3000)	52.8***	33.2***	54.2*	27.5***	26.7	48.0**	51.4
West	58.3	30.8	56.2	21.5	24.5	46.9*	50.9
Mountain	57.0	33.7	53.5	31.8	26.3	59.9	51.2
North Central	56.6	34.3**	58.6	33.8***	28.3	48.1	52.3
South	56.3***	38.7***	51.2	34.9***	26.3	52.5	52.2*
Northeast	50.5	33.7	50.7	29.4	29.8*	45.7	52.9
AMERICAN EVANGELICALS							
(N = 742)	63.0***	40.7***	51.5*	42.6***	29.4ns	53.6**	54.4ns
West	60.2	27.5	49.5	27.2	26.9	55.4*	53.8
Mountain	62.2	40.0	55.6	28.9	24.4	63.0	48.9
North Central	61.5	40.6**	57.8	46.3***	27.5	53.1	54.4
South	66.2***	45.9***	49.1	46.7***	28.7	53.1	56.9*
Northeast	56.0	34.1	49.4	42.9	40.2*	48.8	48.2
ALL CANADIANS							
(N = 3000)	50.3***	35.5	45.5	60.3	26.6	44.0	50.5
British Columbia	49.7	33.8	44.8	38.5	27.1	40.0	50.4
Prairies	54.9	39.4	48.1	74.9	26.0	45.5	49.8
Ontario	52.9**	31.8	47.9	59.8*	26.8	36.5	50.6
Quebec	45.3	37.4*	43.4	56.2	26.7	53.0	50.9
Maritimes	58.1	47.4	36.2	70.3	26.4	52.3	50.4
CANADIAN EVANGELICALS							
(N = 303)	60.9***	40.3	45.0	59.1	27.3	42.6	50.3
British Columbia	57.4	29.5	41.3	31.0	23.3	39.4	49.2
Prairies	57.5	33.8	42.5	69.7	29.1	50.7	48.8
Ontario	67.3**	37.9	50.0	70.6*	28.3	30.6	50.0
Quebec	46.9	68.8*	51.6	37.5	25.8	50.5	51.6
Maritimes	63.6	57.6	37.5	76.0	28.1	57.6	57.6

Source: God and Society Poll 1996.
[1] Rural includes all those who dwell in areas of less than 10,000 people.
Significance indicates a significant difference between evangelicals and nonevangelicals in a given
region. .05* .01** .001***.

match national differences, region is not expected to have a unique demographic effect.

As I note elsewhere (Reimer 1996), the demographic profile of evangelicals
depends on measurement strategy. Hunter used a set of belief items to identify evangelicals and limits evangelicals to Protestants only. Rawlyk used a
scale that included measures for each of "Bebbington's quadrilateral" items
– crucicentrism, activism, conversionism, and biblicism – where about one-

third are Catho-evangelicals. In Smith's 1998 study, where the evangelical category is made up of self-identifying evangelicals and where self-identified fundamentalists form a separate category, evangelicals are not disproportionately poor, rural, uneducated, female, or southern.

In addition, active, or core, evangelicals may have different demographic characteristics than less-active evangelicals. Since this research focuses on evangelicalism as a subculture, variation that exists between core evangelicals in different regions must be noted and may be hidden if evangelicals are analyzed without accounting for variation within evangelicalism itself. Using the same data presented in Table A2, I looked for differences between Canadian and American core evangelicals and found that American evangelicals are slightly more likely to be female. Otherwise, there are no significant differences.

Second, we can compare between regions and between countries. Evangelicals in Canada are not as likely to be employed full time and are more likely to be rural than American evangelicals. The income difference is partly explained by the higher value of the American dollar. Since US $40,000 equals roughly CDN $60,000, we would expect a higher proportion of American evangelicals to make less than $40,000. Regionally, evangelicals in the American West and Quebec show somewhat unique demographics in comparison with other evangelicals, partly because the small sample sizes of evangelicals make for high margins of error (the sample may not be typical of evangelicals in these areas). In the main, I would not expect to find many religious attitudinal differences based on these demographic differences; if demographics seem to account for the differences discussed in this book, I indicate it in a footnote.

In addition to demographics, differences could stem from real or perceived differences in their local context. Attitudes towards racial minorities, for example, may vary on the basis of their presence or perceived threat in the immediate area. Perceptions, in fact, may be more important than reality. Evangelicals may be more likely to resist outside influences if they perceive those around them to be antagonistic towards their views. The core evangelical sample, which is drawn from four unique suburban areas, is particularly well suited to an assessment of the effects of local contextual differences.

To examine perceptions of difference, I asked a series of questions that probed the values and beliefs of the respondents as well as their sense of the values and beliefs of those around them. Specifically, I asked each respondent which values or beliefs they thought their children should be taught, and whether or not they thought others in their community would agree. By examining how evangelicals view the world around them, we gain an important understanding of the effects of broader culture on the evangelical subculture. Table A3 contains the percentage of those who responded positively to each item. It gives us a view of communities where interviews took place through the eyes of the evangelical respondents.

Table A3
Values and Beliefs that Core Evangelicals Think Their Children Should Be Taught

Item	Minnesota (N = 107)	Mississippi (N = 94)	Manitoba (N = 104)	New Brunswick (N = 81)
1 Helping those who are less fortunate				
Important for you?	99.0	100	100	100
Important for other adults?	90.0	88.6	89.6	76.1
2 God exists				
Important for you?	100	100	100	100
Important for other adults?	75.6	92.6	57.3	58.5
3 Those who work hard will get ahead				
Important for you?	87.3	94.5	84.8	84.6
Important for other adults?	95.2	86.3	87.9	91.4
4 Non-Christians will go to hell				
Important for you?	98.1	94.4	81.0	91.1
Important for other adults?	23.4	61.2	10.8	12.1
5 Learning about other cultures				
Important for you?	84.6	87.9	91.1	85.9
Important for other adults?	78.1	62.1	78.9	60.7
6. Sex outside of marriage is wrong				
Important for you?	100	98.9	96.2	100
Important for other adults?	43.2	61.0	34.2	25.8
Average percent difference between respondent and other adult percentages	29.9	20.6	33.4	41.8

Source: CE sample 1995.

Regarding the "important to you" items, the majority of evangelicals answered each item positively, and there is little variation among evangelicals in the regions. This simply means that evangelicals in all four regions hold similar values. (The two items on which there are significant differences – items 4 and 6 in Manitoba – disappear when the liberal Baptist church is removed from the Manitoba sample. Denominational differences are minimal.)

However, there is variation in evangelicals' perception of those around them. It is not surprising that Mississippi evangelicals perceive their communities as more conservative than do evangelicals in other regions (as indicated by their response to items 4 and 6), since they probably are. New Brunswick evangelicals feel most different from those around them, possibly because of the alienation from their community that stems from their lower socioeconomic status. The bottom row of Table A3 shows that Mississippi evangelicals are most likely to feel that those around them share their values and beliefs, while New Brunswick evangelicals are least likely to feel that way. Canadian evangelicals generally feel less like those around them than do American evangelicals. The table suggests that evangelicals feel most unique in areas related to conservative beliefs (item 4) and morals (item 6), based on the percentage gap between their views and their perceptions of the views of others on these items.

In sum, Table A3 indicates that the values and beliefs of people in the sample communities differ in important ways, at least as they are perceived by evangelicals. This could be an important source of variation. As the uniformity of evangelical views in the table indicates, however, we do not expect evangelicals to resemble their greater culture, since evangelicals resist "worldly" influences in many ways.

The community concerns raised by respondents also indicate important differences, which are presented in Table A4. The table gives the percentages of responses of the 118 interviewees when asked what local problems concern them most.

While crime and violence constituted the single greatest concern overall, the concern was most common in Mississippi. In New Brunswick, crime and violence were not an issue, but economic problems were mentioned frequently. The New Brunswick evangelicals I interviewed were also the poorest. Manitobans mentioned economic concerns more often than the Americans as well. The racism and violence of Mississippi, the economic plight of New Brunswick, and the native presence in Minnesota and Manitoba could result in variation in evangelical attitudes. I note these sources of difference in the book.

For the CE sample, differences that stem from church selection and denominational selection are also possible. In each region I discussed congregational uniqueness with denominational leaders, scholars, and local pastors and selected an "average" congregation whenever possible. Of course, choosing a congregation that was unique in some way was unavoidable. In Mississippi, a wealthy Baptist church raised the average Socioeconomic Status (SES) of Mississippi evangelicals, while the Baptist church in Manitoba leaned liberal and the Missouri Synod Lutheran church was on the conservative end of the spectrum of the churches in the area. Another important source of difference may stem from denominational differences. As I noted in chapter 1, the denominations I chose do not perfectly match in each place, mostly because denominations are not uniformly distributed. However, what appears to be a regional difference may be better explained by a significant denominational presence rather than a regional or national cultural difference. I check for the possibility of congregational/denominational uniqueness continuously (by removing a congregation or denomination from the sample or through regression analysis), and these sources of difference are noted when they appear causal.

Table A4
Local Concerns of Core Evangelicals

% who consider this the greatest local problem:	Minnesota [1]	Mississippi	Manitoba	New Brunswick
1 Moral/Spiritual Decline	90	69	56	57
Values decline	6.4	2.6	4.2	0
Family breakdown	6.4	2.6	0	2.7
Crime and violence	16.1	41	23	0
Drugs/alcohol abuse	9.7	5.1	0	2.7
Excluding God from schools	6.4	0	6.3	5.4
Behaviour of youth	3.2	2.6	6.3	5.4
People not saved	9.7	0	0	8.1
Other moral/spiritual	32.3	15.4	16.7	32.4
2 Economic concerns	3.2	18	21	30
Poverty	0	5.1	14.6	13.5
Unemployment	0	0	2.1	13.5
Other economic	3.2	13	4.2	2.7
3 Social/Institutional concerns	6.4	13	23	13.5
Concern for racial minority group or racism	3.2	10.3	12.5	0
Other social/institutional	3.2	2.6	10.4	13.5

Source: CE sample, interviews only (N = 118), 1995.
[1] A few interviewees emphasized more than one problem.

Examination of all possible sources of variation is not the purpose here. Rather, I wish to examine the relative strength of national cultural explanations for variation within evangelicalism. Regional, local, and demographic explanations are important for this discussion because they are alternative explanations that must be considered if an argument for national differences can be made.

Notes

1 According to the best denominational data available, white conservative Protestant affiliates represent 25.7 percent of Americans, a figure
that does not include black Protestants (7.8 percent) who are mostly
evangelicals as well (Kellstedt et al. 1993). The Canadian figure of
10.1 percent (God and Society poll 1996) may underestimate the
number of evangelicals in Canada, since this figure misses some conservatives from mainline Protestant denominations (Moerman and
Hunter 1998; Motz 1990). If Catholics fit in the evangelical category,
then about 14 percent of Canadians are evangelicals (see Rawlyk
1996). Several have noted that more evangelicals attend church on any
given Sunday than do mainline Protestants in both countries (Motz
1990, 68–70; Bibby 1993, 104; Noll, Bebbington, and Rawlyk 1994, 5;
Kellstedt and Green 1993, 67).

2 It is easy to assume that there is something about evangelicalism that
encourages people with certain attributes to join its ranks, or, for those
already in the fold, to develop or maintain these attributes. Niebuhr
(1929), following Weber and Troeltsch, points to the link between
social divergences and doctrinal or denominational distinctions. Using
Weber's terms, it may be assumed that there is an "elective affinity"
between evangelicalism and certain social attributes, whereas in reality these attributes are better explained by a third correlating variable.

3 In his book *Continental Divide*, Lipset states that "knowledge of
Canada and the United States is the best way to gain insight into the

other North American country … The more similar the units being compared, the more possible it should be to isolate the factors responsible for the differences between them" (1990, xiii).

4 I recognize, of course, evangelicalism's significant influence on North American culture, both historically and at present. Since my purpose is primarily to examine the evangelical subculture, I focus on the broader culture's influence on evangelicalism, not vice versa.

CHAPTER TWO

1 Grenville (1995a) found in the 1993 Angus Reid/Rawlyk poll that most Canadians (seventy-nine percent) said "No one" when asked, "Who is the most influential evangelical leader?" This suggests that one would be hard pressed to find prominent evangelical spokespersons in Canada.

2 The best comparative books on evangelical history are: *Aspects of the Canadian Evangelical Experience*, edited by Rawlyk (1997); *Amazing Grace: Evangelicalism in Australia, Britain, Canada and the United States*, edited by Rawlyk and Noll (1994); *Evangelicalism: Comparative Studies of Popular Protestantism in North America, The British Isles, and beyond, 1700–1990*, edited by Noll, Bebbington, and Rawlyk (1994); *A History of Christianity in the United States and Canada*, by Noll (1992); and *The Canadian Protestant Experience: 1760–1990* also edited by Rawlyk (1990).

3 For other comparisons of a religious nature, see Westhues 1976; O'Toole 1982; Bellah 1975; Hiller 1978; Roof and McKinney 1987; Stark and Bainbridge 1985; Bibby 1987. For my list I am most indebted to Kollar (1998).

4 The strongest proponents of what can be called "Competitive Marketing Theory" (Smith 1998, 73) are Roger Finke, Rodney Stark, and Laurence Iannaccone. See Finke and Stark 1988; Finke and Iannaccone 1993; Finke, Guest, and Stark 1996; Finke 1989.

5 Accurate statistics on the number of conservative Protestants in Quebec are difficult to find. Evangelical scholars in Quebec seem to agree the percentage of French evangelicals in Quebec is less than one percent (see Lougheed, Peach, and Smith, 1999; Peach 1990). One scholar suggested a figure of 0.7 percent based on the percentage of French Protestants in Quebec, nearly all of whom are evangelical. In Quebec (including anglophones), Statistics Canada data indicates a population that is about 5.8 percent Protestant (Statistics Canada 1993). Based on a ten-question evangelicalism scale derived from Beggington's quadrilateral criteria, the God and Society poll gives about thirteen percent evangelical, of which only about two percent are evangelical Protestants (Smith 1998).

6 See Hunter's books, *American Evangelicalism* (1983) and *Evangelicalism: The Coming Generation* (1987). See also Quebedeaux's book, *The Worldly Evangelicals* (1978) and Mark Shibley's recent book, *Resurgent Evangelicalism in the Unites States* (1996).

7 Schmaltzbauer and Wheeler find evidence for secularization and "resacralization" (increased orthodoxy) among evangelical college campuses (1996). Jelen (1990) argues that orthodoxy varies with age, and what appears to be linear accommodation to society is better explained by life-cycle effects, where young evangelicals tend to become more orthodox as they age. Finally, Smith (1998) rejects the zero-sum notion of accommodation, arguing that religious traditions like evangelicalism are in a constant process or reformulating and changing in light of their environments.

8 I recognize that the evidence given here can also be used to support differences. For example, much of the border crossing had the effect of strengthening national differences, as when the influx of southern loyalists cemented loyalism in Canada. It could be said that growing similarity (in line with globalization arguments) creates a reaction to preserve differences. However, on the surface, these trends seem to support an argument for similarities.

9 For a thorough critique of Inglehart's theory, see Tepperman 2002.

10 By now, the globalization literature is immense. Works used in this study include Coleman 1993; King 1991; Robertson 1989; 1992; Featherstone 1990; Wallerstein 1991; Waters 1995; Castells 1996; Beyer 1994.

11 Beyer (1994) argues that globalization is the spread of specialized social systems that follow functional lines. These systems (capitalist, scientific/technological, etc.), while totalizing in their areas of specific function, leave people "underdetermined" in mainly private areas of life. It is these "residual" private areas where religion informs. If this is the case, one would predict that evangelicals privatize their faith. They may find it difficult to apply their faith in "public" function areas, such as work and politics, while finding faith salient in the "private" areas of their family and personal lives. I offer evidence of this in later chapters.

12 On cultural production among evangelicals, see Balmer 1993; Moore 1994; Myers 1989; Wheeler 1995; Jorstad 1993; Hunter 1987; Wuthnow 1988; Marsden 1980; Schultze 1990.

CHAPTER THREE

1 Answers to these questions were often condensed or ambiguous. This is not surprising considering the nature of the questions, which probed the basis of the evangelical identity and evoked powerful

religious symbols by which evangelicals understand their world and themselves. Powerful symbols are characterized by condensation (symbols refer to and unify a variety of meanings), ambiguity, and multivocality (symbols mean different things to different people), according to David Kertzer in his study of rituals and symbolism in politics (1989, 11). Responses may also have been condensed because I was viewed by most as an evangelical. No doubt some expected me to be familiar with evangelical identity and language and condensed their responses as a result. Respondents included both dimensions in their answers, implied things that were not stated explicitly, and combined categories. A common response to question 12 (see appendix 1 for question wording) was, "I'm a Bible-believing Christian," which contains both the "content" response of biblicism and the "scope" response of Christian. The common response to question 16, "They must accept Jesus Christ as their Saviour and Lord," implies for the evangelical an acknowledgment of the truth of the biblical account of Christ's life, crucifixion, and resurrection, a belief that Christ's substitutionary death is the only means of salvation, a conversion experience that usually involves verbalizing in prayer an acceptance of salvation through Christ, and a commitment to Christian living. Since it was difficult to code such responses, I coded only those responses that explicitly refer to one of the categories in the table. I coded responses along both dimensions from the interview notes transcribed from the interviews.

2 Missouri Synod Lutherans were somewhat split on the born-again question (see appendix 1, questions 26 and 27). In the interviews, some emphasized that they had been born again at infant baptism, while others stated that they did not consider themselves born again in the popular sense of a conversion experience.

3 An exception to the lack of emphasis on activism arose when I asked pastors to define the tradition they selected. Those defining "evangelical" emphasized not only biblicism, crucicentrism, and conversionism but also activism, especially evangelism. One Manitoba pastor, for example defined an evangelical church as "one where Jesus Christ is central, the word is very much central to the teachings of the church [and there is a] strong emphasis on reaching out." The emphasis on evangelism is not surprising, since, as several pastors pointed out, the words "evangelical" and "evangelize" both have the root "evangel," meaning the "gospel" or the "good news," prompting pastors to emphasize the spreading of the gospel in their definition.

4 Welch, Leege, and Cavendish (1995) use the abortion issue as a case of "symbolic politics" and suggest that the issue has come to symbolize sexual permissiveness for the evangelical.

5 Variamax, Equamax, and Oblimin rotations were performed with fairly consistent results, but since the factors may well be correlated theoretically, the factor loadings below are based on direct Oblimin rotation. Two variables were unstable – homosexuals and Episcopalians change factors in the different rotations; otherwise the factor groupings were identical. Five factors were extracted with eigenvalues of one or more (Kim and Mueller 1978, 29). The factors explained fifty-eight percent of the total variance in the model. Bartlett's Test of Sphericity was highly significant, and the KMO statistic was .80, indicating that the data are good for factor analysis.

6 Stark and Bainbridge's notion of "sectarian tension" (1985:48–62) has three aspects: difference, antagonism, and separation (Bainbridge and Stark 1980; Stark and Glock 1968). Here I use the antagonism aspect as a measure of tension, though I operationalize it differently and use my measures of antagonism to indicate that evangelical distinctiveness is salient because of this tension. Stark and Bainbridge's measures of tension overlap with evangelical commitment or orthodoxy. They do not measure strained relationships or feelings of animosity that is suggested by tension, as my measures do.

7 Smith (2000, 70–2.) found that the evangelicals he interviewed felt tension with the "world" but also felt that they were personally treated with respect and goodwill. It is plausible that the evangelicals I studied would feel that in general, the people around them were considerate and friendly, even though the majority could recall examples of ridicule. For boundary maintenance, perceptions of tension are more important than reality.

8 It should be noted that some evangelicals think the world is deteriorating not only because of the cues they receive from others and the media but also because of their eschatology. Many evangelicals hold the premillennialist view that the world will continue to deteriorate until the second coming of Jesus Christ.

9 See Cavendish, Welch, and Leege (1998) for a review of the research that shows the connection between social networks and commitment. Welch (1993) argues that social integration is the single most important factor in increasing commitment and involvement among parishioners.

10 Smith (1998, 82) found that evangelicals were not more encapsulated than other Protestant traditions (fundamentalists, mainline, and liberals). Nonetheless, two-thirds of his evangelicals said that "most" or "almost all" of their family, friends, and work colleagues were Christian. While mainline and liberal Protestants have similar levels, it could be that a more inclusive definition of "Christian" inflates their levels of encapsulation.

CHAPTER FOUR

1 See Yamane and Polzer 1994; Spickard 1991; Neitz and Spickard 1990.
2 See Yamane and Polzer 1994; Hay and Morisy 1978; Fox 1992; Glock and Stark 1965.
3 See Poloma 1989, 1995; Poloma and Pendleton 1989.
4 See Lofland and Stark 1965; Lofland 1978; Snow and Machalek 1983, 1984; Staples and Mauss 1987; Neitz 1987.
5 Percentages of those who attended church weekly or more growing up: Mississippi, 50 percent; Minnesota, 70 percent; Manitoba, 80 percent; and New Brunswick, 68 percent.
6 Phone interviews with 356 evangelicals were done in a follow-up to the 1993 national Angus Reid surveys. Evangelicals were identified according to the Christian Evangelicalism Scale (CES), which involved getting above a certain score on a series of evangelical tenets (N = 990; see Grenville 1995a). Using the telephone numbers and the demographic information of the evangelicals they identified, Angus Reid staff placed calls to all available numbers asking to speak to the person who fit the demographic profile. All respondents were then rescreened using questions from the CES, leading to the final sample of 365. The experience items measured by the Angus Reid poll include the following questions: 1) Have you ever, as an adult, had the feeling that you were somehow in the presence of God? 2) Have you ever felt you were in close contact with something holy or sacred? 3) Would you say you have ever had a "religious or mystical experience," that is, a moment of sudden religious insight and awakening? 4) Have you ever felt as though you were very close to a powerful spiritual force that seemed to lift you out of yourself? 5) Have you ever spoken in tongues? 6) Have you ever been slain in the spirit?
7 Here I used regression analysis. I created an "experience scale" using the same six variables listed in note 6 as the dependent variable (the scale range from 0, "no experiences" to 6, "experienced all six items," included regional dummy variables, demographics as controls, and measures of commitment (prayer, Bible reading, and evangelism).
8 The General Social Survey (GSS) conducts face-to-face interviews with roughly fifteen hundred randomly selected English speaking, noninstitutionalized adult respondents each year in the United States. The survey contains the following items that tap religious experience: 1) How close do you feel to God most of the time? Would you say extremely close, somewhat close, not very close, or not close at all? (NEARGOD) 2) Have you ever: felt as though you were very close to a powerful spiritual force that seemed to lift you out of yourself? Never in my life, once or twice, several times, often. (GRACE) Regressions

tested the effect of region, demographics, and commitment measures on both of these measures of religious experience. Regional differences were not significant for the NEARGOD regressions, but evangelicals in the American South were more likely to claim an ecstatic experience (GRACE). Prayer was significant and positive in the NEARGOD regression, as was church attendance in the GRACE regressions.

CHAPTER FIVE

1 This point is debated by Stone (1997), who argues that evangelical boundaries follow symbolic, not theological, lines. As I argue below, certain theological boundaries have added symbolic significance.

2 Regarding abortion specifics, Mississippi respondents are consistently more lenient than respondents in other regions (only when the mother's health is in danger are they no more lenient than those in other regions). That is, Mississippians were more likely to feel that abortions should be accessible to women in all but one of the situations mentioned above, and these differences were statistically significant even in regression analysis with demographic controls. This surprising finding is difficult to account for. Church uniqueness does not seem to be the cause, since the pastors of the churches in Mississippi are not more lenient on these items than pastors elsewhere.

3 Chronological investigations of secularism where orthodoxy is assumed to weaken over time have several weaknesses that geographic investigations of orthodoxy do not. First, analyses of change over time can easily confuse lifecycle change or a (brief) period of unorthodoxy with linear secularization (see Jelen's 1990 critique of Hunter's data). Second, analyses of change over time often involve repeated cross-sectional surveys that suffer from changing definitional strategies, sampling strategies, wording changes, and other methodological problems. Finally, analyses of change over time can conflate regional change with overall change. Of course, geographic investigations have weaknesses as well. Besides the obvious weakness of missing change over time, the region of analysis can be too large to accurately investigate change (a problem I examine later in the chapter).

4 For international differences, see Michalos 1982; Lipset 1990; Bibby 1987. For within-country differences, see Bibby 1987; Stark and Bainbridge 1985.

5 While most pastors and denominational leaders stated that perceived theological and moral differences between congregations were mostly a matter of pastoral emphasis, there were some congregational differences in orthodoxy. In fact, differences in orthodoxy seemed to vary more by congregation than by either denomination or region. Canadian

Baptists (members of the Canadian Baptist Ministries) are less orthodox than other Canadian evangelicals according to several belief measures from the Angus Reid data (see also Bibby 1993, 172; Zeman
1980; Burbridge 1987), but this is true neither of Maritime Canadian
Baptists nor of many churches in other regions.

6 The differences discussed here reach standard levels of statistical significance. However, significance tests assume randomized or representative data, which the CE data are not.

7 Several well-educated evangelicals questioned whether either North
American country ever was Christian (according to their definition of
Christian). A few pastors typified America's founders as "deists" or
"humanists" (cf. Noll 1992). Some Canadians felt that early Canadian
settlers came for economic reasons, not religious ones (cf. Berton
1987).

8 As of 5 December 1995, the Toronto Airport Vineyard church was
released from the Association of Vineyard Churches and soon after
changed its name to the Toronto Airport Christian Fellowship (Careless 1996, 1). Apparently, the Airport church's emphasis on manifestations (including such bizarre behaviours as laughing, barking, roaring,
shaking, and "being slain in the Spirit") does not follow the mandate
of the denomination (Koop 1996, 4). The Airport church estimates that
they have had 726,300 visitors, and the renewal has spread throughout Canada, Europe, and around the world. In my interviews, several
pastors, including those in Manitoba, Minnesota, and New Brunswick,
had come in contact with the "Toronto Blessing." The Airport church
also actively experiences prophecies and healings (see Poloma 1995)
but does not emphasize tongues and "the baptism of the Spirit" (Koop
1996, 4). Note that item 8 is not significantly higher in Canada, which
may be partly the result of the Airport church's emphasis.

9 It is recognized that the evangelical column totals in Quebec and the
Maritimes are based on samples that are too small for accurate repre-
sentation. However, the lack of fit between the conservativeness of
evangelicals and that of nonevangelicals in the same region is supported by the 1993 Angus Reid poll as well, which is based on a
sample of roughly six thousand Canadians, giving larger subsamples
of evangelicals in various regions (West = 175; Ontario = 164; Maritimes = 85; no Quebec data). Comparing these three regions on matching questions, evangelicals in the Canadian West are the most
conservative and Maritime evangelicals the least. One wonders
whether these data give a more accurate picture of the evangelicals
particularly in the Maritimes, where a larger percentage of the evangelical population affiliate with the United Baptist Convention (part
of the Baptist Ministries). Some Baptist affiliates in the Maritimes

maintain memberships but many rarely practise (which is more typical of a mainline Protestant church), which may help explain the lower levels of conservatism there. Parishioners who rarely attend are less likely to give responses that accurately reflect the "official" beliefs of the churches or denominations.

10 Even when I combine all the items in Tables 5.5 and 5.6 into one belief scale and look for regional differences using Scheffe's multiple means test, the only region that shows significant differences among evangelicals in Canada is Quebec, which is based on a small sample (N = 31).

11 In the US, statistically significant differences between items for evangelicals are also rare. Items 6 and 7 show a significant difference between the West and the South, and on item 7 the South differs from the Northeast, and the West differs from the North Central region. Using a 1992 survey from political scientists Kellstedt, Green, Guth, and Smidt, from which 1,035 evangelicals can be extracted based on strong denominational measures, I found that differences between southern and nonsouthern evangelicals on thirteen different belief items were minimal. Of the few items that showed significance, evangelicals in the American South were more conservative.

12 A few moral items on the survey brought interesting reactions from those I interviewed. For example, many laughed at the "littering" item, and some at the "overeating" item. I assume that people laughed because the items seemed out of place on a list of moral prohibitions, especially when "littering" followed so strong a prohibition as "homosexual activity" and "overeating" came after "hitting a spouse." Laughter was less common among younger interviewees.

13 Based on regression analysis, I found that education made one more liberal with regard to drinking alcohol, movie viewing, and participating in protests. The independent variables were age, education, income, gender, and region in each equation.

14 There is much evidence from the interviews that the majority of evangelical influences come from the South up. One Canadian Southern Baptist pastor estimated that about half their pulpits were filled by Americans and reported that their "tiny" seminary was funded by the US Southern Baptists. In Mississippi, I found that strong Southern Baptist conventions help weak ones with money and personnel. The 2,048 Southern Baptist churches in Mississippi with some 650,000 adherents give about four million dollars in general offerings per week and were assisting the weaker Alaskan convention at the time of my visit.

15 Several items were not included in the table because item wording or coding changed significantly across samples (belief in God, Jesus is the son of God, how often one reads the Bible, prays, or says grace).

There is no evidence from these excluded items of weakening orthodoxy or orthopraxy among evangelicals.

16 In addition to other methodological differences, the Project Canada
polls use mail surveys while the General Social Survey uses interviews.

CHAPTER SIX

1 Stark and Glock (1968) and, later, Stark and Bainbridge (1985) identified five dimensions of commitment: beliefs, practices, experience,
knowledge, and consequences. However, Kellstedt et al. (1993), suggest that measuring religious commitment includes at least three
aspects of faith – beliefs, salience or importance of faith, and practice –
which I use to measure commitment below. They argue that salience
(the importance of one's religious faith) is a better measure of commitment than knowledge, because it is easier to measure and it is not
specific to religious tradition. In addition, they have found that their
measure had high external and internal validity in a national representative sample of Americans and is one of the best measures of the
affect of religiosity on political attitudes and behaviour (Guth and
Green 1993). My operationalization of commitment matches that of
Kellstedt et al.

2 Prayer walks, like the annual international "March for Jesus," bring
Christians together to march through their city singing, dancing, and
carrying banners. In Canada, some 173,000 Christians in eighty-six different communities took part in the 1994 March for Jesus. Well over
1.5 million took part in the US. Organizers estimated that there were
twelve million participants in 178 nations. In 1997 about twelve million Christians in 185 different countries took part (Drudger, 1998).
The movement was started by an Englishman, Graham Kendrick, in
1987 (Segal, 1994) and the last worldwide march was scheduled for
the year 2000. In similar fashion, concerts of prayer bring a broad
range of Christians together to pray for their city, country, or the world.

3 The Promise Keepers, which was started in 1990 by former University
of Colorado football coach Bill McCartney, had over 700,000 participants in 1995. Canada launched its own chapter of Promise Keepers in
1995 (Derrenbacker 1995). One large American Pentecostal church that
I surveyed planned to send four hundred men to a Promise Keepers
weekend event.

4 It should be noted that responses to the personal evangelism question
indicated that "sharing your faith" was variously interpreted. Some
interpreted the question to mean evangelizing non-Christians only,
others took it to mean anytime they spoke of their faith, whether to
Christians or to non-Christians.

5 I am not assuming that evangelicals have read the books I refer to here. In fact, Sherman and Hendricks (1987) argue that one of the problems is that evangelicals are ignorant of the connection between work and religion. They report that few of the people they polled had ever read a book or heard a sermon, tape, or seminar speaker that applied biblical principles to work issues. Nonetheless, the comparison gives us a lens through which to evaluate the respondent's application of faith at work from their own literature.

6 The books were 1) Bernbaum and Steer, *Why Work? Careers and Employment in Biblical Perspective* (1986); 2) Redekop and Bender, *Who am I? What am I?* (1988); Sherman and Hendricks, *Your Work Matters to God* (1987); Storkey, *A Christian Social Perspective (1979)*; Stott, *Issues Facing Christians Today* (1984); White and White, *On the Job: Survival or Satisfaction?* (1988).

7 As I noted previously, the few evangelicals in Quebec in this sample (N = 31) have lower levels of orthodoxy and orthopraxy than English Canadian evangelicals. The problem may be related to the definitional strategy I used, since nearly half of the Quebec evangelicals put "don't know" for their denomination, and the rest did not name a specific denomination. Only one of the thirty-one respondents attended church regularly. This indicates that the respondents may not be part of an evangelical denomination and thus may be conservative Catholics or other religious conservatives who differ from those embedded in the evangelical subculture. I spoke to evangelical academics in Quebec who argued for a conservative and encapsulated evangelical subculture there, which does not match with this small sample. This unlikely sample of Quebec evangelicals shows a lack of both orthodoxy and orthopraxy, which inflates US/Canada differences, making Canadian evangelicals appear more liberal in this chapter and the next.

8 Commitment is measured by combining seven items into a scale that ranges from four to thirty with a Crombach's alpha of .8762. The variables include measures of church attendance, devotionalism (measured by prayer and Bible reading), salience (measured by the amount of guidance one's faith provides in day-to-day life), and orthodox beliefs (measured by three variables, including the belief that Jesus Christ is the only means of salvation, that Jesus Christ is divine, and that the Bible is inspired). These items were recorded to give each dimension of commitment equal variation in the scale.

CHAPTER SEVEN

1 The most recent examples are the lawsuits stemming from abuses in church- and government-run Indian residential schools, which threaten the financial future of the Anglican Church of Canada

(Fieguth 2000), but which were recently overshadowed by the scandalous behaviour of Catholic priests in US, and the attempted cover-ups by the Catholic church hierarchy.

2 Regarding those who gave inconsistent answers about R-rated movies, there were a few who suggested in their interviews that they were concerned not only about the content of the movie but in particular about going to a movie theatre. For example, one New Brunswick Christian stated that going to a bar or a theatre was always wrong for him. Even if he were to go to a theatre to see a wholesome movie, he explained, someone might see him at the theatre and assume he was viewing some more dubious show. Thus, there may be nothing incongruous about viewing a restricted movie and feeling that "viewing an R-rated movie in a theatre" is always wrong, if the theatre is taboo and not the movie.

3 Then tendency of survey respondents to overreport church attendance has been recently demonstrated by Hadaway, Marler, Chaves, and others in both Canada and the US (Hadaway et al. 1993; Chaves and Cavendish 1994; Hadaway and Marler 1997B; Marler and Hadaway 1999). As I predicted (Reimer 1995), overreporting is higher in the US than in Canada, where 18 percent attended in Oxford County, Ontario, while 30 percent claimed to attend in a poll (a 68 percent overreport). In Ashtabula County in Ohio, 34 percent of those surveyed said they attended church, while only 21 percent did (an 81 percent overreport). However, recent polls in Canada show attendance of around 21 percent, while American claims are normally of around 40 percent, as is the case in the God and Society poll. This makes the Hadaway and Marler survey figures look low in the US and high in Canada, suggesting that Americans might be far more likely to overreport attendance than Canadians.

4 I suggest that this tendency is related to higher civil religion in the US See the discussion below.

5 See Wimberly and Christenson 1981; Christenson and Wimberly 1978; Gehrig 1979.

6 See Westhues 1976; O'Toole 1982; Lipset 1990; Blumstock 1993.

7 Based on a more recent poll of a small number of evangelicals (Ipsos Reid 2001; evangelical N = 66), evangelicals in Canada are still for more likely to vote for the right-wing Progressive Conservatives (32 percent compared to 15 percent nationally) or Canadian Alliance (23 percent compared to 7 percent nationally) than other Canadians, but with the fluctuating popularity of the Canadian Alliance, it is too soon to argue for a politically conservative evangelicalism in Canada.

8 For the strength of the effect of the Christian Right organizations on evangelical voting, see Kellstedt et al. 1996 and Guth 1996.

9 Various studies show evidence of expanding tolerance and comfort zones, at least in the US. Time-series data show growing willingness to grant civil liberties to unpopular groups (Roof and McKinney 1987; Reimer and Park 2001) and some claim decreasing denominational loyalty and increased switching south of the border (Roof and McKinney 1987; Hoge, Johnson and Luidens 1994). Reginald Bibby, however, argues that there is relatively little denominational switching in Canada, since even inactive Canadians show surprising loyalty to the denomination they were raised in (2002).

10 Questions about regional differences were only asked of those who had lived for two years or more in the area they were describing. See questions 78–80 in appendix 1.

11 I have limited my definition to attitudes towards others to avoid the problem of conflating irenicism with liberalism (an obvious problem when dealing with conservatives) and because it is difficult to measure irenic tone (calm demeanour, use of inclusive language, etc.) through quantitative data. For this reason, many possible measures of irenicism were left out. For a defence of this operationalization and more detailed argument for a Canadian irenic evangelicalism, see Reimer 2000.

12 This difference is not reducible to denominational differences between the countries, though the Lutherans vary from other evangelicals in that they feel further from some evangelical groups, among them the National Association of Evangelicals [US]/Evangelical Fellowship of Canada, Pentecostals, and evangelicals in the US.

13 There are at least two other explanations for the differences in Table 7.10. First, a closer ranking could be related to familiarity or contact. The closer ranking for Southern Baptists is largely the result of their higher ranking in Mississippi. Surprisingly, several southern Baptist Minnesotans did not feel close to the Southern Baptist Convention as a whole because they thought it was too fundamentalist or racist in the South. Similarly, certain groups vary in visibility by region, like Anglicans in Canada, and Right to Life in the US, which may lead to more distant rankings. Secondly, the groups themselves may vary by region. New Brunswick respondents told me that they felt close to Anglicans because Anglicans were quite conservative in their area, more so than in other Canadian regions.

14 Other sources of variation also affect responses. For instance, respondents indicated that the Presbyterians were much more conservative in Mississippi than in Minnesota, which partly explains the low percentage in Minnesota on this item. One pastor said that Presbyterians and Baptists in the area share pulpits, and that Presbyterians look for Baptist pastors if a Presbyterian pastor is not available. Similar levels of approval for First Nations people in Manitoba and Minnesota may

actually indicate greater irenicism on the Canadian side because the poverty, alcoholism, and crime attributed to the native Indian community are of a much greater concern in the city of Winnipeg than in Minneapolis, where First Nations people lived outside the city.

15 Evidence from the National Election Studies in the US (Millar 1994) as well as Bibby's Canadian surveys shows that evangelicals are at least as irenic with regard to race and religious irenicism as most North Americans. They distinguish themselves only in the area of sexual/ familial irenicism. As previously mentioned, Hunter's thesis that evangelicals remain staunch in the area of family/sexual morality is supported by these data (1987, 63), for it is only in this area that they emerge as less irenic (see Reimer 2000).

16 While evidence of national cultural influences within evangelicalism does not necessarily mean that evangelical distinctiveness is threatened, certain "unguarded" influences of modernity may nonetheless be detrimental to evangelicalism.

17 One might expect that evangelicals would differ less than mainline Protestants and Catholics on the items dealing with doctrinal belief, because of the type of belief questions used. However, even if we only take those questions where over 90 percent of all committed Christians, including committed mainline Protestants and Catholics, agree (that God exists, that humans are made in God's image, that Jesus is divine, that Jesus forgives sins, and that the Bible is inspired), we find that evangelicals still show for less variation across the countries. The comparative numbers are: all evangelicals, 3.6 percent; committed evangelicals, 0.6 percent; all mainline Protestants, 14.1 percent; committed mainline Protestants, 3.3 percent; all Catholics, 12.8 percent; committed Catholics, 1.0 percent.

18 Self-identified fundamentalists were not common in the Mississippi location. According to this pastor, there were only three other fundamentalist churches in the city, two independent Baptists and one fellowship Baptist church. There were forty-one Southern Baptist churches in the city in 1994 (Annual 1994), and many other types of Baptist churches as well, which indicates that there is a small percentage of fundamentalist churches in that city.

CHAPTER EIGHT

1 Since this research is about the religiosity of individual evangelicals and not about evangelical organizations per se, I recognize that the new institutional theory is not directly applicable to some of the findings. Nonetheless, I argue that the similarities in the individual-level data I have presented reflect a matching similarity in the churches and

denominations through which the viability of the evangelical subculture is maintained and transmitted. Thus, I give reason to believe that
evangelical organizations *supply* a similar evangelical product, just as
evangelicals *demand* product similarity.

2 Since regulations and practice are "loosely coupled," the best way for
organizations to demonstrate isomorphism to the institutionalized
myths of the organizational field is by using the correct vocabulary,
and actual practice may not always match (Meyer and Rowan 1991,
50). In the same way, it is more important for evangelical legitimacy
that the evangelical organization or individual verbalize a commitment to evangelism, family values, and moral orthopraxy; whether or
not one is involved in evangelism or has a traditional family is less
important.

Bibliography

Ammerman, Nancy Tatom.1982. Comment: Operationalizing Evangelicalism: An Amendment. *Sociological Analysis* 2: 170–2.

– 1987. *Bible Believers*. New Brunswick: Rutgers University Press.

Anderson, C. Leigh, Gene Swimmer, and Wing Suen. 1997. An Empirical Analysis of Viewer Demand for US Programming and the Effect of Canadian Broadcasting Regulations. *Journal of Policy Analysis and Management* 16 (4): 525–40.

Angus Reid Group. 1993. Dataset made available by Andrew Grenville, Senior Vice-President, Angus Reid Group.

Annual of the Mississippi Baptist Convention. 1994. Jackson: Mississippi Baptist Convention Board.

Baer, Douglas, ed. 2002. *Political Sociology: Canadian Perspectives*. Don Mills, ON: Oxford University Press.

Baer, Doug, Edward Grabb, and William A. Johnston. 1990. The Values of Canadians and Americans: A Critical Analysis and Reassessment. *Social Forces* 68 (3): 693–713.

Bainbridge, William Sims, and Rodney Stark. 1980. Sectarian Tension. *Review of Religious Research* 22 (2): 105–124.

Balmer, Randall. 1993. *Mine Eyes Have Seen the Glory: A Journey into the Evangelical Subculture in America*. New York: Oxford University Press.

Bebbington, David W. 1989. *Evangelicalism in Modern Britain: A History from the 1730s to the 1980s*. London: Unwin Hyman.

– "Evangelicals in Modern Britain and America: A Comparison." In *Amazing Grace: Evangelicalism in Australia, Britain, Canada and the United States*. Edited by G.A. Rawlyk and Mark Noll, 183-212.

– 1997. Canadian Evangelicalism: A View from Britain. In *Aspects of the Canadian Evangelical Experience*, edited by G.A. Rawlyk.

Beckford, James A., and Thomas Luckmann, eds. 1989. *The Changing Face of Religion*. London: Sage.

Bellah, Robert. 1975. *The Broken Covenant: American Civil Religion in Time of Trial*. Chicago: University of Chicago Press.

Bellah, Robert N., Richard Madsen, William Sullivan, Ann Swidler, and Steven M. Tipton. 1985. *Habits of the Heart: Individualism and Commitment in American Life*. New York: Harper and Row.

Bennett, Colin J. 1991. What Is Policy Convergence and What Causes it? *British Journal of Political Science* 21: 215–34.

Berger, Peter L. 1963. *Invitation to Sociology: A Humanistic Perspective*. New York: Doubleday.

– 1967. *The Sacred Canopy: Elements of a Sociological Theory of Religion*. New York: Doubleday.

– 1992. *A Far Glory: The Quest for Faith in an Age of Credulity*. New York: Free Press.

Bernbaum, John A., and Simon M. Steer. 1986. *Why Work? Careers and Employment in Biblical Perspective*. Grand Rapids: Baker Book House.

Berton, Pierre. 1987. *Why We Act Like Canadians*. Toronto: Penguin Books.

Beyer, Peter. 1994. *Religion and Globalization*. London: Sage.

Bibby, Reginald. 1987. *Fragmented Gods: The Poverty and Potential of Religion in Canada*. Toronto: Irwin.

– 1990. *Mosaic Madness: The Poverty and Potential of Life in Canada*. Toronto: Stoddart.

– 1993. *Unknown Gods: The Ongoing Story of Religion in Canada*. Toronto: Stoddart.

– 1995. *Evangeltrends*. A summary report prepared for Vision 2000. 1995 Consultations on Evangelism.

– 2002. *Restless Gods: The Renaissance of Religion in Canada*. Toronto: Stoddart.

Blumstock, Robert. 1993. Canadian Civil Religion. In *The Sociology of Religion: A Canadian Focus*, edited by W.E. Hewitt, 173–94.

Bogardus, Emory Stephen. 1928. *Immigration and Race Attitudes*. Lexington, MA: Heath.

– 1958. Racial Distance Changes in the United States During the Past Thirty Years. *Sociology and Social Research* 43 (2):127–35.

Bradley, Martin, Norman Green, Jr., Dale Jones, Mac Lynn, and Lou McNeil. 1992. *Churches and Church Membership in the United States, 1990*. Atlanta: Glenmary Research Center.

Bromke, Adam, and Kim Richard Nossal. 1987. *Foreign Affairs* 66 (1): 150–69.

Burbidge, John. 1987. Religion in Canada. *Journal of Canadian Studies* 22: 163–6.

Careless, Sue. 1996. Toronto Blessing Turns Two. *Christian Week* 9 (21): 1, 4.

Carroll, Jackson W., and Wade Clack Roof, eds. 1993. *Beyond Establishment: Protestant Identity in a Post-Protestant Age*. Louisville, KY: Westminster/John Knox Press.

Castells, Manuel. 1996. *The Rise of the Network Society*. Oxford: Blackwell Publishers.

Cavendish, James C., Michael R. Welch, David C. Leege. 1998. Social Network Theory and Predictors of Religiosity for Black and White Catholics. *Journal for the Scientific Study of Religion* 37 (3): 397–410.

Chapman, Mark. 1998. "Evangelical Organizations in One Canadian Community: An Early Report." Unpublished paper. University of Toronto.

Chaves, Mark. 1997. *Ordaining Women: Culture and Conflict in Religious Organizations*. Cambridge and London: Harvard University Press.

Chaves, Mark, and James Cavendish. 1994. More Evidence on US Catholic Church Attendance. *Journal for the Scientific Study of Religion* 33: 376–81.

Christenson, James, and Ronald Wimberley. 1978. Who Is Civil Religious? *Sociological Analysis* 39: 77–83.

Christopherson, Neal. 1997. *Christian Fiction*. Unpublished MA thesis. University of Notre Dame.

Cimino, Richard, and Don Lattin. 1998. *Shopping for Faith: American Religion in the New Millennium*. San Francisco: Jossey-Bass.

Coleman, Simon. 1993. Conservative Protestantism and the World Order: The Faith Movement in the United States and Sweden. *Sociology of Religion* 54 (4): 353–73.

Collins, R., ed. 1983. *Sociological Theory*. San Francisco: Jossey-Bass.

Conover, Pamela Johnston. 1988. The Role of Social Groups in Political Thinking. *British Journal of Political Science* 18 (1): 51–76.

Conover, Pamela Johnston, and Stanley Feldman. 1981. The Origins and Meaning of Liberal/Conservative Self-Identification. *American Journal of Political Science* 25 (4): 617–45.

Dayton, Donald W., and Robert K. Johnston, eds. 1991. *The Variety of American Evangelism*. Knoxville: University of Tennessee Press.

Derrenbacker, Robert A., Jr. 1995. Promise Keepers Launches Canadian Chapter. *Christian Week* 9 (12): 1, 4.

DiMaggio, Paul J. 1983. State Expansion and Organizational Fields. In *Organizational Theory and Public Policy*. edited by R.H. Hall and R.E. Quinn, 147–61.

DiMaggio, Paul J., and Walter W. Powell. 1991. Introduction. In *The New Institutionalism in Organizational Analysis*, edited by Walter W. Powell and Paul J. DiMaggio, 1–40.

Driedger, Sharon Doyle. 1998. "Global Parade of Faith." *Maclean's* June 1, 66+8.

Durkheim, Emile. 1915. *The Elementary Forms of Religious Life*. New York: Free Press.

Elazar, Daniel J. 1966. *American Federalism: A View from the States*. New York: Thomas Y. Crowell.

Elliot, David. 1993. Knowing No Borders: Canadian Contributions to American Fundamentalism. In *Amazing Grace: Evangelicalism in Australia, Britain, Canada and the United States*, edited by George Rawlyk and Mark Noll, 349–74.

Emerson, Michael O., and Christian Smith. 2000. *Divided by Faith: Evangelical Religion and the Problem of Race in America*. New York: Oxford University Press.

Faith Today. "EFC challenges Media on 'Fundamentalism'." January/February 1994, 56.

Featherstone, Mike. 1990. *Global Culture: An Introduction*. London: Sage.

Ferguson, Marjorie. 1993. Invisible Divides: Communication and Identity in Canada and the US. *Journal of Communication* 43 (2): 42–57.

Fieguth, Debra. 2000. Anglican Church faces Spectre of Bankruptcy. *Christian Week* 14 (6): 1.

Finke, Roger. 1989. Demographics of Religious Participation: An Ecological Approach, 1850–1980. *Journal for the Scientific Study of Religion* 28 (1): 45–59.

Finke, Roger, Avery Guest, and Rodney Stark. 1996. Mobilizing Local Religious Markets: Religious Pluralism in New York State, 1855 to 1865. *American Sociological Review* 61 (2): 203–19.

Finke, Roger, and Laurence Iannaccone. 1993. Supply-Side Explanation for Religious Change. *Annals of the American Academy of Political and Social Science* 527: 27–40.

Finke, Roger, and Rodney Stark. 1988. Religious Economies and Sacred Canopies. Religious Mobilization in American Cities. *American Sociological Review* 53: 41–9.

Fox, John W. 1992. The Structure, Stability, and Social Antecedents of Reported Paranormal Experiences. *Sociological Analysis* 53 (4): 417–31.

Garreau, J. 1981. *The Nine Nations of North America*. Boston: Houghton Mifflin.

Gastil, Raymond D. 1975. *Cultural Regions of the United States*. Seattle: University of Washington Press.

Gauvreau, Michael. 1990. Protestantism Transformed: Personal Piety and the Evangelical Social Vision, 1815–1867. In *The Canadian Protestant Experience, 1760–1990*. edited by George Rawlyk.

Gehrig, Gail. 1979. American Civil Religion: An Assessment. Society for the Scientific Study of Religion, Monograph Series, No. 3.

Gerlach, L.P., and V.P. Hine. 1970. *People, Power, Change: Movements of Social Transformation*. Indianapolis: Bobbs-Merrill.

Glock, Charles Y., and Rodney Stark. 1965. *Religion and Society in Tension*. Chicago: Rand McNally.

Goodwin, Daniel C., ed. 2000. *Revivals, Baptists and George Rawlyk*. Wolfville, NS: Gaspereau Press.

Grabb, Edward G., and James E. Curtis. 2002. Comparing Central Political Values in the Canadian and American Democracies. In *Political Sociology: Canadian Perspectives*, edited by Douglas Baer, 37–54.

Grant, John Webster. 1988. *The Church in the Canadian Era.* Rev. ed. Burlington, ON: Welch.

Greeley, Andrew. 1987. Mysticism Goes Mainstream. *American Health* (January/February): 47–9.

Green, John C., James L. Guth, Corwin E. Smidt and Lyman A. Kellstedt. 1996. *Religion and the Culture War: Dispatches from the Front.* Lauham, MD: Rowman and Littlefield.

Green, John C., Lyman A. Kellstedt, Corwin E. Smidt, and James L. Guth. 1994. Religious Commitment and Political Attitudes: A New Look at an Old Subject. Presented at the annual meeting of the Society for the Scientific Study of Religion. Albuquerque, New Mexico, 4–6 November 1994.

Grenville, Andrew. 1995a. Development of the Christian Evangelicalism Scale. Unpublished paper.

– 1995b. The Awakened and the Spirit-Moved: The Religious Experiences of Canadian Evangelicals in the 1990s. Paper presented at the Aspects of Canadian Evangelicalism Conference, Kingston, Ontario, May 1995.

Guiness, Os. 1993. *Dining with the Devil: The Megachurch Movement Flirts with Modernity.* Grand Rapids: Baker Book House.

Guth, James L. 1996. The Bully Pulpit: Southern Baptist Clergy and Political Activism 1980–1992. In *Religion and the Culture Wars: Dispatches from the Front*, edited by John C. Green et al., 146–73.

Guth, James L., and John C. Green. 1993. Salience: The Core Concept? In *Rediscovering the Religious Factor in American Politics*, edited by David Leege and Lyman Kellstedt, 157–76.

Hadaway, C. Kirk, and Penny Long Marler. 1997. The Measurement and Meaning of Religious Involvement in Great Britain. Presented at the meeting of the International Society for the Sociology of Religion, Toulouse, France.

– 1997b. Do Canadians Over-Report Church Membership and Attendance? A Case Study of Religion in a Canadian County. Paper presented at the meeting of the Society for the Scientific Study of Religion, Montreal, November 6–8.

Hadaway, C. Kirk, Penny Long Marler, and Mark Chaves. 1993. What the Polls Don't Show: A Closer Look at US Church Attendance. *American Sociological Review* 58: 741–52.

Hall, R.H., and R.E. Quino, eds. 1983. *Organizational Theory and Public Policy.* Beverly Hills, CA: Sage.

Hammond, Philip E. 1992. *Religion and Personal Autonomy.* Columbia, SC: University of South Carolina Press.

Hammond, Phillip E., and James Davison Hunter. 1984. On Maintaining Plausibility: The Worldview of Evangelical College Students. *Journal for the Scientific Study of Religion* 23: 221–38.

Hart, Stephen. 1987. Privatization in American Religion and Society. *Sociological Analysis* 47 (4): 319–34.

Hay, David, and Ann Morisy. 1978. Reports of Ecstatic, Paranormal, or Religious Experience in Great Britain and the United States – A Comparison of Trends. *Journal for the Scientific Study of Religion* 17 (3): 255–68.

Hewitt, W.E., ed. 1993. *The Sociology of Religion: A Canadian Focus.* Toronto and Vancouver: Butterworths.

Hexham, Irving, and Karla Poewe. 1997. *New Religions as Global Cultures: Making the Human Sacred.* Boulder: Westview Press.

Hiller, Harry. 1978. Continentalism and the Third Force in Religion. *Canadian Journal of Sociology* 3: 189–204.

Hiller, Harry. 1991. *Canadian Society: A Macro Analysis.* 2nd ed. Scarborough: Prentice Hall.

Hodgson, Godfrey, ed. 1992. *Handbooks to the Modern World: The United States.* Vol. 1. New York: Facts on File Publishers.

Hoge, Dean, Benton Johnson, and Don Luidens. 1994. *Vanishing Boundaries: The Religion of Mainline Protestant Baby Boomers.* Louisville, KY: Westminster/John Knox Press.

Hoover, Dennis. 1997a. Conservative Protestant Politics in the US and Canada. Unpublished PHD dissertation, Lincoln College, Oxford University.

– 1997b. The Christian Right under Old Glory and the Maple Leaf. In *Sojourners in the Wilderness: The Christian Right in Comparative Perspective,* edited by Corwin E. Smidt and James M. Penning, n.p.

– 2000. A Religious Right Arrives in Canada. *Religion in the News* 3 (2): 12–15.

Hoover, Dennis R., Michael D. Martinez, Samuel H. Reimer, and Kenneth D. Wald. 2002. Evangelicalism Meets the Continental Divide: Moral and Economic Conservatism in the United States and Canada. *Political Research Quarterly* 55 (2): 351–74.

Howlett, Michael. 1994. The Judicialization of Canadian Environmental Policy, 1980–1990: A Test of the Canada-United States Convergence Thesis. *Canadian Journal of Political Science* 27 (1): 99–127.

Hunter, James Davison. 1981. Operationalizing Evangelicalism: A Review, Critique and Proposal. *Sociological Analysis* 4: 363–72.

– 1983. *American Evangelicalism: Conservative Religion and the Quandary of Modernity.* New Brunswick: Rutgers.

– 1984. Religion and Political Civility: The Coming Generation of Evangelicals. *Journal for the Scientific Study of Religion* 23 (4): 364–80.

– 1987. *Evangelicalism: The Coming Generation.* Chicago: University of Chicago Press.

– 1991. *Culture Wars: The Struggle to Define America.* New York: Basic Books.

Iannaccone, Lawrence. 1990. Religious Practice: A Human Capital Approach. *Journal for the Scientific Study of Religion* 29: 297–314.

– 1991. The Consequences of Religious Market Structure. *Rationality and Society* 3: 156–77.

– 1994. Why Strict Churches Are Strong. *American Journal of Sociology* 99: 1,180–211.

Inglehart, Ronald. 1990. *Culture Shift in Advanced Industrial Society.* Princeton, NJ: Princeton University Press.

– 1997. *Modernization and Postmodernization: Cultural, Economic, and Political Change in 43 Societies.* Princeton, NJ: Princeton University Press.

Inglehart, Ronald, and Wayne E. Baker. 2000. Modernization, Cultural Change, and the Persistence of Traditional Values. *American Sociological Review* 65: 19–51.

James, William. 1902. *Varieties of Religious Experience.* New York: Collier Books.

Jelen, Ted. 1990. Religious Belief and Attitude Constraint. *Journal for the Scientific Study of Religion* 29 (1): 118–25.

Jelen, Ted G., ed. 1989. *Religious and Political Behaviour in the United States.* New York: Praeger.

Jorstad, Erling. 1993. *Popular Religion in America: The Evangelical Voice.* Westport, CT: Greenwood.

Kelley, Dean. 1972. *Why Conservative Churches Are Growing.* New York: Harper and Row.

Kellstedt, Lyman. 1989. The Meaning and Measurement of Evangelicalism: Problems and Prospects. In *Religion and Political Behaviour in the United States,* edited by Ted G. Jelen, 3–21.

– 1993. Religion, the Neglected Variable: An Agenda for Future Research on Religion and Political Behaviour. In *Rediscovering the Religious Factor in American Politics,* edited by David Leege and Lyman Kellstedt, 273–303.

Kellstedt, Lyman, and John Green. 1993. Knowing God's People: Denominational Preference and Political Behaviour. In *Rediscovering the Religious Factor in American Politics,* edited by David Leege and Lyman Kellstedt, 53–71.

Kellstedt, Lyman, John C. Green, James L. Guth, and Corwin E. Smidt. 1993. Religious Traditions and Religious Commitments in the USA. Paper presented at the 22d International Conference of the International Society for the Sociology of Religion. Budapest, Hungary, 9–12 July 1993.

– 1996. Grasping the Essentials: The Social Embodiment of Religion and Political Behaviour. In *Religion and the Culture Wars: Dispatches from the Front,* edited by John C. Green et al, 174–92.

Kertzer, David. 1989. *Ritual, Politics and Power.* New Haven: Yale University Press.

Kim, Jae-On, and Charles W. Mueller. 1978. *Factor Analysis: Statistical Methods and Practical Issues.* Newbury Park, CA: Sage.

King, Anthony D. 1991. *Culture, Globalization and the World-System.* New York: Macmillan.

Kollar, Nathan R. 1998. Facing North; Facing South: Two Religious Perspectives – Canada and the United States. Paper presented at the Annual Meeting for the Society for the Scientific Study of Religion. Montreal, Canada, 6–8 November 1998.

Koop, Doug. 1996. Toronto Airport Vineyard Release to Fly Solo. *Christian Week* 9 (18): 1–4.

Lamont, Michele, and Marcel Fournier, eds. 1992. *Cultivating Differences: Symbolic Boundaries and the Making of Inequality.* Chicago and London: University of Chicago Press.

Leege, David C. 1993. Religion and Politics in Theoretical Perspective. In *Rediscovering the Religious Factor in American Politics,* edited by David Leege and Lyman Kellstedt, 3–25.

Leege, David, and Lyman Kellstedt, eds. 1993. *Rediscovering the Religious Factor in American Politics.* Armonk: M.E. Shape.

Lenski, Gerhard. 1961. *The Religious Factor: A Sociologist's Inquiry.* Garden City: Doubleday.

Lieske, Joel A. 1992. Political Subcultures of the United States. *The Journal of Politics* 55: 888–913.

Lipset, Seymour Martin. 1990. *Continental Divide: The Values and Institutions of the United States and Canada.* New York: Routledge.

– 1996. *American Exceptionalism.* New York: Norton.

Lofland, John. 1978. Becoming a World-Saver Revisited. In *Conversion Careers,* edited by James Richardson, 10–23.

Lofland, John, and Rodney Stark. 1965. Becoming a World-Saver: A Theory of Religious Conversion. *American Sociological Review* 30: 862–74.

Lougheed, Richard, Wesley Peach, and Glenn Smith. 1999. *Histoire du Protestantisme au Québec depuis 1960.* Quebec City: Éditions de la Clairière.

Luckmann, Thomas. 1967. *The Invisible Religion.* New York: Macmillan.

Maclean's/Decima Poll. 1989. Separate Identities. *Maclean's* July 3: 32–3.

Maclean's Special Report. 1993. God Is Alive. *Maclean's* April 12: 32–50.

Malcohm, Andrew. 1985. *The Canadians.* New York: Times Books.

Marsden, George M. 1980. *Fundamentalism and American Culture: The Shaping of 20th Century Evangelicalism, 1870–1925.* New York: Oxford University Press.

Meyer, John W., and Brian Rowan. 1991. Institutionalized Organizations: Formal Structure as Myth and Ceremony. In *The New Institutionalism in Organizational Analysis,* edited by Walter W. Powell and Paul J. DiMaggio, 41–62.

Michalos, Alex C. 1982. *North American Report.* Vol. 5. Dordrecht, Holland: D. Reidel.

Millar, Warren E., and the National Election Studies. 1994. *American National Election Studies Cumulative Codebook, 1952–1992.* 7th release. Ann Arbor, MI: University of Michigan, Center for Political Studies, Interuniversity Consortium for Political and Social Research.

Moerman, Murray, ed. 1998. *Transforming Our Nation: Empowering The Canadian Churches for a Greater Harvest*. Richmond, BC: Church Leadership Library.

Moerman, Murray and Lorne Hunter. 1998. Church Planting: Key to Discipling Our Nation. In *Transforming Our Nation: Empowering the Canadian Churches for a Greater Harvest*, edited by Murray Moerman, 51–88.

Moore, R. Laurence. 1994. *Selling God: American Religion in the Marketplace of Culture*. New York: Oxford University Press.

Motz, Arnell, ed. 1990. *Reclaiming a Nation: The Challenge of Re-evangilizing Canada by the Year 2000*, Richmond, BC: Church Leadership Library.

– 1990. The Condition of the Canadian Church. In *Reclaiming a Nation*, edited by Arnell Motz, 13–34.

Myers, Kenneth. 1989. *All God's People and Blue Suede Shoes: Christians and Popular Culture*. Wheaton, IL: Crossway Books.

Neitz, Mary Jo. 1987. *Charisma and Community: A Study of Religious Commitment within the Charismatic Renewal*. New Brunswick, NJ: Transaction Books.

Neitz, Mary Jo, and James V. Spickard. 1990. Steps Toward a Sociology of Religious Experience: The Theories of Mihaly Csikszentmihalyi and Alfred Schutz. *Sociological Analysis* 51 (1): 15–33.

Neuhaus, Richard John, ed. 1987. *The Bible, Politics and Democracy*. Grand Rapids: Eerdmans.

Nevitte, Neil. 1996. *The Decline of Deference: Canadian Value Change in Comparative Perspective, 1981–1990*. Peterborough, ON: Broadview Press.

Niebuhr, Richard H. 1929. *The Social Sources of Denominationalism*. Hamden, CT: Shoestring Press.

Noll, Mark A. 1992. *A History of Christianity in the United States and Canada*. Grand Rapids: Eerdmans.

– 1997. Canadian Evangelicalism: A View from the United States. In *Aspects of the Canadian Evangelical Experience*, edited by George Rawlyk, 3–20.

Noll, Mark A., David W. Bebbington, and George A. Rawlyk, eds. 1994. *Evangelicalism: Comparative Studies of Popular Protestantism in North America, the British Isles, and Beyond, 1700–1990*. New York: Oxford University Press.

Olson, Daniel V.A. 1993. Fellowship Ties and the Transition of Religious Identity. In *Beyond Establishment: Protestant Identity in a Post-Protestant Age*, edited by Jackson W. Carroll and Wade Clark Roof, 32–53.

Ostling, Richard.1994. Laughing for the Lord. *Time* 15 August 1994: 38.

O'Toole, Roger. 1982. Some Good Purpose: Notes on Religion and Political Culture in Canada. *Annual Review of the Social Sciences of Religion* 6: 177–217.

Owen, Carolyn A., Howard C. Eisner, and Thomas R. McFaul. 1981. A Half-Century of Social Distance Research: National Replication of the Bogardus Studies. *Sociology and Social Research* 66 (1): 80–98.

Peach, Wesley. 1990. Evangelism – Distinctly Quebec. In *Reclaiming a Nation: The Challenge of Re-evangelizing Canada by the Year 2000*, edited by Arnell Motz, 153–76.

Penning, James M., and Corwin Smidt. 1999. Back to the Future?: A Longitudinal Analysis of the Symbolic Boundaries of Students Attending Evangelical Colleges. Paper presented at the annual meeting of the Society for the Scientific Study of Religion. Boston, 5–7 November 1999.

Plaxton, David. 1997. "We Will Evangelize with a Whole Gospel or None": Evangelicalism and the United Church of Canada. In *Aspects of the Canadian Evangelical Experience*, edited by George Rawlyk, 106–22.

Poewe, Karla, ed. 1994. *Charismatic Christianity as a Global Culture*. Columbia: University of South Carolina Press.

Poloma, Margaret. 1982. *The Charismatic Movement: Is There a New Pentecost?* Boston: Wayne.

– 1989. *The Assemblies of God at the Crossroads: Charisma and Institutional Dilemmas*. Knoxville: University of Tennessee Press.

– 1995. Charisma and Institutions: A Sociological Account of the "Toronto Blessing." Paper presented at the annual meeting of the Society for the Scientific Study of Religion. St Louis, Missouri, October 1995.

Poloma, Margaret, and Brian F. Pendleton. 1989. Religious Experiences, Evangelism, and Institutional Growth within the Assemblies of God. *Journal for the Scientific Study of Religion* 28 (4): 415–31.

Posterski, Donald C., and Irwin Barker. 1993. *Where's a Good Church?* Winfield: Wood Lake Books.

Powell, Walter W., and Paul J. DiMaggio, eds. 1991. *The New Institutionalism in Organizational Analysis*. Chicago and London: University of Chicago Press.

Quebedeaux, Richard. 1978. *The Worldly Evangelicals*. San Francisco: Harper and Row.

Rawlyk, George. 1984. *Ravished by the Spirit*. Montreal and Kingston: McGill-Queen's University Press.

– 1990. *Champions of the Truth*. Montreal and Kingston: McGill-Queen's University Press.

– 1994. Who are these Canadians who call themselves Evangelicals? *Christian Week* (15 November 1994): 5.

– 1996. *Is Jesus Your Personal Saviour? In Search of Canadian Evangelicalism in the 1990s*. Montreal and Kingston: McGill-Queen's University Press.

Rawlyk, George, ed. 1990. *The Canadian Protestant Experience, 1760–1990*. Burlington, ON: Welch.

– 1997. *Aspects of The Canadian Evangelical Experience*. Montreal and Kingston: McGill-Queen's University Press.

Rawlyk, George, and Mark Noll, eds. 1994. *Amazing Grace: Evangelicalism in Australia, Britain, Canada and the United States*. Grand Rapids: Baker Books.

Redekop, Calvin, and Urie A. Bender. 1988. *Who am I? What am I?* Grand Rapids: Zondervan.

Reed, John Shelton. 1972. *The Enduring South: Subcultural Persistence in Mass Society.* Lexington, MA: Lexington Books.

Regnerus, Mark D., and Christian Smith. 1998. Selective Deprivatization among American Religious Traditions: The Reversal of the Great Reversal. *Social Forces* 76 (4): 1,347–72.

Regnerus, Mark D., David Sikkink, and Christian Smith. 1999. Voting with the Christian Right: Contextual and Individual Patterns of Electoral Influence. *Social Forces* 77 (4): 1,375–401.

Reimer, Sam. 1995. A Look at Cultural Effects on Religiosity: A Comparison between the United States and Canada. *Journal for the Scientific Study of Religion* 34 (4): 445–57.

– 1996. North American Evangelicalism: A Look at Regional and National Variation in Religiosity. Notre Dame, IN: Unpublished PhD Dissertation.

– 2000. A More Irenic Canadian Evangelicalism? Comparing Evangelicals in Canada and the US. In *Revivals, Baptists and George Rawlyk*, edited by Daniel C. Goodwin, 153–80.

Reimer, Sam, and Jerry Park. 2001. Tolerant (In)civility? A Longitudinal Analysis of White Conservative Protestants' Willingness to Grant Civil Liberties. *Journal for the Scientific Study of Religion* 40: 735–45.

Richardson, James, ed. 1978. *Conversion Careers.* Beverly Hills, CA: Sage.

Robertson, Roland. 1989. Globalization, Politics, and Religion. In *The Changing Face of Religion*, edited by James A. Beckford and Thomas Luckmann, 10–23.

– 1992. Globalization: *Social Theory and Global Culture.* London: Sage.

Roof, Wade Clark. 1993. *A Generation of Seekers: The Spiritual Journeys of the Baby Boom Generation.* San Francisco: HarperSanFransisco.

Roof, Wade Clark, and William McKinney. 1987. *American Mainline Religion: Its Changing Shape and Future.* New Brunswick: Rutgers University Press.

Rousseau, Jean-Jacques. 1966. *The Social Contract.* New York: Hafner Publishing.

Schmaltzbauer, John A., and C. Gray Wheeler. 1996. Between Fundamentalism and Secularization: Secularizing and Sacralizing Currents in the Evangelical Debate on Campus Lifestyle Codes. *Sociology of Religion* 57 (3): 241–57.

Schultze, Quentin J., ed. 1990. *American Evangelicals and the Mass Media: Perspectives on the Relationship Between American Evangelicals and the Mass Media.* Grand Rapids: Zondervan.

– 1991. *Televangelism and American Culture: The Business of Popular Religion.* Grand Rapids: Baker Book House.

Scott, W. Richard, and John W. Meyer. 1991. The Organization of Societal Sectors: Propositions and Early Evidence. In *The New Institutionalism in*

Organizational Analysis, edited by Walter W. Powell and Paul J. DiMaggio, 108–40.

– 1994. *Institutional Environment and Organizations: Structure Complexity and Individualism*. Thousand Oaks, CA: Sage.

Segal, Karen. 1994. Marching in "the Hat." *Christian Week* 8 (7): 1.

Sherman, Doug, and William Hendricks. 1987. *Your Work Matters to God*. Colorado Springs: Navpress.

Shibley, Mark. 1996. *Resurgent Evangelicalism in the United States: Mapping Cultural Change since 1970*. Columbia: University of South Carolina Press.

Smidt, Corwin, and Lyman Kellstedt. 1987. Evangelicalism and Social Research: Interpretative Problems and Substantive Findings. In *The Bible, Politics and Democracy*, edited by Richard John Neuhaus, 81–102, 131–67.

Smidt, Corwin E., and James M, Penning, eds. 1997. *Sojourners in the Wilderness: The Christian Right in Comparative Respective*. Lauham, MD: Rowman and Littlefield.

Smith, Christian, with Michael Emerson, Sally Gallagher, and Paul Kennedy. 1996. The Myth of the Culture Wars. *Culture* 11 (1): 1.

Smith, Christian, with Michael Emerson, Sally Gallagher, Paul Kennedy, and David Sikkink. 1998. *American Evangelicalism: Embattled and Thriving*. Chicago and London: University of Chicago Press.

Smith, Christian. 2000. *Christian America? What Evangelicals Really Want*. Berkeley and Los Angeles: University of California Press.

Smith, Glenn. 1998. "The Québec Protestant Church." In *Transforming Our Nation: Empowering the Canadian Church for a Greater Harvest*, edited by Murray Moerman, 203–66.

Snow, David A., and Richard Machalek. 1983. The Convert as a Social Type. In *Sociological Theory*, edited by R. Collins, 259–89.

– 1984. The Sociology of Conversion. *Annual Review of Sociology* 10: 167–90.

Soper, Christopher J. 1994. *Evangelical Christianity in the United States and Great Britain: Religious Beliefs, Political Choices*. New York: New York University Press.

Spickard, James V. 1991. Experiencing Religious Rituals: A Schutzian Analysis of Navajo Ceremonies. *Sociological Analysis* 52 (2): 191–204.

Spilka, Bernard, Ralph W. Hood, and Richard R. Gorsuch. 1985. *The Psychology of Religion: An Empirical Approach*. Englewood Cliffs, NJ: Prentice Hall.

Stackhouse, John Jr. 1993a. *Canadian Evangelicalism in the Twentieth Century: An Introduction to Its Character*. Toronto: University of Toronto Press.

– 1993b. More than a Hyphen: Twentieth-Century Canadian Evangelicalism in Anglo-American Context. In *Amazing Grace: Evangelicalism in Australia, Britain, Canada and the United States*, edited by George Rawlyk and Mark Noll, 375–400.

Staples, Clifford L., and Armand L. Mauss. 1987. Conversion or Commitment? A Reassessment of the Snow and Machalek Approach to the Study of Conversion. *Journal for the Scientific Study of Religion* 26 (2): 133–47.

Stark, Rodney, and Charles Y. Glock. 1968. *American Piety: The Nature of Religious Commitment*. Berkeley, CA: University of California Press.

Stark, Rodney, and William Sims Bainbridge. 1985. *The Future of Religion*. Berkeley, CA: University of California Press.

Statistics Canada. 1993. *Religions in Canada*. Ottawa: Industry, Science and Technology Canada. 1991 Census of Canada. Catalogue number 93–319.

Steensland, Brian, Jerry Park, Mark Regnerus, Lynn Robinson, Bradford Wilcox, and Robert Woodberry. 2000. The Measure of American Religion: Toward Improving the State of the Art. *Social Forces* 79: 291–318.

Stone, Jon R. 1997. *On the Boundaries of American Evangelicalism: The Postwar Evangelical Coalition*. New York: St Martin's Press.

Storkey, Alan. 1979. *A Christian Social Perspective*. Downer's Grove, IL: Intervarsity Press.

Stott, John. 1984. *Issues Facing Christians Today*. Hants, UK: Marshall Morgan and Scott.

Swenson, Don. 2000. The Dilemma of Interpretation. Paper presented at the annual meeting of the Society for the Scientific Study of Religion. Houston, 19–22 October 2000.

Swidler, Ann. 1986. Culture in Action: Symbols and Strategies. *American Sociological Review* 51: 273–86.

Tajfel, Henri, ed. 1982. *Social Identity and Intergroup Relations*. New York: Cambridge University Press.

Taras, David. 2000. Swimming against the Current: American Mass Entertainment and Canadian Identity. In *Canada and the United States: Differences That Count*, edited by David Thomas, 192–208.

Tepperman, Lorne. 2002. The Postmaterialist Thesis: Has There Been a Shift in Political Culture? In *Political Sociology: Canadian Perspectives*, edited by Douglas Baer, 15–36.

Thomas, David., ed. 2000. *Canada and the United States: Differences That Count*. 2d ed. Scarborough, ON: Broadview Press.

Troeltsch, Ernst. 1931. *The Social Teaching of the Christian Churches*. Vol. 2. Translated by Olive Wyong. New York: Macmillan.

Turner, John C. 1982. Towards a Cognitive Redefinition of the Social Group. In *Social Identity and Intergroup Relations*, edited by Henri Tajfel, 15–40.

Tweed, Thomas A., ed. 1997. *Retelling US Religious History*. Berkeley and Los Angeles: University of California Press.

Wagner, Melinda. 1997. Generic Conservative Christianity: The Demise of Denominationalism in Christian Schools. *Journal for the Scientific Study of Religion* 36 (1): 13–24.

Wallerstein, Immanuel. 1991. The National and the Universal: Can There Be Such a Thing as World Culture? In *Culture, Globalization and the World-System*, edited by Anthony D. King, 91–105.

Waters, Malcohm. 1995. *Globalization*. London: Routledge.

Watkins, Mel, 1993. *Handbooks to the Modern World: Canada.* New York: Facts on File Publishers.

Weber, Max. [1904–05] 1958. *The Protestant Ethic and the Spirit of Capitalism.* New York: Charles Scribner's Sons.

Weber, Timothy P. 1991. Premillennialism and the Branches of Evangelicalism. In *The Variety of American Evangelicalism,* edited by Donald W. Dayton and Robert K. Johnston, 5–21.

Welch, Michael R. 1993. Religious Participation and Commitment among Catholic Parishioners: The Relative Importance of Individual, Contextual, and Institutional Factors. In *Church and Denominational Growth,* edited by David Roozen and C. Kirk Hadaway, 324–35.

Welch, Michael R., David C. Leege, and James C. Cavendish. 1995. Attitudes Toward Abortion among US Catholics: Another Case of Symbolic Politics? *Social Sciences Quarterly* 76: 143–57.

Westfall, William. 1997. Voices from the Attic: The Canadian Border and the Writing of American Religious History. In *Retelling US Religious History,* edited by Thomas A. Tweed, 181–99.

Westhues, Kenneth.
   1976. Religious Organization in Canada and the United States. *International Journal of Comparative Sociology* 8: 206–23.

Wheeler, Barbara. 1995. You Who Were Far Off: Religious Divisions and the Role of Religious Research. *Review of Religious Research* 37 (4): 289–301.

White, Jerry, and Mary White. 1988. *On the Job: Survival or Satisfaction.* Colorado Springs: Navpress.

Wilkinson, Michael. 2000. The Globalization of Pentecostalism: The Role of Asian Immigrant Pentecostals in Canada. *Asian Journal of Pentecostal Studies* 3 (2): 219–26.

Wilson, Charles Reagan, and William Ferris, 1989. *Encyclopedia of Southern Culture.* Chapel Hill: University of North Carolina Press.

Wimberley, Ronald C., and James A. Christenson. 1981. Civil Religion and Other Religious Identities. *Sociological Analysis* 42 (2): 91–100.

Wuthnow, Robert. 1988. *The Restructuring of American Religion.* Princeton, NJ: Princeton University Press.

– 1994. *God and Mammon in America.* New York: Free Press.

Yamane, David, and Megan Polzer. 1994. Ways of Seeing Ecstasy in Modern Society: Experiential-Expressive and Cultural-Linguistic Views. *Sociology of Religion* 55 (1): 1–25.

Zeman, Jarold K. 1980. *Baptists in Canada: Search for Identity Amidst Diversity.* Burlington, ON: G.R. Welch.

Zhu, Chenggang. 1992. Regional Subcultures and Attitudes toward Abortion. Unpublished PHD dissertation. University of Notre Dame.

Index